THE WORLD'S EDITION

OF THE

GREAT Presbyterian Conflict

PATTON VS. SWING.

BOTH SIDES OF THE QUESTION.

With Portraits of Profs. Patton and Swing,

And containing a full outline of the circumstances which preceded the trial, many of which are not known to the public. Pulpit sketches of Profs. Swing and Patton, by the Rev. Chas. L. Thompson, of this city. Also, the fourteen famous sermons preached by Prof. Swing, "for utterances in which" the prosecution has based its charges of heterodoxy.

THE CELEBRATED "CHARGES AND SPECIFICATIONS;"

Prof. Swing's Declaration; Prof. Patton's famous argument; the answer to the same by Prof. Swing and his counsel; the closing argument by Prof. Patton, and the verdict of the Presbytery.

CHICAGO:
GEO. MACDONALD & CO.
1874.

PUBLISHERS' NOTICE.

In presenting this volume to the public, the publishers desire to call attention to the fact that they have named this issue "THE WORLD'S EDITION," and at the same time think it proper to explain their reasons for doing so. The contents of this work, with one exception, have been free to the world from the time they were written or spoken. The entire report of the "Trial of Prof. Swing for heresy," has been published in all the leading newspapers of this city, and the same may be said of Prof. Swing's celebrated Sermons, they having been printed in "*The Chicago Times*," "*Chicago Tribune*," "*The Inter Ocean*," "*The Chicago Pulpit*," "*The Alliance*," and other journals, all of which are free from copyright and trade monopoly. Considering, therefore, that the matter herein contained has been ***spoken to the world*** by Prof. Swing, Dr. Patton and others, and *published to the world* through the journals here named, the publishers think that "THE WORLD'S EDITION" is a fitting title for the present issue.

While the publishers make a claim of the title page, by copyright, for their own protection, they unhesitatingly proclaim to the world that the entire contents of this work (with that exception) belong to the world, and can be published by any person or firm throughout the globe, as free from copyright as the Constitution of the United States.

The publishers embrace the present opportunity for tendering their sincere thanks to the members of the Chicago Press for the interest they have manifested in the present volume, and for the valuable assistance they have lent them in furnishing carefully corrected reports of the speeches and proceedings of the Presbytery during the trial.

LAKESIDE BUILDING, CHICAGO, MAY, 1874.

INDEX.

A REVIEW OF THE CONFLICT.

Before perusing this work, it may be of some interest for the reader to know some of the circumstances which preceded and produced it. They are simply these:—

For the past few years Professor Swing's sermons have attracted considerable attention, and have been quoted by the secular and religious press throughout the country; some praising him for his broad views and eloquent expression of the gospel, while others, commenting on his eloquence, expressed their doubts as to the orthodoxy of his views.

Matters stood in this way until last summer, when the Pittsburgh *Presbyterian Banner* published an article reflecting upon Mr. Swing's orthodoxy. This article was copied by the *Interior*, which is edited by Dr. Patton, and he made some able comments on it. To this Professor Swing, by way of exculpating himself from the charges of the *Banner*, and to rebut the comments of the *Interior*, wrote a letter on the subject. This called forth an editorial in the *Interior*, which was followed by another letter from Professor Swing.

This newspaper war at once attracted attention, and ministers and people began to look into matters for themselves. Professor Swing's sermons were read with special interest. Some thought them orthodox; others were of the opposite opinion.

The Presbyterian clergymen, of Chicago, meet together once a week (on Mondays), for the exchange of thought and religious conversation. In one of these meetings, held in April, the subject of Dr. Patton's criticisms on Professor Swing's sermons became the theme of conversation, which soon assumed the features of a warm discussion. Some expressed themselves as to Dr. Patton's action being unwarrantable and unjust; others took an entirely different view of the subject; and it was evident when the meeting broke up that the matter would result in serious consequence if its discussion were renewed.

On the following Monday, the meeting was remarkably well attended, and every member seemed ready for discussion on the Swing-Patton affair should opportunity present itself. At length one of the members presented a resolution indorsing an article which appeared in the *Interior* on February 12th, to the effect that "there are those who doubt, and we among them, that Professor Swing believes that Christ is God: that the death of Christ was an expiatory sacrifice; that men were justified by faith alone; that the punishment of the wicked is eternal; and that he believes in the Church doctrine of the Trinity, and in the regenerating influence of the spirit;" and stating that it was the duty of the author of the article to bring the subject matter thereof under the notice of the Presbytery, with a view of its determining, on inquiry, whether said doubts were well or ill-founded. There then ensued a sharp debate, and the resolution was withdrawn by general consent. At a meeting of Presbytery shortly after, Dr. Patton gave notice that he would prefer formal charges against Professor Swing at the meeting of the Presbytery in April.

On April 14th, the Presbytery of Chicago began its annual meeting. Dr. Patton presented two charges. The first charge, which was supported by twenty-five specifications, set forth that Professor Swing had not been zealous and faithful in maintaining the truths of the Gospel, and had not been faithful and diligent in the exercise of the duties of his position. The second charge, supported by four specifications, set forth that Professor David Swing did not sincerely receive and adopt the Confession of Faith of the Presbyterian Church, as containing the system of doctrines taught in the Holy Scriptures. The strongest points urged in the charges were that Professor Swing had shown himself in his sermons to be guilty of Sabellianism and Unitarianism; that he had used unwarrantable language about Penelope; that he had preached in aid of the Mary Price Collier Unitarian Chapel, and had totally rejected three great Presbyterian tenets.

After a warm debate, it was decided to refer the matter of the charges to the judiciary committee, who, on the Monday following, presented a majority and minority report. After discussion, the reports were recommended, and the modified specifications were ordered to be presented to the meeting the following day. On account of the illness of Professor Swing, the Rev. Mr. Noyes, whom he designated as his counsel in the trial, was appointed to that office by the Presbytery. The revised charges of Dr. Patton were reported back to the Presbytery April 22, and were accepted, and the time for the commencement of proceedings was fixed for Monday, May 4. On this day the accused was called upon to plead, which he did in a statement in which he set forth that he was a New School Presbyterian. He submitted a number of observations setting forth his Christian creed, and showing that the Presbyterian Church had slipped, and was slipping, away from the religion of despair, and had come unto Mount Zion into the atmosphere of Jesus as He was in life and death, full of love and forgiveness.

Dr. Patton made a strenuous but unsuccessful demand for a continuance, and on the following day the examination of witnesses for the prosecution commenced. Among those were Dr. Patterson, who expressed his conviction of Professor Swing's orthodoxy; Mr. W. C. Goudy, who held a different view; and Dr. Swazey, who helped the defense with his testimony concerning an alleged heretical sermon. Thursday, May 7, the examination of Judge H. G. Miller was proceeded with, who told what he remembered of the sermon on "Ministerial Calling," and Mr. Shufeldt, who strengthened the prosecution by asserting that he considered Professor Swing to be unsound on the question of infant damnation. This closed the testimony for the prosecution, after which a motion for continuance was made by Dr. Patton, on the ground of the absence of an important witness, the Rev. Laird Collier, and refused, the vote of the maker of the motion being the only one recorded in its support. The defense then began the production of testimony, their first witness being Horace F. Waite, who declared the utmost confidence and belief in Professor Swing's orthodoxy. On the fifth day of the trial the testimony of Messrs. O. H. Lee, H. W. King, and Horace H. Hurlbut was added to that already given in support of the defense by Mr. Waite, and closed the case for the accused.

The counsel for the defense then expressed a readiness to waive argument, but Dr. Patton declined to consent, and the Presbytery adjourned until Tuesday, May 12, in order to hear the arguments of the prosecutor and defendant. On this day Dr. Patton commenced his argument for the prosecution, which was both lengthy

and exhaustive.* The Rev. Mr. Noyes followed with his defense of the accused. Unfortunately, he was deterred by sickness from speaking longer than an hour.

Saturday, May 16, Professor Swing took up the argument for defense.‡

Saturday, Mr. Noyes closed his argument for the defense, and Dr. Patton put in a replication for the prosecution, in which he urged that Professor Swing did not stick to the Confession of Faith, and that, therefore, the Presbytery were bound to find him guilty.**

Monday, May 18, the issue of the trial was further discussed by the Rev. Dr. Patterson.

On Tuesday, several of the Presbyters delivered speeches; some on his guilt, and others on his innocence.

Wednesday, it was apparent that the close of the trial was near at hand. On this day twenty-nine Presbyters gave their opinions in the case. After the Presbyters had spoken their views, the question arose as to how they should vote.

Rev. Dr. Hurd moved that the vote be taken on the several charges and specifications by the calling of the roll, each member, as his name is called, to vote to "sustain" them or "not to sustain" them.

After a warm discussion, the motion was carried.

Rev. Mr. Brown moved that the members vote on each specification in its moral sense, as sustaining or not sustaining the guilt charged on the accused.

After a long discussion, this motion also prevailed.

Rev. Dr. Blackburn moved that those who desired be allowed to vote "sustained in part," in reference to the specifications.

The motion provoked considerable discussion, Professor Swing's friends opposing and Dr. Patton's favoring it. After the members had all spoken their views, the motion was laid on the table—ayes, 30; nays, 21.

Rev. Mr. McLeod did not think it right to prohibit any member from voting as he pleased, and he proposed to give in his vote with the clerk in part where he desired on certain specifications, despite the action just taken. Several members declared similar intentions.

After discussion, the Presbytery reconsidered their vote, and then passed Blackburn's motion.

THE ROLL CALL.

The roll was then called on the final vote, and the members answered either by a single "no" on sustaining the charges and specifications, or by singling out the specifications that had not been sustained. The result was as follows:

NOT SUSTAINED.

R. W. Patterson, Arthur Swazey, A. H. Dean, W. N. Blackburn, N. Barrett, W. Forsythe, J. Covert, E. R. Davis, E. L. Hurd, W. F. Brown, E. Schofield, J. B. McClure, J. Post, B. S. Johnson, J. Otis, O. H. Lee, J. E. Fay, A. L. Winney, S. B. Williams, R. E. Barber, A. H. Merrill, W. H. Dunton, W. P. Caton, J. H. Taylor, J. H. Burns, J. H. Trowbridge, J. H. Walker, M. M. Wakeman, W. R. Downs, J. T. Matthews, C. L. Thompson, C. Wisner, A. E. Kittredge, Glen Wood, L. H. Reid, D. H. Curtis, E. W. Barrett, J. S. Gould, E. Smith, F. A. Riddle, H. A. Hopkins, D. R. Holt, J. H. Hurlbut, A. Dreysdell, G. H. Leonard, A. Mitchell.

* See Dr. Patton's argument for the Prosecution.
‡ See Prof. Swing's Argument.
** See Dr. Patton's Replication.

SUSTAINED IN PARTS.

L. J. Halsey, W. F. Wood, J. McLeod, D. J. Burrell, R. K. Wharton, J. M. Wharton, J. D.Wallace, H. Warden, J. M. Ferris, Ben. E. S. Ely, E. L. Carden, W. Brobson, W. C. Young, T. King, M. Lewis.

Total not sustained, 46. Sustained in parts, 15.

The moderator said the next thing in order, according to the programme, was the rendering of a judgment by the judicatory.

Rev. Dr. Hurd moved, in order to facilitate business, that a committee of three be appointed to prepare a minute to express the finding of the court.

The motion prevailed.

The moderator appointed Rev. Dr. Patterson, Elder Barber and Rev. Mr. McLeod as such committee.

A recess was then taken until 2:30 o'clock.

Afternoon Session.—The afternoon session began at the stated hour. The moderator asked for the report of the committee on a verdict, and Dr. Patterson submitted the following:

The Verdict.—The committee find from the record of the clerks that the vote of the Presbytery in this case stood as follows: Sixty-one votes were cast, of which 15 were in favor of sustaining the first charge, and 13 for sustaining the second charge; 46 against sustaining the first charge, and 48 against sustaining the second charge. We therefore find that the accused has been acquitted of both charges by the judgment of this court aforesaid.

R. W. Patterson.
James McLeod.
R. E. Barber.

Rev. Dr. Swazey moved that the report be adopted.

The motion prevailed, after which the Presbytery turned its attention to the transaction of miscellaneous business.

They had not proceeded far, when Professor Patton rose and said that he was not present when the report of the committee was presented in reference to the finding of the court, but he had since learned its nature. He now begged leave, at this point, to give notice that it was his intention to appeal—with all due deference to this body—to the synod of Northern Illinois, which meets next October, and he would file his appeal within ten days after the Presbytery adjourned, according to the rules of that body. [Applause.]

Some objection being offered to the brevity of the report of the committee on the verdict, the motion to adopt was reconsidered, and a new committee was appointed to bring in a verdict and reasons for the finding of the court.

At a subsequent meeting of Presbytery, May 25, the report of said committee was presented and adopted. See report of committee on verdict, page 163.

TRUTHS FOR TO-DAY.*

Spoken in the Past Winter by David Swing.

[Cut from "The Chicago Alliance."]

To say that these sermons are thoughtful, eloquent, scholarly productions of a devout mind, would very imperfectly express their character. If, in addition to this, they should be described as combining great tenderness with intellectual force, poetic felicities with logical power, broad Christian sympathy with solid sense and holy motive, then their main features only would be indicated. As religious writings they have decided and valuable characteristics of their own. In style they are as unlike Bushnell as Arnold, no nearer Robertson than Beecher, no more like Phillips Brooks than George McDonald. Swing reminds you of these influential names, not because he is an imitator, but because with them he recognizes the divine constitution of things, respects human nature, and pleads for the practical in religion. But Prof. Swing could not write as he does without a gift of his own, for it is not his learning, or culture, or piety, that can explain his peculiar persuasiveness. We have elsewhere, in an analysis of his genius, ascribed his power to a very happy and rare blending of heart-force and brain-force—spirituality and imagination—sensibility and good sense. With such a nature, he can never be a sectary—can never devote himself to the promulgation of one idea. No one can read his sermons without recognizing their catholicity of spirit, their gracious aim, the fertility of their matter, and their helpfulness to souls that recoil from the formal and arbitrary in religion. As sacred compositions, they captivate by a sweetness that is as natural to them as tints to the rose or flavor to the strawberry. They are logical without a display of argumentation, and poetical without any sacrifice of directness and sincerity. While one's reason is appealed to all along, the language of the appeal comes up all blossoming and fragrant with the heart. It would be hard to find in the same compass so much real poetry and logic in vital union as in these discourses. And here is the secret of their power.

His volume does not pretend to be a formal commentary, nor a body of systematic divinity. It is simply one harmonious note in the great plea of the Gospel for charity, and brotherhood, and noble living, and a loving following of the Lord Christ. It is just as absurd to criticise Prof. Swing for not writing and preaching in the Pattonian vein, as to complain of a meadow-lark for not being a hand-organ, or a clear, free, mountain streamlet, singing among the ferns and mosses, for not sounding like a coffee mill. He has his place to fill among the children of men. Not all are called to the same service. There are diversities of gifts, but the same spirit; differences of administrations, but the same Lord. No one supposes that he is called to preach Calvinism, but in the great procession of our humanity, so sad with its burdens, and sins, and burials, and tears, if he can encourage any to take hold of the Infinite hand that is so near them, and to rest on the Infinite heart that yearns over them, if he can beget in any a hunger for the eternal Righteousness, and teach sorrowful eyes to see, in the glory of the Lord, the majestic meanings of life, and to strive for the fruition, as we believe he is doing, then he does not preach in vain nor labor in vain. H. N. P.

* The title of a work by Prof. Swing, published by Jansen, McClurg & Co., Chicago.

Rev. DAVID SWING.

Rev. FRANCIS L. PATTON, D. D.

ST. PAUL AND THE GOLDEN AGE.

Paul a servant of Jesus Christ. *Romans i: 1.*

The immense amount of attention given, within recent years, to the relation of Paul to Christianity, warrants us in drawing some inferences regarding that prominent character, at least justifies us in making him a theme of brief remark. It will be years yet before the position of St. Paul can be fully defined, and for this closing up of accounts none of us can afford to wait. It is the privilege of each year to gather up the approximations of truth that appear within its own bounds, and, pending the final decision, to derive what cheer or help it may from the evidence rendered up to the passing hour.

As in the trial of some great personage, the public does not await in solemn silence the closing of the case and the decision of the court, but irresistibly follows each witness and weighs the testimony each hour; so, in the progress of moral inquiry, one cannot sit down and wait for the end, but by the mind's nature is led along through a series of weights and measurements in succeeding days. There is no provision made in the mind for perfect repose. It is commanded us by nature to go on. Like the Wandering Jew, in the fable, we must march, march, march!

But the following obligation should be confessed, namely, that the newer the inquiry, the greater the number of facts not yet brought in, the greater should be the modesty and charity of the wondering crowd, hoping, longing, fearing, as they stand around the witnesses and the box of the accused. Before the vast inquiries now opening up like a river that approaches the sea, — inquiries rising under the name of Darwin or Huxley, one need not sit down in silence, but may only proceed with the charity and humility of children diffident in their helpless youth. If inferences must cease until inquiries are wholly ended, life is reduced to a sleep that needs waking only once in a hundred years.

In all the present inquiry about St. Paul there is no vital idea involved. Hence, nothing is to be feared, even if not much were to be hoped. How far he differed from the other apostles, how far he was designed of God to give shape and tone to the Church, how far he has done so, what were his views, what his genius, how far his teachings were local, how far universal, are inquiries that involve no calamity, and hence need produce no passion, no trembling among Christians, nor boastings among infidel hearts. The inquiry promises good to the Church far more than it forebodes any evil. Paul seems a power only half-weighed, half-prized in the past. The new attention of the present seems to be the return of the Christian mind to a better estimate of its own outfit and resources.

An age afar off may better read a man or a system than an age that was near, because it may bring to the task a more congenial mind and heart. That the Church has reached a point eighteen centuries away from St. Paul is no proof that it ever exhausted, or even fully studied, the details of the doctrine, or spirit of the apostle. It often happens that a thousand years come between an event and any careful study of the event. Men are diverted by some new issue, and then by some other issue, and for hundreds of years make no sign of return to any objects that stood by their starting point. Thus Aristotle unfolded the inductive philosophy, but men turned away from it and never came near it again until in the far-off days of Lord Bacon. Astronomy flourished in old Egypt, and was quite complete and truthful; but the public mind deserted it and returned not until in modern periods. Thus men are always making long and great wanderings, and great and beautiful returns.

In Mexico and South America there are old mines of silver and gold where, thousands of years ago, shafts were sunk and furnaces were busy separating the metal from dust. But upspringing war, or decay of industry, or growth of vice drew away the toilers and left the mines to the silence of a thousand years. Now the new status assumed by the nineteenth century sends men back to the mines, and new shafts are sunk, and new furnaces blaze in the long deserted valleys of the precious ores.

In religion, the ages desert rich veins, and, after decay has hung for centuries about the old shafts, back come their remote children, and with double energy and intelligence make the gold and silver distill from the old earth. They return with better science and secure a richer yield.

The early tendency of the Church toward temporal power, drew away from the spirituality of Christ and from the broad republicanism of St. Paul. The fact that Peter was represented as having the keys, and being the rock upon which the Church was founded, drew the attention of the early half-barbarous Church toward that one apostle, and for fifteen hundred years Peter was the ideal genius of the Christian establishment. Not the absolute Peter of the Testament, but the idealized Peter of Romanism — Peter with human embellishment, Peter, transformed into a colossus. One can perceive this transformation and enthronement of this apostle, not only in the fact that he was made pope and was followed by a regular succession, but even in the sculpture and painting of the middle ages in which arts Peter always enjoyed the richest colors and robes, and the whitest blocks of marble. Moses, David, Peter, were the favorites of the artists.

Innocently, and even unconsciously, St. Paul was left under a cloud. He was so world-wide, so separated from forms and from localities, that, to the half-civilized ages, he was almost invisible, while Peter with keys in his hand and with the suspicion of being a rock upon which a Church could be built for the keys to lock and unlock, became very visible indeed. That which men wish to see is always the most visible. With the ideas that Paul held, that forms were of little value, that neither circumcision nor uncircumcision availed, that neither meat nor no meat, holy days nor no holy days, contained any merit, that nothing was of any value except the new creature, the new soul within, it was impossible for him to rise into first notice and first love in an age to which forms had been the dearest and best thing. The world was oligarchic, despotic, aristocratic, in all its education and hopes. Empire was its largest idea. Peter supposed to be a rock of government, and supposed to possess keys, was, therefore, worth a thousand times more than St. Paul, who was an exponent of man universal and of a religion of only the heart. Peter stood for empire, Paul for the soul.

Such an age did not, and would not, calmly weigh the two ideas, the Paul and Peter, and declare Peter to suit and delight it the more. It would simply grasp

Peter by its instinct. It would not deliberately reject Paul. It would never dream of his being anything valuable. When Indians select colored beads and ribbons from white explorers, they do not condemn the books, the laws, the schools of the white race. They do nothing and think nothing on the subject. They grasp by instinct and lay hold upon gaudy colors and objects of sense. So the early Church did not rationally condemn Paul; it reached out its arms by instinct and grasped the man that possessed the keys of power. The act was that of a child, not that of a philosopher. Accustomed to an empire, it grasped for a sword as did the infant Achilles.

In this unconscious neglect Christ Himself suffered, not a little, along with his apostle. It was, of course, impossible for any age wholly to overlook Christ. Paul was one of twelve and could be escaped, but Christ was one of one. He was alone. But what was denied the age in the power to ignore, it atoned for in the power to interpret badly. Compelled to see Christ, it interpreted Him by its own instinct, and made of Him a regal prince anxious to grind to powder many enemies and to exalt a few friends. The monarchic instinct that doomed Paul to obscurity, doomed the Christ to the similitude of a rude King, rather than clothe Him with the beauty of a Saviour. And thus the great cloud of keys of empire, of material things, of forms, of thrones, of princes and slaves, of pomp and circumstance threw its shadow far down the valley of human life, even down to the Pilgrims and Puritans.

Paul and his Master, belonging to a new era, to one of spirituality and human equality, it was necessary for them both to lie in partial shadow until their new era should come. If there was an instinct that could grasp the literal keys and local empire, so there would be an instinct that would grasp a new life and a kingdom of man universal. Paul, along with his Saviour, must wait for this. Fitted for a spiritual life they must stand until the pageant of Peter had passed by.

Another great shadow followed the Church. It was that of the Mosaic age. Moses and David were grand monarchs. Their brilliant power and severe institutions have haunted the Christian era in all its long career. Notwithstanding the sermons of Christ and the terrible eloquenee of St. Paul about the dissolution of the Mosaic economy, the empire of the Hebrew State was so deeply in harmony with the taste of bishops and popes that the laws of Moses carried away the study and love that belonged to the Sermon on the Mount and the new truths of the Pauline letters. The Mosaic age died slowly. As by long paths ages come, by long paths they depart. This shadow of Hebrew power followed the Church, not only up to the reformation of Luther, but up to the Pilgrim fathers, who still wished to seize upon some country as Moses had seized upon Palestine, and to banish Quakers and Hugenots, as Moses had silenced the Philistines and Amorites.

The fact that the Westminster Assembly passed an edict as to what is required and what forbidden in the ten commandments and neglected to inquire was is enjoined and what forbidden in the Sermon on the Mount, shows that the empire of Moses was still intruding itself upon the presence of Christ. It is not to be wondered at that in all these long centuries the more spiritual and liberal ideas of St. Paul lay in the oblivion of neglect. Full of universal love, reckless of geographical lines, hostile to the outward, devoted to the new life, wholly separate from earthly power and kings, living beyond Moses as manhood outranks infancy, and rapt in the vision of Jesus Christ, Paul was compelled to wait until the rise of liberty should destroy alike the sceptre of Moses and the sceptre of the pope. He waited the time to lead mankind to a religion of the spirit, and to the Sermon on the mountain side.

Luther unveiled the image of Paul. That hand lifted some of the heaviest drapery. A thousand material things were consumed by his touch, and the faith of the soul in Jesus Christ became brilliantly visible. Luther thundered against penance and works just as Paul thundered against the outward forms of the Jews; and against popes and states just as Paul had declaimed against an earthly Jerusalem and the caste of the Hebrews. Luther was one of the first flowers of the seed sown by the Saint. Then followed the wide German and English efflorescence. In such mortals as John Wesley and Whitfield and Duff, and almost the whole school of those men, the soul of Paul beams forth, a sun that had been long clouded. They are all the abandonment of the papal idea and are the escape from the shadow of the Mosaic age. They are a reproduction of Christ; an acceptance of the Church of Jesus and Paul.

Paul's ideas, those of democracy, of spirituality, instead of ceremony, of attachment to Jesus Christ, were too great for the first fifteen centuries. They must needs lead a semi-life until the spread of intelligence and republicanism should help abolish rites, and place all men upon one level, not only before God, but, what is more difficult, before men.

An age will never accept anything at discord with itself. An aristocratic State will demand aristocratic religion, schools and amusements. An ignorant, superstitious country will require a superstitious literature and religion. The stories they tell their children will be about ghosts and wonders. As an iron magnet will not attract gold dust, nor brass, nor silver, will gather up nothing but the dust of itself, will lift nothing but kindred iron, so an age will lay hold of no idea out of harmony with its heart. Monarchy grasped Moses and St. Peter, and let fall all else. Universal liberty reaches out for its own children and draws to its bosom Christ and His large souled apostle. The development that has plucked iron crowns from the foreheads of kings has plucked them from the foreheads of priests, and has given us not only a people's government, but a people's Saviour.

But for Paul, it is thought by many students of history that Judaism would have carried its circumcision and seclusiveness and awful despotism right forward for perhaps a thousand years. It would have wound the thorns of the State laws around the body of Christ, a wreath of pain and despair around a symbol of hope. The revolt of St. Paul weakened the old dispensation, and led John and the subsequent Christians into the beginnings of a new career. Paul's steady light abates the Mosaic shadow.

All history, profane and sacred, contains proofs that God embodies His truth in some human heart, buries it there and commands it to blossom as fast as men give it sunshine enough, and only so fast.

In the bosom of Moses there lay ideas beyond his people. They laughed them and him to scorn. But in a few centuries, the Hebrew commonwealth grew grand all over with the outgrowth of Mosaic truths. Not grand compared with a modern ideal, but compared with what was and had been. In the outset Moses was too great for his people. In the end the people had caught up with their leader. No phenomenon is more frequent. In St. Paul was buried the gospel of spirituality, of all humanity, of a pure heart and of Jesus Christ.

The first idea of spirituality sounded the death knell of forms. Circumcision or uncircumcision would avail naught, but the "new creature."

The second idea, "all humanity," abolished popes and powers, fagots and proscription, the exaltation of the creed of Apollos or Cephas, and raised a slave to the rank of a son of God.

The third idea of a pure life announced the end of a salvation by means of a complex machinery of doctrine and the dawn of a new era of honesty and piety.

The fourth idea, Jesus Christ, yesterday, to-day and forever, cast Christianity into the form of a personal friendship and love for the divine Saviour. For Paul to live was Christ,—to die, gain, because death sent him to Christ. The world resolved itself into the presence of the Saviour.

In Paul's bosom, more than in any other human heart, were planted these four ideas—four rivers in the paradise of religion. As when Moses came down from the mount his face was radiant with a light not visible to those around him, but streaming off to beat upon shores five hundred years away, as Galileo and Bacon spoke words that were unheard by those nearest, but were borne by some strange reverberation to a multitude afar off, so Paul, more divinely, carried in his bosom truth-germs destined to blossom far away from the tomb of his dust. Perhaps these seeds are now disturbing the soil of this century.

Think of these four great ideas. Spirituality! This is nothing else than a divineness of soul, a rising above things material, gold and lands and raiment, and living for the soul in its relations to time and eternity. God is called a spirit because there are characteristics in all material things that separate them from perfection. The word spirit is the ideal for the everlasting. It is an embodimen. of love, and of thought, and of truth, and of life, and hence is felt to be immortalt The spiritual man is hence a soul not wedded to dust, but to truth, love and life. To be spiritually minded is life. In Paul's grand religion, rites availed nothing. Circumcision, baptism, set days, sects of Paul and Apollos, were all of no moment compared with that spiritual cast of the soul, able, like angels' wings, to bear man to immortality.

Look at his second idea. The oneness of humanity! Oh sublime sentiment! Had Catharine de Medici known it, she would have clasped the Hugenots to her bosom and said, "I love you all." Had Calvin felt its infinite tenderness, he would have thrown his arms about Servetus and said, "Live and be happy, my brother. I differ with you, but love you." But this idea must await the birth of democracy.

Look at Paul's third idea. A new life, a new creature! It will be the development of this idea that will announce the dawn of a perfect civilization and a golden age.

The church has tried the religion of dogmas. The Scotch churches reached a creed of four thousand articles, but that church, and all branches of all churches, have furnished thousands of men for every branch of dishonesty and crime.

The men that commit acts of crime and dishonor, the men who commit frauds in the money circles, come, in part, from the multitude that carry a catechism or a Book of Common Prayer. All this because religion has been a form of argument rather than a shape of the inner life. Oh blessed age will that be when a holy life shall be the aim and significance of religion, and when it shall be universally confessed that unless one has the spirit of Christ he is none of His.

But, passing all these, look at Paul's fourth passion. Love for Jesus Christ! I shall say little here because the measurement of words fail.

In sounding the sea, places were found where the lead failed, and for hours the vessel would sail with the sounding line coiled on its bow, there being no use for it in the awful silence beneath. Paul's attachment to Jesus Christ is beyond our cold, feeble measurement. For him to live was Christ. To die was gain, for the soul joined its Friend. As children live for the happiness that spring and summer and winter promise to their glad hearts; as they long for the morning because of the new pleasure it will bring; as for them to live is pleasure; as Pitt and Burke and Webster lived for country, and honor, and human law; as for them to live was fame and greatness, so for Paul to live was Jesus Christ. He slept and awoke in that sacred prepossession. To die would be gain because the great golden cloud that enveloped him did not belong to earth, but was only the outskirt of a radiance that threw its sheen forward from the vast sea of endless life.

My dear friends, measure these four ideas of Paul and behold in them the coming glory of Christianity and the coming blessedness of man. Liberty and intelligence are the conditions of society that are able to accept of these four ideas of religion. And as liberty and intelligence are gradually advancing, so these essentials of Christianity are rising more and more upon the soul's horizon. Science cannot injure them. The welfare of society will make men always return to them. They will always prove too useful to be destroyed, too truthful to be denied, too comforting in life and in death to remain unloved.

A BROAD ORTHODOXY.

"To the intent that now unto the principalities and powers in heavenly places might be known by the Church the manifold wisdom of God."—*Eph.*, iii: 10.

The theme drawn from this text for your thought this morning is contained chiefly in the words "manifold wisdom of God." The other ideas of the passage may be alluded to after this one thought shall have been studied.

If, as some suppose, Christianity is to be all summed up in any one doctrine, then the Bible is an unusually large book for so simple a purpose. But if God has made the Church and the Bible a mirror in some sense of His vast and varied thought as to the duty and destiny of His children, then the Bible in its immense store of truth between Genesis and the Apocalypse is only a picture of the manifold wisdom of its author. Whoever reads the oracles of religion as contained in our Scripture must feel how fitted they are to the many forms of human want and character. If there are minds fond of symbols, they may find all through the Old Testament or in the vision of St. John a statement rendered almost wholly in the language of symbolism. When we remember the happiness and the knowledge which the buoyant, poetic years of youth reach through figures of speech drawn from the material world, we must rejoice that the book which is to influence their moral career is so full of figurative language from the Psalms of David to the last chapter in John's revelation. Although an immense amount of time and labor has been wasted over the effort to make literal prophecies out of John's poem and to find fulfillment along the path of history, yet, notwithstanding this long error, the poetic part of the world has extracted a great amount of good theology from those pages so terrific as to the wicked, so glorious as to the righteous. From that book comes the New Jerusalem, the White Throne, the River of Life, the Pearly Gates, the Crystal Sea. When we remember also what a multitude there is of less poetic and more formal minds, we feel the value of the great apostle who spoke always as a solid reasoner with definite premises and definite conclusions. In the world everywhere there is a group, more limited indeed, but powerful, who study questions of duty as between man and man, and man and God, and to these what an exhaustless fountain of thought is opened up in the sermons and words of Jesus. Here the Quakers exhaust their life and love. This many-sided wisdom of God has, however, another significance at which it is our purpose more particularly now to refer. There is a many-sidedness of doctrine just as marked as the variety of literary or logical style. We come along with our ardent desire to form a catechism or a formula that shall include and evermore contain the wisdom of God to men, but no sooner do we close up our estimate and prepare to rejoice over our work, than along comes some new student or some new age and reminds us of something important left out. In his history of Christian doctrine, Dr. Shedd alludes to perhaps a score of catechisms, all which sprang up within a small area of space, and all which compilations differed from each other. The variations of Protestants formed the theme of a long and once called powerful argument against the Protestant sect. So numerous had catechism become before the day of John Knox, and as varying as numerous, that he announced when he published his, that if any friends discovered some point wherein it seemed to come in contact with Scripture he would change it in the next edition. This multiplicity of confession of faith must descend from the fact that the study of God is too high and too broad for man, and that after his most patient effort he must sit down over the result saying, "Hast thou by searching found out God? Canst thou find out the Almighty to perfection?" And next to the infinity of God as rendering incomplete the theologies of men comes the wonderful scope of human want and character. There are myriads of hearts and myriads of minds, and large must be the volume of truth which shall offer food for all at all times. There have been timid, distrusting souls which have gone through life feeding all the way upon a score of truths culled from the Bible, which truths would have been of little price had they been repeated to the ear of the extreme egotist. There have been sorrowful souls, such as Cowper, and pensive souls, such as Fenelon, over which has daily passed like an autumnal sigh the breath of only a few sad doctrines, as if the gorgeousness of summer had gone by and nought remained but for her faded leaves to fall. When Maria de-La-Mothe read the Bible she never passed away from the New Testament, and seldom from the story of Christ as related by St. John, for her religion being one of love to Christ, she passed her life where He was nearest in His words and character. For her to live, was Christ.

This immense scope of the Bible, and this similar breadth of human life, are facts which render it a vain attempt to gather up Christianity into a catechism, and thus treasure it up for ourselves and our children. A "Confession of Faith" can be only an imperfect index of the book. In some editions of Homer and Virgil there stands an argumentum at the head of each canto to tell us what the next thousand lines are all about; but, oh! how dead that statement to the mind that knows what a world of beauty and sentiment, and of joy and suffering, is beyond, flashing in the sunshine of genius, and arrayed in the full verdure of the heart and the drapery of language.

When we behold the magnificence of the world and the greatness of man, and then turn also to the throne where He sits, to whom earth and man are both as nought, we realize how vain must be the desire of the spirit to find some symbol in language which shall carry in it the meaning of the great book of religion lying open for the guidance and salvation of society. It is amid some of the manifold shadings to doctrine Paul stands in the letter to the Corinthians, and at the close of a most eloquent review he names three virtues, and then declares charity to be the greatest of the three. Whether it is the euthusiasm of the orator or the calm reason of the philosopher which speaks is uncertain, but this we know, that he places faith and hope both in the second place compared with the heart's love. It would seem to us un-Presbyterian in any way to slight the faith which has so covered itself with glory since the reformation, but who ever reads the Bible with any thoughtfulness will often find his favorite word quite overthrown and the substance of things put in its place. The worship of words is wonderfully overthrown in that book, and go to what term you please you will soon hear the commandment, "Thou shalt have no other gods before me." No sooner have you concluded that there is nothing valuable but faith than along comes the same Paul and says, "We are saved by hope;" and before your soul becomes fitted to this surprise or can call a council together to announce "hope" as a *saving* doctrine, the same Paul has declared that charity is better than either hope or faith; and while you stand amazed amid these heresies James comes along, and declares that "by works are ye saved."

Now these are not contradictory voices, but harmonious tones. Each one of these terms presents a phase of Christian experience. They are colors in gorgeous moral landscape. As among the hills in autumn a company of rambling friends will say to each other, "What a blue in that sky! what a russet on that oak! what a crimson in those leaves! what a saffron here, what a purple there!" so in the words of God the free mind turning its pages must say, "What faith! what hope! what works! what baptism! there is in these rules of life and death." A faithful reading of the Bible is the death of all words worship. The life and salvation portrayed in it are so Godlike that they elude exact definition and pass and repass before us as the heavens move over us by night, with depths we cannot measure, and with stars we cannot count. Our books of doctrine are valuable as outline indices of a volume too large to be fully mastered or retained, but compared to God's word they are as a skeleton of the dead body compared with that body itself when, robed in beauty, it greeted its friends in the street or was the life of the sacred home.

The Baptist is a person who sat down to read the Testament, and who came to four or five passages which informed him "that he that believes and is baptised shall be saved," but who paused before he came to the sixth statement, which would have omitted the immersion and have said, "He that believes shall be saved." The Solifidian is nothing but a Bible reader who, having found five texts that give salvation to faith only, went away and made up his creed without waiting for any remarks from any quarter about good works or immersion. The Fatalist is a mortal who has turned the sacred book over to find passages that should indicate the absolute empire of God and the abject humility of man, and fixing his whole gaze at last upon the figure of "clay in the hands of the potter," has announced the dogma "that man is predestined to his condition on account of nothing he has done or ever could do, but solely by the will of God; while the Arminian is one who has read all such words as "come unto me," "seek and ye shall find," "whosoever will let him take the water of life freely." Hence, much of each creed is only an indication to the world as to what part of the Bible the makers of it had canvassed. When a ship anchors at New York, and begins to unload a cargo of oranges and pineapples, you perceive at once that that vessel does not come in from all nations, from Greenland and England and Germany, but from some island or port in the Southern sea. It is thus in the world of theology When you pick up a confession of faith of any Church and read a few pages, you perceive at once that the book has not come in from all the great Bible of the Almighty, but that this particular ship has received its cargo at Dort, or Nice, or Geneva. Far be it from you, I hope, to despise these human compendiums of truth, for a book is valuable if, in condensed form, it makes only a tolerable estimate of the divine truth; for going to the Bible yourself alone you would not be able to deduce so full or true a philosophy of life and salvation. When the Westminster assembly sat in council for four years, it is fairly presumable that they summed up the doctrines of the Bible, as would have been impossible to the world that stood in vast multitude without. Hence it would be folly and vanity not to confess the value of their great digest. But after all this admiration, we know that creeds are not the places where divine wisdom fully expresses itself, but are the places where the human mind fails, places where the mind gives up and seeks rest. The creed of the Baptist only informs us where the student paused; and the creed of the Fatalist only tells us what verses he read. Thus paused; and the creed of the Fatalist only tells us what verses he read. Thus all these compendiums are marks set up to tell us where the toiler quit work.

Do you recall to mind, my friends, how weary Dr. Chalmers became of these human forms in his later years? After he had preached his astronomical sermons, and had by scientific study begun to see how vast a thing the universe is, he seems to have outgrown the mediæval theology, and to have placed great stress upon the general but unpopular idea of being a good Christian. In Dean Stanley's "History of the Church of Scotland," the historian says, "Even late in life he, Chalmers, was accused by *suspicious zealots* of being an enemy to systematic theology, and his reply was certainly not calculated to allay the alarm." I omit the reply. It was in brief that he preferred "the New Testament." Who those "suspicious zealots" were, Dean Stanley does not state, and perhaps it would be impossible for any historian to separate their names from the oblivion which comes soon and deep to minds that are only "suspicious zealots" in the great battle of life.

The accusation brought about no reform, for in the debate over the "Sustentation Fund" Dr. Chalmers exclaimed, "Who cares about the Free Church compared with the Christian good of the people of Scotland? Who cares about any Church but as an instrument of the most Christian good? For, be assured that the moral and religious well being of the people is of infinitely higher importance than the advancement of any sect."

Chalmers in one of his broad discourses quoted this little fragment of verse:

"The man
That could surround the sum of things, and spy
The heart of God and secrets of His empire,
Would speak but love. With love, the bright result
Would change the hue of intermediate things,
And make one thing of all theology."

These thoughts and this poetry from Dr. Ghalmers, too, in his glorious old age! It is not to be wondered at that under the leadings of such hearts the Free Church of Scotland sprang forward to a great career. His was not the only wide soul of that day. The almost equally great Dr. Duncan expressed ideas equally heretical and alarming. He said: "There is a progressive element in religion. It is a mistake to look upon our fathers as our seniors. They are our juniors. The Church has advanced wonderfully since its foundations were laid." * * * "I am first a Christian, next a broad Christian, thirdly a Calvinist, and fourthly a Presbyterian."

I have drawn these illustrations from history to remind you that the manifold glory of God is too varied and too vast to be caged up in the phrases of a few men at some given time and place. Say what we may in our condensed formulas, the glory of God will flash on in the New Testament as though we had taken nothing away from its profusion. Our creed is a few flowers plucked from the vast prairie between Lake Michigan and the Missouri.

After you have declared that one is saved by only the deity of Christ, I turn to the book of books and find the disciples all busy with His humanity alone. And after you have cried out "faith alone," I find Magdalen much forgiven because she had loved much, and Peter forgiven because of his tears of penitence, while the woman who emptied the alabaster box seemed blessed on account of her good works done in the name of Jesus. The truth is, salvation seems like the city of Thebes, entered by any one of a hundred gates, all beautiful portals of marble or bronze, or glittering brass, but all opening from the dreary, lonely country into the splendor of society and art and government. But come in by any gate, it was Thebes you perceived and reached. So in religion, be the golden gate, faith or hope, or charity, or penitence, or virtue, it opens out upon the presence of Christ. He must be the central object, the motive of the footstep, the vision before the eye, whether the eye is radiant with a saving hope or bedimmed with penitential tears.

Now we are informed in the text that the Church was organized to make known to principalities and power this many-colored wisdom of God. To the raptured vision of St. Paul, to his elevated mind, which never took a common view of any subject, but to which all the truths of religion loomed up toward the very throne of the Almighty, it seemed that the Church was established that it might unfold the glory of God before all the potentates of earth and heaven. So grand was this redemption of a world to be, that it seemed to Paul even the very seraphim in heaven would look down upon earth and see God's love pouring forth through Jesus Christ and flooding the earth, not in wrath as in the days of Noah, but with the windows of heaven open for a new outpouring—that of infinite grace.

As in presence, therefore, of an august company which Paul calls "principalities and powers," and to which we, less poetic, less divine, and more earthy, add the nations of the earth, the heathen world, the educated world, the skeptical world, as being the "principalities and powers" that plainly encompass us all,—in such a presence, let us make the Church a place not where the narrowness and vanity of man are unfolded, but where all eyes looking may catch glimpses of the manifold wisdom of God. The manifold discords of man have already made sad havoc of this manifold wisdom of the Creator and Savior. The Church has been so narrowed that it would seem not ordained as a gate to heaven, but as a wall to keep the world away from its bliss. The principalities and powers looking down from heavenly places must see the tumults of sects rather than the sparkling sea of redeeming love. Oh, may these scenes hasten away from earth, and may the Church throw open all the gates of life, that future ages may see the world coming to salvation by many roads, some by faith, some by love, some by hope, some by charity, but all by one Christ as He is freely offered to all in the Gospel.

INFLUENCE OF DEMOCRACY ON CHRISTIAN DOCTRINE.

One generation passeth away, and another generation cometh; but the earth abideth forever. *Ecclesiastes 1 : 4.*

This verse from the Bible is read, not as a text out of which a discourse may be developed, but rather as a pensive thought, which suggests a line of reflection, perhaps beyond the meaning of Solomon, and hence beyond the warrant of the passage. All we claim for the words is that they invite the heart to mark how generations come and go, bearing away with them their customs and thoughts in part, and leaving the stage of action clear for a new scene. Paul also said, "The fashion of this world passeth away." Cicero said, "The times are changed, and we are changed in them." Paul in his Corinthian letter confesses that his teachings were modified by the times which he described as being a "present distress." The greatest Being of earth declared that some Mosaic customs were authorized on account of a local and temporary "hardness of heart." Thus by these voices, sacred and profane, we are reminded of the changes taking place in the internal and external appearances of society, in its dress, machinery, arts, beliefs, sentiments and hopes.

There are a few mortals who, by some strange fatality, have escaped learning this lesson of a changing world, and who are ready to denounce as infidel, the mind that presumes any part of the past to have become the subject of repeal. Antiquity is their test of truth.

From this bondage to that which has nothing to recommend it but its dust, the majority of the public, especially in cities, has escaped, and in their presence there is no longer need for proof that the times are always busy reshaping the ideas and the things of yesterday. The same activity and progress that are shaping the implements of industry and the material pursuits of men, are shaping also their thoughts, beliefs, motives and hopes.

The whole Mosaic economy was an adaptation of moral teachings to a particular condition, and hence, when the Saviour came, His first work was to remove ideas that had lived beyond their proper time. The law of eye for eye, tooth for tooth, the law of divorce, the law of caste, were all repealed or modified in answer to the demands of a new era.

We have thus the highest authority of a personal nature for confessing and expecting all the ideas of men to be modified, repealed or enlarged, by the influence of new times and places. To this authority of person, we add the facts of human life, which go to show that ideas are modified by climate, and government, and by the popular education. What has been useful in one age has been useless in another, not because the idea has ceased to be true, but because it has ceased to be pleasing to the public heart. The doctrine of God's absolute sovereignity is just as true as it was in the days of King Œdipus or of Calvin. It will always remain a confessed fact, that God's will must be the supreme will of the world, but while this is confessed, yet we do perceive that our age as a fact, passes over the great absolutism in silence, compared with the age of Athens or Geneva, and God's love and sweet Fatherhood become more visible than His absolute despotism.

To pass by a truth, is not to contradict it, nor despise it, any more than to study the law is to despise or deny the claim of science or theology. To pass by a truth is often nothing else than to sail by England when your destiny is France, or to omit France when your errand is to England. It is not a condemnation, but a selection. It is not possible that any one age shall make use of all known truths at once and equally, for truth is like a grand armory where are stored all the equipments for warfare, but from which it is not to be expected that every arm and flag and chariot and signal shall be withdrawn at any one time. The armory is a place to draw from, but not to exhaust.

The world of truth is always greater than the world of men, and hence there will always be great truths lying in silence and in neglect, like fields in fallow waiting for some future season that shall demand them for a new sowing and harvest.

In the realm of principles, as in the old world of the classics, there are great silences and solitudes. In our American continent there are vast countries from which man in his civilized state long since departed, leaving behind him ruins of former magnificence, now overgrown with the ivy and the cactus. The vales are richer than New England, and the climate fairer than that which roars about these lakes, but yet man has gone away, leaving traces of his heart and mind in the carved rocks, and terraced gardens. Thus society marches away from one part of the dominion of truth, and, dying, leaves its children to roam to some other shore, perhaps more bleak, perhaps more like to paradise. When one generation passeth away, it will nearly always be found that it took a great deal with it, movable property, gifts, relics, household gods. And when the other generation cometh, lo! in its arms are strange new things, very sacred, and the centres of new hopes and action. Fugitives from famine or fire, try to carry with them household divinities. Exiled generations going from life, have their arms full of customs and ideas that never are seen again on our shores — customs which they could assimilate into healthy food for the soul, but which were rejected by their children.

Next to the supersedure of truths, comes the expansion or contraction of ideas that remain. About many moral statements there hangs always an indefiniteness that makes it possible for each era to expand or contract them. Physical truths may be retained in one form. At our national Capitol there are standards of the inch, the bushel, the quart, the pound, so that the silk or grain of this year may be bought and sold by the measurement agreed upon in the past. It is said that the old kings of Egypt became so anxious that measurements in that kingdom, should forever remain the same, that they built the pyramids, that upon their immovable sides, and in their minute recesses, the empire might always find the standard of all surveys and measurements, from the miles of the highway, to the smallest measure of wheat and wine. When we come to moral ideas, however, we are compelled to do without any standards. There is no stone pyramid to which we can go to adjust our line, no hollowed rock in which we can pour our quart of wine to see if it corresponds to the quart of the Egyptian kings of four thousand years ago. There are thousands of people who will not confess this to be true, and who will contend that they do possess a stone pyramid upon whose sides they can measure all the ideas of religion and duty, but after years of careful search, you will find yourself unable to discover their pyramid in the objective world. It is only a mental structure, a life long hallucination.

To illustrate this part of our discourse, let us take the idea of "Church." Let the Episcopalians define it, and certain demands are essential that are rejected by the Presbyterians. Let the Presbyterian define it, and he has come into conflict with the Baptist and the Covenanter. Along come the Plymouth Brethren and define the Church to be a body of men assembling, for the hour, to worship. They may never assemble again, but while they were together they were a Church. Dr. Hodge, the most learned thinker the Presbyterians have in this age, declares the Church to be in the heart, and that each soul that loves Christ, is a member of the Church.

Now this is what I mean by the elasticity of a moral idea. These notions are enlarged or contracted, according to the genius of the generation that comes to them here or there. All moral ideas, from the conception of God, to the most humble duty, all doctrines from faith, hope and charity, to the notion of heaven and hell, suffer or undergo this sliding form of measurement, and baffle all attempts to render a final and exact expression. They are infinite in the mathematical sense of the term.

Having now seen that ideas are wont, in some instances, to withdraw from the human arena, and in other instances to undergo limitation or expansion, let us inquire what influence we should expect our land to exert upon the Christian ideas that have invaded it from foreign shores. That no changes would be wrought, could be believed only by those who suppose themselves to possess the standards of measurement, to own a pyramid of solid rock. This is a small multitude, indeed not a multitude at all, but a group. That no changes would be wrought might be the opinion of persons giving no thought to the matter. Of these, the multitude is large indeed. That changes, many and valuable, should be expected, is certainly the conclusion of all who, with free minds, pay any attention to the common influence of government and climate and race over the thoughts of mankind. Just what and how many these changes are, time would fail us here to inquire. You may at your leisure carry forward the task we begin, and you will find the whole matter to a high degree, pleasing and useful.

Coming to a land of gigantic human industry, where the motto is, each one is the builder of his own fortune, to a land where a farmer boy in Kentucky bears himself forward to the place of chief orator, or where a penniless youth lifts himself up to be a millionaire, and a noble citizen; and where this is occuring all the time, the daily phenomenon of the last fifty years, Christianity must expect its fatalism to be shaded, and its doctrine of human freedom and responsibility to stand forth in a more brilliant light. The surrender of all things to God, the resolution of life into a waiting for fate, or into a machine that was powerless to go or to stop of itself, was a conception of God suited to an age when citizens possessed no liberty as to their state, and no industry as to changing their fortune or fame or happiness. An idle country, and an oppressed, powerless country, always underrate the human will, and overstate the Divine interference. Having been denied the privilege and opportunity of toiling for self, men have at last resolved self into despair, and God into an absolute despot.

A free country where the human will and personality rise up into such grand proportions, is the land that might be expected to transform man into a being of personal power, and God into a Father, acting in harmony with His children. The monks in their cells, the middle ages in their bondage to kings, priests and ignorance, possessed no great consciousness of free agency, and hence that was the generation to ignore man, and to enthrone a pitiless fate under the name of God; but the age which, in a perfectly free country, permits every man to carve out for himself a happiness, and education, and fame, is the age to develop the consciousness of free agency, and hence the age to bind more nearly together, man and God, as acting in concert. Political freedom develops the human consciousness of free will and responsibility.

This perpetual industry amid external pursuits, also diverts the mind from the study of mysteries, to the acceptance and enjoyment of facts, and hence the public mind turns away from predestination and reprobation and absolutism, not simply because it has developed a consciousness of freedom, but also because in the long association with facts, it has lost love for the study of the incomprehensible, in both religion and philosophy. In this casting off of old garments, it no more cheerfully throws away the inconceivable of Christianity, than the inconceivable of Kant and Spinoza. In this abandonment, there is no charge of falsehood cast upon the old mysteries; they may or may not be true; there is only a passing them by as not being in the line of the current wish or taste, raiment for a past age, perhaps for a future, but not acceptable in the present.

Out of this enlargement of the office of man's free will, have come the great missionary movements, and the Sunday and ragged schools of our land. The philosophy of waiting for God has been quite superseded by the enormous development of industry and free-agency that our land has produced. Man is raised, not to a state of vanity, but of responsibility. He feels that God waits for His children to come to His help against the mighty. Here and there a fatalist remains to remind us of the stupor and palsy of antiquity. A Cincinnati clergyman has recently published a labored article to show that Christianity is spreading as rapidly as God desires, and that all human efforts to hasten the world's evangelization are vain and presumptuous; but this ignoring of man's office as a co-laborer of God on earth, this assumption of man's living death is a phenomenon appearing but rarely on the horizon of our republic. Types of men, like types of birds or beasts, pass away slowly, as sometimes an individual creature is found after science has declared the species to have become entirely extinct. Thus types of belief die slowly.

That God has assigned man a work to do here in this vale, and that He has equipped man for doing it, is an idea cast forward greatly by a republic full of human freedom and human achievements. A religion of repose is killed by a politics of activity.

Permit me, therefore, to assume that our republic has tended toward the overthrow of the ideas of human insignificance and of fatality, and of simple divine despotism; and, transforming God into a Father, has made man a co-laborer without whose assistance the moral world pauses just as the plow stands still when man deserts the field for a life of indolence. Man's relations to morals and to agriculture are the same so far as human vision can scan the landscape.

Passing by this illustration of the influence of our land upon religious ideas we may find another example in the distinction now made between doctrines, a discrimination that divides them rapidly in essential and non-essential ideas. In the past, not remote, not only was there a vast multitude of dogmas, but they were all deemed very vital. To hold to apostolic succession or to immersion, or to psalmody, or to infant baptism, or to the divineness of slavery, was deemed a large part of soul salvation. A free soil politician was an infidel, and on the opposite a slave-holder had a poor prospect of heaven. Here we need not particularize. You all know by heart all this black page in church history.

Well, along came a country in which everything was destined to be vast. It embraced every climate, every wood, every ore, every grain, and fruit. Its waters assumed every shape from ocean to lake, from mighty river to mountain brook. Its railways were to run three thousand miles in a straight line, and, starting among New England pines, to end among Pacific orange groves. All nations were to meet in the citizens of this new world. Over this land so vast there was to float a banner of freedom and equality, education and industry. Such was to be the character of the new realm except that words are not able to paint the image in the prophecy. In the gradual fulfillment of this prophecy, which has already gone beyond the promise, it readily came to pass that all that is small in religion began to become manifest as such. The daily struggle amid great things, with the heart full of only leading ideas, built up early a special sense that could discern the large and the small in wealth, in machinery, in agriculture, in character and in Christianity. Ideas that had once been immense underwent great reduction in this uprising of thought, and ideas in themselves infinite, such as Christ, and worship, and faith, charity, virtue, these, vast as the oceans around and the continent between them, came at once into power, not by accident, but by the command of a land of vast spirit and destiny. The whole drift of the country was toward a sifting of thoughts.

Not only did the vastness of the land toil towards this result, but the internal genius of it by which a hundred nations were contributing different races and tongues to be moulded into one brotherhood, made it essential that ideas in which the multitudes differed should be speedily forgotten, and that those in which they agreed only should be remembered and cherished.

Now, the essential ideas of morals and salvation, are the ones in which only most minds agree, and hence the nature of the case united with the vast spirit of the country in exalting the great truths of Christianity and in lulling to sleep the infantine dogmas. These are not condemned as wholly useless, much less as false, but are passed by as if in a sweet sleep, which it were cruelty to disturb.

There are truths in Christianity of infinite worth. Without them, the soul is lost. With them it passes along the paths of usefulness here, and comes beyond to paradise. It ought to have been anticipated that a land like this, trained in an air of greatness, and seeking also a brotherhood that would bind many minds in its silken links, would find the absolute essentials in Christian doctrine and give them its hand and heart. It has done so beyond anticipation, and in its arms, loving and omnipotent, it is bearing us along, compelling us to accept of her destiny as our own. It is vain we were taught the Calvinistic creed, for we perceive the Arminian is borne along equally toward heaven. It is vain we were taught the Arminian creed, for we perceive the Calvinist is just as far toward God's love and bliss. O beautiful disregard of names! The country in declaring all men to be one, and in its greatness and in its effort to make a brotherhood in society, has invaded the domain of the spirit, and, plucking our badges from our bosom, has whispered, "You are all one brotherhood, also in religion." Thus have we built up a state whose soul has outgrown the body politic and has marched into the temple of God. We remember now the German cottager's dream. His humble cot, while he slept, lifted up its rafters and became a cathedral. The chimney became a spire. The windows became gothic and filled with colored glass. His fireplace became an altar, and his children, living and gone, became seraphim bending over that mercy-seat.

Thus while you and I sleep our state becomes a sanctuary. Its liberty, its free will, its greatness of idea, its equality of man, its brotherhood, all enter our once humble abode and lift it all upward and outward as in the transformation of that German dream.

It is impossible for the state to be engaged making us brothers and the church to be engaged making us enemies and strangers. One of the other effort must abandon the field. The church bows justly to the spirit of the Republic. In India, two communion tables are spread so that the converted Brahmin may not touch the cup the poor native of low caste has polluted. This is an easy result in India, but where the state makes all one, then religion also hastens to accept of the harmony.

You may, my friends, at your leisure, seek and find further instances of this modification of Christian belief by the new surroundings of government. Christian customs will also be modified along with the creed. Not that something absolutely better will always be found, but something more demanded by the accidents of the time. The themes of the pulpit will always be assigned afresh by each new generation. When our catechisms were being written, the chief enemy upon the horizon was the Romanist full of error and cruelty, and hence many are the darts aimed by the Westminster soldiers at the papal hosts. With the overthrow of the papal throne new arrows and armor are demanded for new foes. The field of battle shifts from Paul to Genesis. The thumb-screw of the inquisition is not so much feared as the spade of the geologist. The mass and prayers for the dead are not so alarming as the crucible of the chemist. It is not Arius and Arminius now that we fear. It is Darwin and Buckle. New methods also arise. Once it was enough if the pulpit brought out to the multitude the statements found in the Holy Scriptures, but now the public has learned what is in the Scriptures, they ask us to prove that the Scriptures are holy. To unfold the text was the easy task of our fathers; to find the warrant of the text is the more difficult work of their children. A new method divested of authority and weighed down with rationalism and doubt, has gradually displaced the authoritative declaration and warning of yesterday. Christ comes not announced by a simple herald, but led by a spiritual and intellectual philosophy. The soul is asked to receive its own in the name of virtue, pardon and future life. The banner of the cross is borne by the impulse of its own fitness and beauty, rather than by the command of Buller and Paley. When Tyndall flies to the light, and heat, and dust, Christianity flies to the soul. Thus you will find that the public education has awakened a broader inquiry into branches of learning connected in some way with theology, and hence the pulpit is compelled to discuss themes that were foreign to its office a few years since. With the growth of rationalism, it must more carefully separate the true from the false to meet the new love of the real truth and the new ridicule of all superstition and folly. The truth will no longer bear a great admixture of falsehood.

In this republic of equality that places the rich and poor, the laborer and the clergyman, upon one plane, the whole language of abuse and denunciation has been banished from the sacred desk, so that Thomas Paine, if now alive, would enjoy the undreamed of pleasure of hearing his objections met by hearts of sympathy and tenderness, rather than by the hisses of an age full, equally, of vanity and revenge. Compared with former generations this one, most of all, discards the power of personal egotism based upon peculiar training in peculiar lines of thought, and, offering the right hand, says with a friendship that would have melted an old infidel to tears, "Come let us reason together."

But time fails me. There are some general statements I desire yet to make.

There need be no alarm about this abrasion of an old shore by a new wave, for we know that what the waters are stealing from some old bank where men have ceased to live, they are depositing elsewhere and making new homes for a better race, new streets for greater cities. The wave that carries something away always gives something back elsewhere to mankind. The coast changes, not the sea. And furthermore the abrasions upon the old shore are limited, for the encroaching sea deals only with alluvium or drift, and, having swept this clean by a hundred years' toil, it finds at last an admantine rock—an iron-bound coast where the waters cease their destruction, and, their work done, praise God in peace or storm.

"And all through winter's storm and summer's calm,
They rise and fall an everlasting psalm."

Thus Christianity possesses within itself, in its central Christ and doctrines, a coast, iron-bound, where all waves of thought must pause and become an anthem of divine praise, full of human hope and human gratitude.

In this rise and fall of ideas it is not very wonderful that we perceive no great commotion, and nowhere in orthodox denominations perceive any arraignment of individuals for departures from the faith. This absence of trials for heresy comes, not simply from the fact that there is little heresy in the case, for this has never been an influential fact, but this wide and deep peace comes from two other facts, first, that the age bears all its ministry toward the essential ideas and absorbs them at these points; and, second, that so far as there are any new departures they are universal rather than individual. If they were the new departures of one man there would be trial and discord, but they are the modifications of a whole generation, rather than the light of any individual. Whatever there is of the new in the present it has come to all equally and gently as the dew in the night. The jury is *particeps criminis* in the great case.

So far as my own vision can penetrate, and judgment infer, the pastors of this city in the denomination to which I belong, are of one mind in theological questions. It may be that some surpass others in admiration of the German maxim that "Silence is golden," and hence, have a better developed virtue of reticence, but to me, in an intimate acquaintaince with all, they seem all borne along in the wide arms of a country that has been the instrument under God, of revealing to them all the breadth and kindness of the Christian religion.

Generation passeth away, and generation cometh. This means that you will all soon become dust. The great invisible arms that are carrying religion and all ideas along, are carrying your body to its place in the waving grass, and your spirit back to God. Oh my friends, love that religion, that by command of God, fits itself so well to our country, our happiness, our life, our death. Say not it was for the past. Its superstition was for that, its truth is for the present and future. It assumes the image of the soul, and hence, was made, not for woman and for childhood, but for the human race. Our state builds up liberty, Christianity absorbs the idea and advances to freedom of the spirit. Our state demands public virtue. Christianity's favorite maxim is, "Blessed are the pure in heart." Our state loves humanity. Christianity silently points to Jesus Christ. Pass it not by. Oh may this generation, while it is passing along, number among its transformations, the transformation of your hearts into the image of the Saviour, that when, after a few years, it shall have strewn all your bodies like autumn leaves upon the earth, it may waft your spirits, redeemed and sanctified, back to your Maker.

THE WORLD'S GREAT NEED.

Ye must be born again.—*John* iii. 7.

The great pursuit of the wisest and best men that have ever lived, has been to help onward and upwards the morals of the people. By common consent the names of Socrates, Seneca, Marcus Aurelius, Luther, Calvin, Knox, Penn, George Fox, are the grandest of names. Besides such stars of fame, the lustre of a captain in bloody war, or of a Cresus, or Rothschild, fades away as glow-worms at sunrise. Nations have always looked with love and confidence upon their moralists. Mark the Chinese love for Confucius, and American love for the morals of Washington and Franklin. There is a common feeling that in such men lie the reasons for national success, and the basis of security. Out of them seem to issue the nation's moral life, as the tree grows from rich soil.

Now what is it that exalts these few moralists? What is it that determines at once that such men are the jewels of their century, or State?

Morals do not please as does music, painting, or eloquence. Morals do not make us laugh or weep; and hence, Paul, and Daniel, and Luther, and Fox, must be lifted up in the world's esteem by some new and peculiar kind of fact.

It seems to me we find this fact in the public conviction of the utter depravity of the masses, and in the public approval of any soul that can or will help a depraved race upward. Paul is loved the more because the world feels deeply that such morals are a stranger to it, and yet are its only hope. Suppose the world to have been quite free from sin, Paul's moralizing would have been without significance. Martyn's trip to Persia would have been only the roamings of a traveler.

It is the world's confessed wickedness, it is the world's universal and inborn depravity that makes the Christian and moral leaders flame like suns in the human sky. The fame of every such man as Paul, or Socrates, or Seneca is a public confession of depravity. Those men are thrown up by a great want. Their fame is the confession of old sorrow, old grief, old tears. It is the awful fact of universal sin that renders these names so precious. Their wreaths are woven by the fingers of sorrow. What rendered the life and words of Marcus Aurelius so beautiful? It was the fact that not a living mortal known to the whole Roman world had lived, or could live after that fashion. He was bright by reason of the dark background.

It is not worth while, therefore, to quarrel with the Bible when it says, "I was born in iniquity;" "the heart is deceitful:" "the heart is desperately wicked;" and "man must be born again." The conspicuousness of Christ, of Paul, of Penn, of the great Elliott among the Indians, shows that the Bible is only a picture of human life, and that men do need to "be born again." You may quarrel with theologians if you wish, who have taken Bible texts into their labratories, and have re-appeared after long stirring of the crucible, having in their hands some strange compound of mysterious color and questionable use; but with the plain Bible—with its words, "Ye must be born again"—let us have no debate. It was the effort of the old chemists to turn all things into gold, but the old theologians seemed to have possessed the faculty of changing gold into all things else; and taking a pure, priceless truth from the Bible were wont, unconscious of its worth, to join it to their amalgam, and then emerge with a poor oroid—their very faces meanwhile crying out the old, "Eureka." With these, one may dispute, but as for the simple words of the Bible, they are the picture of the world's facts. They are the mirror, which reflects back to us nothing but our face with no deformity, or charm left out. Those words are deeply written on all the generations, and their meaning is only too vivid. It makes the heart, and the head to ache. Let us confess that one of the most prominent facts of society is its moral weakness, its depravity. It *ought* to "be born again."

It is generally assumed that a child is born with certain mental predispositions; with a gift for language, for mechanics, for poetry, for reasoning. Hence it was said thousands of years ago, "A poet is not made by study, he is born." The great English dramatist says, "How hard it is to hide the sparks of nature." Another says, "Nature may lie hid for a time, but at last she will reveal herself." Thus it has always been assumed, that when one is born he is hurled into a certain orbit where he must journey forever, as calmly, and resistlessly as the planets.

This sentiment is not true to the letter, but it shows what Christ meant when He said, "Ye must be born again." He meant that the soul must be hurled into being a second time. Its first life was a failure. It ought to be reborn so that a new genius, a new drift might be possible.

Oh! what a vast change is here indicated—a change in the depths of our nature—a tearing down and re-building of the very soul.

Now the world's greatest *fact* being its degradation, its greatest *want* is to be expressed by the word "recreation," or "reborn."

This is the world's great *want*. It is its *greatest* want—this reconstruction of the human soul so that it will no longer love to lie, nor cheat, nor sin in any form, but will love God, and all moral beauty. Even old Egypt, thousands of years ago taught her citizens that after death the soul stood before God, and a Council of two and forty just men, and had to make the following statement: "I have not blasphemed. I have not stolen. I have not stirred up strife. I have not slandered any one. I have not practiced any crime. I have given food to the hungry, drink to the thirsty, clothes to the naked." Unless the soul could make this statement truly, it was at once stricken from existence; but if it could make this statement truly it went to heaven. These creeds Champollion has deciphered from old carved rocks unread for years, far in the thousands.

Yes, the great want of earth is a society living in honor, and virtue; loving God, and mankind. Such a result would be Heaven. To approach it, and finally reach it, is the mission of religion.

There are several Christian sects that do not sufficiently magnify this idea of conversion, or new life. They believe in it, but do not make it the great central thought of their teaching. With the Methodists, and Presbyterians, and their kindred schools, the first effort is to help convert men, and hence their great question to the candidate for membership is, "Do you feel that you have undergone a change of heart; do you hate sin; do you love holiness?" And persons enter the Church, or remain out, according to the responses to these inquiries. It matters not if some assert a change who have really met with none, and if some assert a falsehood knowingly. The questions are exactly in the line of the world's reform; they are the great questions to be asked, and hence the religion that most patiently asks them, and most lovingly seeks affirmative answers, will always secure better results than a Church that passes them by in silence, and assumes that all is well in the soul.

The perpetual effort to build up a new spiritual life, the unchanging conviction that soul needs a profound reform now, and the accompanying belief that such a new drift of being may be found by the heart, has all the advantage to be found in all direct effort toward a result. The pure rationalist will assure you, that the quantity of education, or wealth in a land will be, as the quantity of zeal, and longing, and will-power in those two directions. We are informed, that the good elocution of a Greek orator, was the result of long conflict with a natural foe, and that the culture of all Greece, was the result of a national zeal along one narrow channel of feeling, and thought. From the universality of such facts, has grown up the maxim that "the gods help those who help themselves." In a world subject to such a law, it is cruel to strike from religion the intense longing for a new heart, and the absorbing belief in its necessity, and then wait for moral progress to come in by some unknown gate.

It has counted wonderfully in the race of usefulness that the Methodists, for example, have for one hundred years, turned their longings and efforts toward the immediate reconstruction of the human spirit. Notwithstanding the weakness of shoutings, and the frequent discord in their old hymns, the long pursuit of a better life has given at last to our land, millions of the best citizens. The Presbyterians present a similar spectacle. Guilty often of fanaticism—guilty of midnight meetings, and of falling to the floor in the struggle with the old Satan, they have nevertheless surpassed rationalistic methods in the great work of recasting the soul. In some of the villages of Persia, there is to-day a sudden, and vast reform taking place under the mission banners, in the name of the actual pursuit of a egenerate heart. What men seek, they find. Only that gate opens at which men knock.

It is useless to reply, "We do not believe in a miraculous conversion of the soul, but only in a conversion brought about by study, will-power, hymns, and prayer;" for it is of a change of *heart* only I speak. I have said nothing about the agent in the new creation. The pure rationalists believe in a "changed" heart, and would seem bound, therefore, to make this "new heart" a vital thing in their Church life. For it is the world's greatest want, its greatest longing, its only hope. Some orthodox sects pursue with more zeal this one object—the transformation of the heart—and hence seem to be more in the path of the highest human duty—more fully in the path of reform.

From Dr. Ryder's* letters, you will perceive that his philosophy believes in a new heart, but in securing this new heart, instead of increasing the labor, and

* Referring to a correspondence in the *Chicago Tribune* between Wm. Ryder, D. D., of St. Paul's (Universalist) Church, and E. O. Burgess, D. D., of the Christian Church, growing out of a sermon preached by the former on Rev. George H. Hepworth's renunciation of Unitarianism.

whole pressure in *this* life, he prolongs the time. He diminishes the power, and doubles the time. He allows us future centuries upon the other shore in which to come to a harmony with God. But the orthodox limit us to a few years here, and hence pursue with more enthusiasm, and with deepest feeling the work of reforming their fellow men. They shorten the time, and double the impulse; and when we remember that what this world needs is good men on this side of the grave, rather than saints on the other, we cannot but feel that orthodoxy is the best friend of the life that now is. When we consider that the great enemy of society is sin, the religion that makes a change of heart its chief object, seems evidently the better one for the great end. Only those efforts count in the progress of the centuries, which harmonize with the world's great need—which become parts of God's work—parts of the development and growth of humanity.

It is to be admitted that education, books, art, reason help to convert the soul—to change it—hence all enlightened pulpits are full of usefulness. But when to these influences a Church adds an additional effort, pointed and urgent to convert the heart, it may well claim a special usefulness. A Church will be useful according to the depth of its realization that men must "be born again"—not hereafter, but in these passing days.

Let us come now to a comparison of the means for creating, or producing this new heart.

There are sects that expect a new heart to come from the common means of civilization. A new heart as to sin, is just like a new taste as to learning, or music—a simple result of culture. They call in no special agents, no superhuman influence.

The truly orthodox, to the influence of all natural means, add the special influence of God's Spirit, and of a divine Christ. In the very outset one might conjecture that a religion claiming help from God, and from a divine Savior, would most powerfully affect the heart. None of the influences of civilization are left out, but in addition to these the heart opens up a communion with God; opens up a study, and soul-communion with Jesus Christ, and thus casts itself into the presence of infinite purity, power, justice, and goodness. What are the ordinary forces of civilization compared with such a fellowship as this? The element to be eliminated from man is sin. Now civilization bears within itself a great remnant of sin. Civilization is not holy. It is not infinitely just, and pure. But the Spirit of God is the very opposite of sin. The soul, therefore, coming to God, comes to perfect purity, and sees its own wickedness as it can never see it in human culture. Before this soul-communion with God, the influence of human agencies fades in feebleness.

It may be that, here and there, an individual might seek moral perfection, without being influenced by the idea of God. In sober years, here and there a soul might seek what might be called morals, as being a refined temperance of life. I think Stuart Mill has said, he could imagine a religion of humanity, where man would seek uprightness from a love of himself, and of society's peace; but these possible theories, count nought in presence of the sweeping fact, that all morals have revolved around the idea of God. God renders virtue necessary, and beautiful, and is to be its reward. As the eyes of servants look unto the hand of their masters, as the eyes of the maiden unto the hand of her mistress, so our eyes, wait upon the Lord our God, until He have mercy upon us.

While God is Creator of material worlds, yet the heart feels that they are but decorations of His temple, and that the rational soul is the chief end of the world in its height, and depth. Hence the greatest relation of Deity, is the relation to the soul. Hence God must be the God of morals more extremely than the God of matter. If, as Hamilton says, "there is nothing great on earth but man, and nothing great in man except his soul," so we suspect, that there is nought so great in the sky as God, and no attribute in that blessed One so vast, as His moral beauty. When, therefore, the heart thinks of its sin, it must at once, in fear, or in hope, feel the weight, sweet, or sorrowful, of that sinless One, all around like the air, or sunshine.

In seeking a new moral nature, the soul must fly to this vast bosom, and seek its new life there—

> "Go when the morning shineth,
> Go when the noon is bright,
> Go when the eve declineth,
> Go in the hush of night."

Hence, when we seek the conversion of the human race, give me that religion which leads the wicked heart up to a communion direct with God, and with Jesus Christ. Where God is, there is no sin; and the heart that believes most in God, and looks most to Him for help, will become separated most widely from the love, and pursuit of vice.

It is an attribute of human nature, that it is educated by objects outside of self. Before each scholar, there stand some great scholars of the past alluring, and detaining, and transforming the mind of to-day. We are all lesser lights, revolving around some central sun of immense light, and heat. Without this influence we make no progress.

In religion it is not otherwise, and hence, most useful must be that form that makes of Christ a divine Being, and invites the heart to move about such a centre of power, holiness, and love. Its theory would seem at the outset to promise most for society. The moment you declare Christ only a human being, you have weakened His influence upon the soul. The light, and warmth are eclipsed, and the poor soul gropes about, and tries to find in civilization a power denied it in the realm of the divine, and infinite. To part with ignorance, let us go to the learned; to part with sin, let us go to the presence of the holy.

As the planets get further from the sun, their light and heat diminish. Their flowers, and fruits lose sweetness; their summers shorten. What must it be in the most remote Neptune—three hundred times as far away as our earth! Oh, star of perpetual ice, and winter; without bird, or flower, or leaf! But to chill the central sun would give the same result. Now in the soul's universe, there is a scene as dreary. Christ is declared to be only man—only falliable man. And thus the human race is crowded back, far away from the old centre of Divine warmth, and light; and many is the soul which this theory has left without a flower, or leaf, or trace of summer time.

Mr. Hepworth excites hope only in this, that he has kindled a little better central sun for his heart—has declared Christ to be Divine, above other measure of divinity believed in by many of his sect. He redoubles the radiance, and the warmth of that character that has always shone in rejuvenating, converting power upon the heart. Men looking upon civilization, or culture only, may not be reborn in spirit; but looking upon a divine Christ in love, their souls are affected by the holiness, and immortal life in the great vision.

Instead of man's revolving around humanity, Mr. Hepworth invites him to revolve about the Divine. It is a step upward, but not an espousal of orthodoxy, not even a departure from the old Unitarian Creed. To preach fully his gently orthodox ideas it seemed not necessary to withdraw from associations long and sacred; able in themselves to clothe his words with power—for the creed of his denomination embraces his ideas in its grandest books, and many are the hearts in his Society that are willing that the soul of Channing should come back to the half-desolate home. I feel that there are thousands in the Unitarian body who are willing, even anxious, to have a common, fallible man plucked from the centre of their system, and to see replaced there a divine Savior, drawing all hearts by His love, and heavenly attributes.

The world will, sooner or later, be compelled to go to the Divine presence—not to human presence—for its new heart. Mankind has not holiness enough to entice any hearts from its sins—has not love enough to persuade, nor power enough to alarm. It is the conception of an ever-present God; it is the sublime divinity of Jesus; it is communion with these characters; it is a belief in the infinite love, and power, and justice, and in the all-pervading presence of Deity, that can give to this world noble, converted hearts, and can bear earth along toward the new birth—the new genius of human life.

THE VALUE OF YESTERDAY.

For ask now of the days that are past. *Deuteronomy*, iv: 32.

Time is one of the incomprehensible things. If we gaze up into the blue sky, and thus shut out all lowly objects, and then repeat the word time to our soul, we will find ourselves absorbed in a deep mystery. Each breath we take lies partly in the past, partly in the present, partly in the future. One of the most beautiful sentences uttered over the name of Jesus Christ is that one of Paul—"Christ, the same yesterday, to-day and forever.

Time divides itself into these three continents — yesterday, to-day, and to-morrow, each grand, and each peculiar—and each measureless. The divinity that presides over to-morrow is called Hope; the present has no guardian by name, and the divinity of yesterday is called Memory. There is no eloquence, no poetry, no process of reasoning that can do justice to the beauty and influence of any one of these periods. Looking backward and forward the heart becomes overwhelmed with the weight and mystery of the theme.

The study of the distances in the heavens in which we find that there are suns whose light could not have reached our world in less than a million years, is scarcely less bewildering than this contemplation of the yesterday and the to-morrow. Led by its own impulse the human heart has always prized the morrow more than the present, or the yesterday, and hence has written the most of its poetry in the name of Hope. Hope has always been the popular goddess of earth's children. When all other shrines are vacant, this one receives its daily offerings of flowers. When the seven classic philosophers were holding a banquet together, it was asked of them, "What is the most universal possession?" The reply agreed upon as most accurate was the word hope, for he that has nothing else has hope.

But this extreme popularity and worship of futurity constitute a reason why the mind should guard against a total oblivion of all else and form an excuse for reading before you this morning the words of the text, "Ask now the days that are past." For the hour let us oppose the orators and the poets and the youth and beauty of the realm, and speak in behalf of yesterday. We shall not find the same loveliness of person that belongs to Hope, but what is wanting in bloom and smile may find compensation in wisdom and pensiveness.

The days that are past are like a mother whose youth and powers of mind and affections have all failed in the life-long devotion to her children. The marks in her forehead, the whiteness of her face, the solemnity of her heart are only proofs that her bloom and vivacity have journeyed over to her loved ones, and their life, their love, their works, their language, their song are a direct inheritance from the one who is soon to be recalled from their sight. Thus yesterday, going back to the tomb of Solomon or Moses, or in that longer journey proposed by recent sciences is, whether we go back a thousand or a million years, the mother of us all, and the tomb, and ruins of all the nations are only marks upon the forehead of this great parent; they are the whiteness of that face which faded in behalf of new life and new happiness. The lonely silent pyramids, the brilliant ruins of the Acropolis, of Palmyra, of Thebes, the deeply entombed streets of old Jerusalem, all the ivy-covered minsters of Europe, Catholic or Protestant, are fragments of that home where Yesterday lived and taught the new generations playing about her feet.

The greatness of man as pictured in the future may be a dream so far as our life, or our nation's life is concerned, but the past is a great fact of which nothing can rob us, and whose worth no fancy can over-estimate. In order to behold the presence and kindness of God, it is not necessary to draw upon the powers of hope any more than upon the powers of memory. It is a confessed truth that by nature we look for the most and highest good in the future, and, since God is the ideal of goodness, the soul beholds Him unveiling himself in days that are to come. We say, "Our father in Heaven," more in anticipation of what He will be than in confession of what He has been; for the sin and suffering of earth make it logically necessary for us to select the future as the arena of the Creator. But, having confessed this logical superiority of the future, the past yet remains a vast field of religious truth and sentiment.

Let it be granted that there is a personal God whom we define as the sum of all perfections, yet we could not prove that it was necessary that this God should have expressed all His attributes in the very first years of human life. If it was lawful for the human race to begin in a childhood that could neither speak nor walk, and if it was lawful for all science and art to begin with simple lessons and slowly work forward, it would seem equally lawful that the Creator should not unfold all His glory to the first generation, but should strew it along for a ten thousand or million years period. All the beauties of earth are progressive beauties, all the arts are progressive arts, all the sciences are progressive sciences—and hence one might expect that the infinite love of God would be subject to a slow manifestation of itself. A *priori* reason would suppose, perhaps, that a God of love would be found proceeding as such from the outset in the history of a creature like man, and that man would never know a year or a moment of sin or pain, that barbarism and depravity would be impossible for a day or an hour. But being driven by the facts away from the use of a *priori* logic we must fall back to the second best logic, and, following the phenomena of science and art and all human activity, must suppose that God selects not a day or a year for His own full emblazonment, but a vast epoch such as is demanded by geology or the study of the stars. With this confession in our minds we can "ask now the days that are past," and see in man's face and language and laws and arts the gradual unfolding of divine wisdom and love.

A child taken from our public schools at the age of twelve years and examined in reading, in conversation, in knowledge, in music, will be found to possess a language that consumed six thousand years in its construction; it will be found to possess knowledge that has been wrought out by the toil and perhaps sorrow of a hundred generations. It will sing perhaps a song, "My Country 'tis of Thee," or "Home Sweet Home," that is the upshot of thousands of years of sentiment and thought about liberty and home. What then is a bright pure school child to-day, but a place where God's love and wisdom in days that are past have treasured up their tenderness as the earth treasures up the dust that for millions of years has filtered down upon it out of the invisible either in which the worlds all float?

But pass from the school child to all the school children, and to all the adult minds and hearts that move upon the earth, listen to all their wisdom and music and industry and eloquence, and do you not feel that this multitude measures a great revelation of God above that day when earth possessed but one man or family, and that one without language and without learning and without virtue?

There are two theories about the origin of man. The one that he was made in his present form by the Creator by a simple instantaneous command, the other that man is the result of a long development and mutation of species. Thus the only dreamed of theories give us only one human being in the outset, and that one a human being defective in language, in art, in learning, in hope, in memory. Defective in language because there was nothing to be said; in art for there was no one to admire the skill; in learning because there was no language in which to express facts; in hope because there was no realization of any imperfection or death; in memory because there was nothing to be remembered.

In the first human being therefore, God could no more display His perfections than a musician like Mozart could unfold his genius to an infant, or to a South Sea Islander. Could the divine virtue be perceived by a being that had not perceived sin? Could the divine immortality be appreciated by an individual who was a stranger to death? Could the divine omniscience be felt by a being that had not yet learned or developed the love of knowledge? By no means Could the sun reveal its power and beauty if it had nothing but a clod to shine upon? Give it a planitary system, skies, stars, clouds, continents, seas, fruits, flowers, and it possesses then an arena for its play of color and light.

In order that God should reveal himself, a race was necessary, not only moving in vast multitudes, but moving along vast periods of time; and hence, recalling the days that are past, the heart in the least religious may perceive a Creator scattering the attributes and truths of His own being.

You tell me God is sinless. Looking into the future we perceive only a dream, and turn away uncertain, but, looking into that vast realm called Yesterday, and perceiving that sin has always brought sorrow, and that virtue has brought beauty of face, and life and peace of heart, I come back from that survey feeling that righteousness is a divine attribute. The sins of men are so inwoven with the sorrows of men that this very tumult and perpetual weeping are only an announcement of the benediction, "Blessed are the pure in heart, for they shall see God." But it is impossible to descend to particulars. We can only say that the immense past of humanity may be viewed as a field in which the arts and the industries and the philosophies and religion, taking the form at last of Christianity, have gradually found opportunity for the revelation of their glorious natures.

But, turning aside from thoughts about God's own emblazonry, think of man himself and his immediate personal relation to the days that are passed. As we said in the outset, great is the office of hope. We have no word too good or extreme for that faculty, but we would enter a plea in behalf of the value of yesterday in its relations to mind and heart. Hope is a grand sentiment, but it conveys no information. All the information of the soul comes up from the days that are gone. Hence one of the best thinkers said, "Not to know history is to be always a child." The value of the ideas that enter into human life is chiefly to be learned by watching their evolution and workings in that great workshop called Yesterday. Take the idea of liberty, and no dreamer who looks into the future can behold its length and breadth, but he alone can measure the import of the term who hears the cry of the slave from the days of the Romans down to the career of our own land, and who sees the prosperity of freedom from Athens to Florence, and from Florence to England and America. Take the idea of home, and if you would feel the import of the word, look not forward into poetic haze, but back into human experience, in the tears of sadness and joy that have fallen by the feet of any exile going away or coming back; or look into your own childhood and consult its memories and then the term unveils itself with no light or shadow left out.

Beyond the unfolding of truths Yesterday possesses another power—that of softening and modulating the mind and heart. Egotism draws its vanity from a perfect forgetfulness of yesterday. Self-consciousness and coming greatness erase all else from the mind, and the egotist stands great in his possibilities. He is just about to conquer a world or greatly surprise one. Any deep study of his own or of the world's yesterday would drain his heart of the last drop of personal vanity, for there was an arena and he did not conquer nor astonish a world—and there all those who were more highly endowed are sleeping in forgotten dust. If the past utters anything that is of value it is that all self-worship and glorification are the weakest shape human nature can assume, and that there is nothing worth living for except the general mental and moral progress of self and of mankind. The great graves are those which cover the dust of hearts that did some work that entered after them into the public welfare and happiness.

There is no vanity away from man. The sea gives us her music without egotism. The rainbow spreads out her gorgeous lines without boasting. The nightingale sings her notes herself unseen among the wild thorn, in the silent night. The floral world in June fills the air with perfume, and the sight with her indescribable tints, but without any ostentation. Man alone has vanity; not because man alone has soul, for this would be to degrade soul below the standard of dumb life; but because man alone has wandered from the divine path. This wandering has been aided and abetted by his blindness to yesterday, and by living only in the proud thrones and crowns and glories of to-morrow. Vanity draws its chief nutriment from the future. This is, perhaps, the reason why nearly all of us pass through a vain period in early years. Fortunate is the heart that did not, in early life, pass through a score of years of personal greatness. The animal spirits and poetry of youth make it despise the past, and dwell only in the land of hope, and as the future contains nothing that can humiliate, contains no tombs, no disappointment, no dust of the heart, it carries the young soul away from truth and decorates it in its own regal and gaudy drapery. But when the past begins to be recognized by the mind, when the soul looks back at its own path and the great path of mankind, a spirit rises from that wide, silent ocean that drives away all self-worship and makes man stand up in a combined strength and humility—the only combination worthy of man or his Maker.

It may, perhaps, be a beautiful providence that young persons look only into the future, for there certainly should be some years of life set apart for a happiness without much alloy—and such a joy does come from a steady gaze toward that realm whose gates are not only always garlanded; but are always open. But if this be so, then I know there is another providence also that makes man as he draws near the noontime of life, labor and usefulness, begin to look back and find in the history of man a sober truth and a self-forgetfulness and love of mankind which the rosy future could not give. Hence despise not the years when you find your reflection begins to look back, for God has not without reason placed behind the human race a long five or ten thousand years, and it is not without reason that this past is constantly becoming more immense and more varied. It is the soil out of which man grows and is to grow, and the longer the rains wash down the mountain sides, and the more of yesterday's leaves and grasses mingle with the mold, the greater will be the productions of to-morrow.

Yesterday contains all the battlefields in which freedom was gradually wrought out from many threads all dipped in blood. Yesterday contains the experiment and the failure of all despotisms. Yesterday contains the onset and defeat of every form of sin and vice. Yesterday holds the ashes of all beauty, and of all life except that of the soul with God. Yesterday is full of past usefulness and of its ways and means, full of tears and their causes and cures. In that shadowy domain there stands the cross, and there is the Saviour dying for the vast myriads of a race. God has not without reason thrown such an immense history behind His children of to-day. It must be that out of the world that has been there is always flowing down to those who are living a stream of wisdom and character that bears onward to a sacred destiny.

The past is the long, uniform trade-wind that bears the spirit along toward its far off haven. The ship striking those winds has around it a friend that shall for days and nights and for weeks, without calm or storm, bear it along over the wide sea. The human spirit, if it will guide its course properly, may pass into such a moving air, that, without storm or calm, will day and night throw it along toward a better, nobler home.

The poet Dryden bequeathed us a poem upon this great dream of to-morrow:

> Trust on and think the morrow will repay,
> The morrow's falser than the former day;
> Lies worse, and while it says you shall be blest,
> Steals all the pleasure that you once possessed.

Aware of the value and beauty of hope, and not daring to depreciate it in the least, yet I do wish you all to feel that there are two other powerful influences in human life, in each individual life, to-day and yesterday. A bad yesterday is the saddest condition of the soul. If one can only look back on a good yesterday, the future need not be feared; but if yesterday was marked by a great crime or folly, I do not see how there could be an eternity long enough or purifying enough to wash it white. There may be some river Lethe known only to God and created by His mercy, dipped into which the soul may forget its vice and crime, but reason looking upon the Catherines de Medici, or upon the violet murderers of our own land, cannot see anything in the countless years of eternity that could erase the vision of memory of the black spot. "Things past," Livy says, "may be repented of, but never erased." Yesterday is nothing but to-day passed over by our mind and heart. The great duty of the hour is, not to gaze with poetic rapture into the future, but to weave out of the present a glorious past.

One of our poets says: "To-morrow do thy worst for I have lived to-day." And the old Martial says: "Didst thou say thou wilt live to-morrow? He is the wise man who lived yesterday." To-day is the sublime part of life because it is continually making that yesterday which will always follow us go where we may in this life or one to come. Aristotle says there is one thing which God cannot change and that is yesterday. If this is so and we all feel that it is, then there is one thing better than all high resolve—namely noble deeds already done. Better therefore than hope of great things to come is the memory of good already performed. Shakspeare says:

> "To-morrow and to-morrow and to-morrow,
> Creeps in this petty pace from day to day
> To that last syllable of recorded time;
> And all our yesterdays have only lighted fools
> The way to dusty death."

Oh my friends before whose feet the stream of life is running sweetly to-day, and above all oh ye young hearts who have as yet no yesterday, but in whose hands its destiny is lying all untouched and ready to be formed for joy or grief—do not despise to-day, and fill your eyes with only the vision of glittering hope; do not sit upon the banks of this stream waiting for its waters to run by and bring you the beautiful future, but pour out your heart's powers and life upon the present, because it is creating a Yesterday whose smile, if it wears one, will never perish, and whose tears of sin, if it has them, not even a merciful God can wipe away.

The chief part of your life is not that which spreads out before you, but it will soon be that which shall lie back of you. The impulse of a river is not in the broad expanse where it emerges into the sea, but is far back of that in the table lands and mountain ranges of a vast continent, all which, having caught the rains and having dissolved the snows of yesterday crowd the stream foward in a majestic sweep. The wide mouth of the Amazon is the result of the storms and snows of a thousand winters. Thus life should not go on allured only by poetic hope, but pressed forward by the momentum and majestic flow of days that are gone. Heaven is a height to which men climb on the deeds of his life. Hence the Bible speaking of the dead coming to heaven, says: "Their works do follow them." Oh yes, these works make the soul; they weave its life out of their golden threads; they fill it with wisdom and love and humility, and then throw it forward to heaven as the south wind carries northward in spring the song of birds and the garlands of flowers. Hope is herself founded upon the past. It is a glorious past only that produces a serene, glorious hope. Yesterday is the foundation of the Heavenly City. Hope is the sweet blue sky in which the structure rises. Oh friends, combine both hope and memory. Coming to the grave he only can look forward with joy who can sweetly look back.

SOUL-CULTURE.

For what is a man profited if he shall gain the whole world and lose his own soul?—*Matt.* xvi. 26.
And the Child grew and waxed strong in spirit.—*Luke* ii. 40.

The words soul and spirit are sprinkled over the pages of the Bible as thickly as leaves upon the ground in autumn. There is no evident difference in the signification of the two words. A book has been published within the past two years, whose object is to teach that man is composed of three elements—mind, soul, and spirit; but most readers rise from the book entertained to some extent, but to a greater extent untaught and bewildered.

Beyond the grand divisions, mind and soul, it is difficult to pass. And these two continents are not marked out by definite coast lines and separated by great neutral oceans, but rather lie contiguous, like the two tints of a flower, with a beautiful middle ground, where the spectator loses power to announce which color is more vivid.

But for our purpose we do not need a definite mapping out of mind and soul, intellect and spirit, knowledge and character; we need only the general truth, that man possesses a certain soul-life, that can grow and can rise and fall like the waves of the deep.

It is wonderful how much the Bible uses this word spirit. If you will open your Concordance and see what an array of texts there are in which this word is master of the proposition, you will ever after think more highly of the soul within your own bosom. You will there see set in order the "spirit" of wisdom, the "spirit" of love, the "spirit" of charity, of peace, the "spirit" of God, the broken "spirit," the faithful "spirit," and, according to Peter, the glorious "spirit." Reading over this grand catalogue, made up out of all the deepest thought of Job and St. John, you cannot but feel thankful that the Creator has poured into your bosom a portion of that soul without which the whole world would profit nothing.

I have read these texts, not for the purpose of leading you again over the estimate of that deliverance of spirit announced by Christ, but for the purpose of uttering some thoughts that ought to be held as preliminary to all consideration of that blessed redemption revealed in the New Testament. If there is offered the world a Saviour of the soul, the world may well inquire what the soul is, and whether it is desirable that it struggle much, or long, for a friendship with that great Soul of Nazareth. Our inquiry is not a direct application of the text, but a preliminary reflection.

If one might dare find a defect in the method of preaching the gospel, it would seem safe to declare that the method is one of endless assumption of preliminary thoughts, and endless repetition of final truths and conventional terms. In place of any discussion of the nature of sin, we are warned simply as sinners, and the punishment is daily re-announced. The nature of faith is passed by in our zeal to urge men to believe; the philosophy and analysis of repentance are crowded out of the world by the perennial command to repent; and instead of defining or measuring the inspiration of the sacred Book, it is enough if we say daily that all Scripture is given by inspiration.

Whether this avoidance of preliminary questions is to be attributed to a want of courage, or want of industry, or to a long prevalence of dogmatism which is too vain to admit the importance of an inquiry, we cannot venture to affirm, but must content ourself with the conviction that there is need of reform in the topics and mode of the sacred desk. When, however, we all remember with what labor, and with disappointment often, men have sought the foundation truths of life, we cannot but palliate the sin that gives up this path of pursuit, and accepts of a final word and no questions asked.

All thoughts about the soul must indeed lead us to a wall at last, which we cannot undermine or scale; but such is the common destiny of truth-seekers that our tears of sorrow will fall no sooner here, and no bitterer, than along any path our foot may choose. It is said that Aristotle grieved all his life that he could not explain the tides of the sea that washed the shores of his country. The pursuit of knowledge, like the pursuit of any pleasure, is a chase of both joy and grief. All the nets that drag through the sea of life draw out the good and bad at last to the shore. All the seventy years are a constant effort to sift the varied sorrow out of those seventy years; and when at last we fall, the winnowing fan will be found in the right hand, trying still to separate grain and chaff. But, unreadable as all things are in the world, there are always approximations to truth possible on all hands, and with these our hearts must learn to be content.

In this matter of intellect and soul, it is not otherwise. Though there are places where colors blind and are lost, or where light ends in shadow, yet there is some color and some light. I am inclined to think that the soul is the conscious life or being of man, and that intellect is simply its grandest servant, its daily purveyor. A new fact is valuable because it feeds this inner life. It helps the soul to some new motion or deed of joy. Knowledge is fuel for this warm flame. The Psalmist says that while he was musing the fire burned—not the fire upon the hearth—but the flame in his bosom. He says, "My heart was hot within me," and while he mused the fire burned the more intensely. That is, as the facts passed along in review before his intellect, his soul within him increased the flow and power of its life.

Knowledge is said to be power. It is indeed power, for the soul converts it into all manner of action—joy, charity, worship, love, eloquence. As the rich earth drinks in simply water and light and heat, and then sends forth all manner of fruit and blossoms, so the soul receives the facts of the intellect, and makes them the basis of a vast creation, varied as that which came from the Almighty.

To the poor negro, lying on the banks of the Niger, what a narrowness of soul! What a perpetual stupor! But how could his soul live or move? The facts of the world have never fallen upon it, as dew upon drooping grass. The vast culture of the world, the vast arts useful and beautiful, its immense history, running back through thousands of years and over vast empires, have never passed into his brain, and the soul, having no purveyor, starves within its silent dungeon. The spirit of this poor savage is a seed that has fallen upon a rock. There is nothing to nourish its mysterious germ. Tendrils thrown out could grasp nothing; hence there is no unfolding of leaf or flower.

Compare with this desolate soul a Burke that was cast among the facts of England, or a disciple that leaned upon the heart of the world's Lord, and saw truths turning into soul. The facts of earth are only the food ordained of Heaven for the life of the spirit. Besides the common five senses, there is an innumerable army of purveyors—history, science, art, religion—whose only calling is that of adding to the emotions and impulses of that mystery called soul. The truths of this whole career are only the soil of that strange but beautiful growth, the spirit.

Truth, therefore, sought through simple desire to increase one's store of acquisition, truth pursued only to learn what comes next, must be much like the miser's pursuit of gold—a fatal transformation of a means into an end. As money is worthless, only so far as the blessings of life are bought with it, so the acquisition of knowledge must have its value measured by the outgrowth of sentiment.

The decoration and enlargement of the heart are the direct end of truth, and, without this result, knowledge is not power, but is treasure buried and forgotten—like the fabled gold of Capt. Kidd—by some unknown sea. Florence Nightingale is all the prison truth and battle-field truth of the world turned into divine soul. Those gloomy facts were converted into an infinite love by the strange machinery of man.

A Christian's creed, therefore, is only a first step toward being a Christian or even a good man. He has facts, just as a successful speculator has money, but whether the man will be a Christian is as uncertain as whether the gainer of money will be a noble man or a despicable miser. It is the fire which truth kindles in the soul that determines the value of all study and experience and reflection. Hence the grand men of the world have never been those who have acquired most truths, but those with whom the world's experience and events have hastened to put on the garments of divine spirit, those with whom truth has been only a hand to strike afresh each day the spirit's harp. Hence it has easily come to pass that the most useless and forlorn men who have lived since the world began have been the professional heresy-hunters in the Church. Living for a certain assemblage of words just as the miser lives for his labeled bags of gold, they have always left their souls to go dressed in vile rags and to die of famine in absolute sight of a land of milk and honey. Not knowing "that an ounce of life is better than a ton of knowledge," they are but clerks who file the business transactions of yesterday and await calmly the arrival of some morrow of dispute. These having read a page, or having had an opportunity of hearing a discourse, do not open their souls to admit any new warmth, but with Shylock begin to read the record, and to mutter that "it is not so stated in the bond." The idea of character never disturbs their brain, but man's prospect of heaven is learned wholly by a comparison of antique bonds. Instead of seeking the grandeur of man in the soul's alembic, where truth is passing over into the realm of spirit, they locate salvation in their forty articles, and give to prejudice and to memory the heavens that God made for the heart. These have never been the useful or loved men of history. They are the misers of Christianity. But when there has come along a being with whom a single fact in morals has fallen in upon that holy place called the soul, and burst forth into some sweet sentiment, there has come along a being that was both earth's help and earth's joy.

In Wilberforce, the fact of negro bondage fell in upon his heart like a flower seed falling into the warm black earth of Italy or Florida. His one truth produced a tear. His tear increased into a river of eloquence. The river widened into the modern Sea of Liberty. His soul absorbed that truth of suffering and became all colored with a Christ-like humanity, as the snow white wool drinks in the Tyrian dye. Alongside this Wilberforce, place a score of professional heresy-hunters fresh from their victim, and how wretched they all appear in presence of such an uprising of a single heart!

There is no doubt the notorious Catherine II. held more truth and better truth than was known to all classic Greece—held to a belief in a Saviour, of whose glory that gifted land knew nought; and yet, such is the grandeur of soul above mind, that I doubt not that Queen Penelope of the dark land, and the doubting Socrates, have found at Heaven's gate a sweeter welcome sung of angels than greeted the ear of Russia's brilliant, but false-lived queen. Penelope knew little about our God, nothing about our Saviour; but what truth she knew was transfigured in the white raiment of life—the garb of immortality.

"Virtue is knowledge applied," says a thoughtful writer. And Cicero says· "Why should I study unless to prepare myself for my associations with my fellow men?" Beautiful thought of that unrivaled man! Why read the history of liberty unless I intend to grasp it with a firmer hand, and seek to break the chains of humanity? Why study the flowers of the field unless I am to come home tenderer to my children, and a better believer in God? Why read over the world's charity unless I am myself henceforth to be of kinder heart?

Thus the Christian creed is valuable only so far as the soul can and does draw it into its crucible and transform it into life. The variations between Methodist and Calvinist go for nought, because the variations are over ideas that are incapable of being made into the fibre of soul. They count nothing because they do not reach the realm where God stretches at last the line of measurement.

It is not the Trinity that moulds human life, but the doctrine of God. It is not the eternal possession of the Holy Spirit that may shape the human soul, but the fact of an ever-present spirit. That Christ was eternally begotten of the Father is a doctrine that cannot be appreciated in any way by man's heart, but the Christ of the New Testament can be grasped and loved; and hence the responsibility and success and beauty of human life will be all related to the latter of these statements, and be wholly discharged from all the former, without penalty or costs.

That truth alone is valuable and filled with responsibility, which might make our life deeper and better. To slight this is to lose that soul, than which one would better lose the whole world. Those are the responsible facts which lie above our hearts as the pure snow on the mountains lies ready to bless in summer time the fields beneath.

Intellect is said to be cold. So it is by itself. But complain not at the snow that reposes upon the Rocky or Alpine range. Cold? Yes. But all summer long, and long is the summer at their bases, the vineyards and fields and orchards draw their clusters, their golden harvests, from the kind melting of these treasures of the frost. Cold, indeed, but all of France and Italy are made a paradise beneath.

Truth in itself is cold, but in the design of the Creator its white treasures falling as softly as snow, and falling through many centuries, daily dissolve and transform the spirit beneath into a never-fading paradise.

Our material earth is built by many layers wrapped around it in its long history. Geologists dig to great depths or go where the earthquake has made openings miles in depth, and lo! the lowest ground or rock is found to have been formed by the falling of leaves and grasses, and by the varied wrappings of the ages gone. It is now known that the atmosphere is raining forever an invisible dust upon this ball, making it larger and warmer and more beautiful. The rock scraped by a glacier becomes covered, and invites moss and lichen to its breast.

The human soul is such a world. The truths of to-day, of yesterday, of the whole past are settling down upon it a golden rain from the hand of God, making the glorious wrappings of time and of the great futurity. Thus the dark facts of earth, its slavery, its suffering, its sickness, its calamities, its burned up cities, its solemn cemeteries of the dead, all may be transformed into human spirit and make the soul come to heaven at last rich in its tenderness and love. The earthly knowledge is made into never dying power. Bulwer says, "Oh how much greater is the soul of one man than the vicissitudes of the whole globe!" And elsewhere he says, "Not in the knowledge of things without, but in the perfection of the soul within, lies the true empire of man."

From considerations such as these, I am inclined to think that mystery is also a servant of the soul trying to give it some shade of beauty which no plain fact could even paint upon it. To eliminate vanity, to overthrow egotism, to check the footsteps in the path of sin, to keep the soul tender, to bring the king down to the level of his servant, I can conceive of nothing more powerful than the mystery of death. When the mother thinks of it she bids her children good night with a deeper love and with a more intense prayer that God will be an angel over them by night. By mystery our philosophers are made to be as children, and, indeed, the hearts of all educated beings are lifted up by its sad but strong arms above the dust of earth, and are borne nearer the infinite throne. As though the events of earth were insufficient to exalt us, realms are created where unseen hands smite the heart strings, and where the air trembles with a grand unknown melody.

It is not probable that the Creator has poured out darkness around man only to harrass him on life's march. All things are ordered for good, and it must be that to the facts that educate mankind, mystery adds the shadow of facts, to carry this education along some new paths. When the world sums up educational influences, it enumerates success, and acts, and languages. But this estimate is too rude and coarse, for a human friend, deeply loved and long known, often casts over the soul a culture which all schools would have failed to bestow. Indeed, from the closets of the great schools, we go forth with empty hands, compared with the treasures which we carry from the bosom of the noble mother, where we spent all early years, and from the earth and sky that were the oceans of our island childhood.

Into any survey of educational forces, we must admit, therefore, elements that escape the first rude estimate, and find room for those shadows of awful facts that perpetually hang their dark curtains before us.

As the depth of mystery is only felt by the most civilized and advanced soul, and is a cloud of which a savage knows nothing, it may be inferred, that it comes not as a penalty of culture, but as a delicate hand to lead it to a still better being. The solemn question of Hamlet, "To be, or not to be," surpasses the books of the school-house in shaping the spirit of man. The willow and cypress, that mourn over the tombs of our dead, impress our hearts the more deeply, because the wind that sighs through them, and the somber shades they cast, help us to pass over into the unknown world. Thus, by fact, and by the wandering shadow of fact, the soul of man is perpetually fed. They are the only manna that falls for it, in this wilderness march.

To the natural power of the world's truths it pleased God to add the "truth as it is in Jesus." The soil of earth was too poor to nourish a great soul. Into the common thoughts of society the heavens opened and poured out the vast truths of penitence, faith, charity, purity of heart, and heaven beyond. To live a life amid such surroundings as earth now possesses must be only to live a career of preparation for a world more blessed. To lose one's soul must be to pass through this sublime temple without drinking in its virtue and holy worship, and not only to have rejected the true, but to have suffered the falsehoods of society to rush upon the delicately-strung harp of the spirit, and break its strings, and hush its melodies. "Truth," says the great dramatist, "are the wings wherewith we fly to heaven."

O friends immortal! earth will soon disappear. You will soon pass from its varied scenes. While you walk yet on this mortal land, hold most dear those truths that may be embodied in the heart. Let your creed be measured by the need of your inner life, and let all the duties and joys and grief of life only wrap some more beautiful garment around your spirit. Then, called to go hence, you will bear away with you the good of earth, as the sun, rising from the sea, draws up after him its whitest mist and most delicate colorings.

VARIATION OF MORAL MOTIVE.

The love of Christ constraineth us.—*Corinthians v.: 13.* Love is the fulfilling of the law.—*Romans xiii.: 10.*

The world is so vast that no human foot can travel over it, and no heart occupy all places with its home. Going to Florida in winter, or Switzerland in the summer months, or to the New England hills in autumn, one feels that in each of these wonderful kingdoms of nature, he should build his home, and live his whole life. Coming to the borders of a sweet lake in our own Northwest, looking down from a silent forest into the waters that are clear as glass to the depth of hundreds of feet, the heart suddenly feels that it is good to be there, and wishes to build three tabernacles for self and friends, upon the spot where such divine beauty seems transfigured. We forget our limits of space and enjoy a feeling of infinity of space and of perpetual life.

Then the thought comes that one cannot live everywhere. Do all we may, there will be beautiful spots where we can possess no house. There will be waters we cannot look into, bird songs we may not hear. Is is sorrowful that there are seas whose waves do not beat for us. Building by the lakes, a voice comes up from the Mexican gulf inviting us to its early spring. Building by a mountain solitude, the city sends out to us its joyous shout, its music, its art, its eloquence—and the mountain home is tempted even to ruin by a counter charm. Sad warfare between finite man and infinite beauty!

In this bewilderment of the beautiful there is no alternative left the heart but to conclude that the world is too large for it. It cannot go all over it, cannot hold it all in its arms. Life is too short for the enjoyment of all the grand days that open their morning portals between the St. Lawrence and the Amazon, between the Black Sea and the Golden Gate. There is a tomb in the grass that cuts short this wandering from joy to joy. The tomb is the author of all eclectism. With traces of sorrow perhaps, but with resignation, the limited mortal heart must say, the world is too large for me, and must select its spot for life and for death. It must plant a few vines and trees and make the most of its narrow realm. We cannot pluck all roses, the hand being made for but one.

So the moral world of our God is too large. It outreaches our mind and affections. It hath motives too many for any one, but just enough for all; too many for a life, but enough for all lives. All mankind make up a kind of infinity of mind and heart, and an eternity of time, and in this vast sea of humanity all God's moral beauties and forces find demand. But in any one soul fluttering along over only a few years, as a winged butterfly flits only over one summer's foliage, the divine motives cannot all find full field of action. The heart not being able to live everywhere must contentedly pitch its tent in some vale, and say, "Here will I live and die." We would not narrow down life from choice, but accept the order of necessity. We would struggle to grasp as much as possible, but with the full assurance that to comprehend and enjoy all is denied us in God's decree.

The text, embody one of the fragments of the great realm of motive. Christ's love of man and man's love of Christ, cause and effect, make up a grand incentive to virtuous action. These are not the whole of truth. They are golden branches plucked from a great tropical wilderness. For the love of Christ is not the only thing that restrains, nor is love the only fulfillment of the law. In Oriental language a part is a whole, and one beautiful thing is a complete world. The fear of punishment also restrains. The fear of Christ restrains, and love is often found in great depth and yet the law is not fulfilled. Paul had just said, "Knowing the terror of the Lord we persuade men," and, "We must all appear before the judgment seat of Christ." Such souls as Peter, had loved deeply, and yet had fallen into sin; so that love did not fulfill the law. The "terror of the Lord" was invoked to help restrain, and yet, amid these phenomena come the words, "Love is the fulfillment of the law" and "The love of Christ constraineth us." Beautiful transformation of what we love into a whole universe.

The philanthropic leaders in our age are wonderfully constrained by the love of mankind. Pity for the poor human race, daily moves the best hearts that have ever lived. Before this immense influence hundreds of our best men bow as before a divine command. Thus we perceive that the world of moral motives is as rich as the world of physical beauty, and if a single heart cannot build its home by every beautiful vale, but must go from the many to the one; so, in the world of morals, the heart cannot but retreat from the whole universe, to take refuge in a part. Its house must be by this river or lake, but not by all waters that sleep or run. The love of Christ is a beautiful part of the moral world. It is stated as if a universe; but this is a statement of love, rather than of logic. Love always confuses its dream with the picture of infinity. "Love is the fulfilling of the law," is also a sublime part of the moral world. It is quoted as being the whole, but this too, is the language of admiration rather than of logic; for if this were the whole truth, it would only be necessary for men to be sincere in sentiment, and their love would be the same as perfection. In the midst of a universe so vast, what can the poor limited heart do, but accept of some one great impulse an impulse acquired by taste, by locality, or by inheritance, and build there its earthly house for its few years here below?

There is a sect of Christians now rising up in our land, or rather coming into the world a second time, who have reached what they call the higher life. Led by such noble minds as Professor Upham and Dr. Boardman, and Inskip, they have developed a piety, which has eliminated, not only all doubt from their mind, but all care and sorrow from their heart. To them no pain can come. They are glad when their friends die, for they see heaven so near, and they say that God is so with them, that this earth is a border of Paradise. They have reproduced with additional beauties the quietism of Madame Guyon of the seventeenth century Turning their gaze upon only peace in God it has become a universe and all else has faded from their horizon.

Thus in tranquility of soul there is found a motive of life, a power that hurls into the sea of oblivion the sin that comes from this world's temptation, and the sorrow that comes from its physical pain and death. The grave is the cradle from which earth turns away and leaves the sleeping child to be rocked of angels and to awake with God. These fresh hearts may be in error to-day, as that woman and the great Fenelon were two hundred years ago; but they illustrate the general fact, that one or two motives are all that the heart can carry, and these become to that heart a whole world. They are to it immensity and eternity.

To the city of God there are many paths, paths for different centuries, different meridians, and different individuals. There was something in the times of Calvin and Luther and on to Jonathan Edwards, that enabled the motive of punishment to be very influential for good. To inquire whether anything would have done as good service, would be about like the inquiry, whether some other method of light and heat might not have been resorted to by the Creator, that would have made our existing sun unnecessary. It is certain that "the terror of the Lord" wielded a mighty influence on the past centuries; and the same impulse of virtue will always be extant and active; but to the millions of a subsequent age a new impulse is liable to arise, and, expressing itself in the words, "the love of Christ constraineth us," may, for a time, be a complete universe to the existing heart. The horizon is daily swept for new clouds.

New motives are always unfolding and blossoming with new colors. Our fullest roses were once single leafed. Some seek riches for fear of a poor-house at last, or the jail for debt. Nobler minds seek wealth, because of the education and beauty it will buy for the dear loved ones, or for the brothers in the street. Each age and each form of government is fashioning a religious argument for itself, despotism admitting the element of authority, republicanism admitting the sweeter influence of good result, caring less for *ipse dixit* than for the fitness of things. Motives come and go along with the coming and going of new times and new men. The arguments for a holy life change. The old ones do not become false, but they fail to please. New ones are demanded by the new minds and hearts coming into life. In the childhood of you in this hall, who are oldest to-day, it was customary to frighten young hearts into virtue. We little children feared a dark room for reasons good then, but poor now. All misfortunes were the vengeance of our Heavenly Father following some bad act of the past week or day. We did not hear much about the text, "Whom the Lord loveth he chasteneth." But the Christian children of to-day, are led along virtue's path, by being shown the lovely side of Christianity. Music, books, Christmas festivals, tender Sabbath-school teachers and a thousand inventions of love, draw their spirits up toward that Being, who gave existence and name to Christianity. The new motive rises like a star. The love of Christ constrains them.

There can be no one impulse to virtue that shall monopolize all souls and all times. Mind is too full of variety. The times change too much and we are too much changed in them. If there be one word deeply carved upon God's works that word is *variation*. In the strata of the earth, on its surface, in the faces of men, in the pursuits of society there is the record of a God who is infinite in forms and qualities. Next to the beauty of God's unchangeableness in principles, comes the beauty of His variety in non-essentials. The laws of vegetation are perpetual, but the leaves and flowers and fruits vary. The peach was born yesterday, but trees, in the eternity past. God is fixed as to righteousness for himself and for His children; but the motives to it among men assume new shapes with the shifting time and place. It is always purity that lies before the soul; but whether the heart shall be led to it by the intrinsic goodness of the object or by the fear of punishment for seeking the opposite, are details that admit of variation. A deliberative mind will be influenced by both ideas; the passionate heart by only the goodness of virtue, seeking it as the hungry child seeks food; the cowardly, timid nature will seek it from fear. The variety of motive will be demanded by the variety of mind.

A deeply religious woman objects to the hymn,

> "Prone to wander Lord I feel it
> Prone to leave the God I love,"

saying that she feels no proneness to wander, none to leave the Good she loves. She says, "How would it sound in our ear for a mother to sing to her child,

> "Prone to wander child I feel it
> Prone to leave the child I love?"

To a nature of this kind the motives of Christian life are formed on Christ himself. All considerations of perdition are out of the question. The love of Christ constraineth. Love is the fulfilling of law in all this passionate heart. It was so in the school of Madame Cuyon and Fenelon and the Wesleys—and will always be so whenever the soul rises to a passion in love and faith. Perfect love casteth out fear.

The higher life of religion will find its motive in religion itself. As the musician finds his motive, not in the pain of discord, but in the sweetness of music, so the higher order of Christian life will find its impulse, not in any fear of hell, but in the beauty and good of Jesus Christ. As art is not the avoidance of deformity, but the study of positive beauty, so Christianity is not a flight from wrath, but a loving development and enjoyment of the more perfect life. God is not to be sought because there is a Satan, but because there is a God.

When patriotism runs low and there is impending war it is necessary for the State to repeat the law that treason is death. This law is a perpetual fact. This law will never be repealed, but it is kept in existence only by the low form of patriotism possible here and there. But the true citizen lives above it, and ignores it, and wholly forgets it, for his positive love of his native land constrains him. It fulfills the law. Behind the mercenary Persian troops went the driver with his whip, a man with a whip behind each squad, and the victory came not from love of country, but from fear of the scourge; but the moment a country becomes worthy of love and its citizens become intelligent enough to love it, the whip behind the soldiers is superceded by the honor and happiness in front. The flag overhead with its red, white and blue carries a divine impulse in its waving folds. Its threads are the threads of life—its red is the blood of men's hearts. Before this banner of beauty the fear of a Persian whip falls out of all use and even remembrance.

It would be dreadful if Christianity were less noble than patriotism and must be expected to draw its activity from a whip on the field of battle. The banner of salvation is grander than any that ever waved over bloody fields, even of human liberty. It rustles in the winds of immortality. It is not the flag of a transient state full of the graves of our children, but the flag of that great Fatherland where there is no death and no tears. Under its snowy white and its heavenly azure, soldiers in the higher life need no impulse but the love of their passion-full hearts.

Hence the better men become, the more Christ-like Christians become; the more will the world of punishment give place to the world of peace and joy in the presence of Jesus Christ, and the more intelligent and cultivated men become, the more will they be moved by the positive side of religion; by its excellence rather than by its penalties.

But amid all the fluctuations of patriotism the law of death for treason remains written on the statute book of nations. And so in Christianity however any class or any age may rise above the influence of penalty for sin, yet punishment remains a perpetual fact in the ecomony of our God. Its dark cloud will rise or fall according to the quality of humanity. Wherever there are hearts that can see no goodness in holiness, none in honesty, and in charity, none in Jesus Christ, none in the worship of God, wherever there are minds incapable of being led by the intrinsic good of religion, there this dark cloud of divine wrath is ready to descend and to envelop with its thunders the soul that cannot and will not be enveloped by love. The result of sin expressed in all religions by the word "hell" is a perpetual influence, liable to go and come as humanity advances or retreats in the path of intelligence and morals,—but it must be a perpetual fact in a world of beings capable of being immoral. A world of sin must be a world of penalty.

As we said in the outset, one heart cannot live in all the beautiful places of earth, neither can it be led by all the motives of entire humanity. What is true of a mind may be true of an age. It is possible for a whole age to become like Guyon and Fenelon, enamored of one idea, and, forgetting the gloomy hell, draw all its spiritual life from a vision of Jesus Christ and of His redeemed earth and happy paradise. The love of Christ may constrain a whole age. This ought particularly to become the case in an age of unusual education and culture, and in an age that develops the goodness and benevolence of Jesus Christ. An age that loves the poor, that feeds and clothes the destitute and famine-stricken, that pours out millions upon a burned up city, that governs its children by love instead of torture, that enthrones kindness in public schools and even in prisons and jails, and that does all these new things in the name of a positive study of Christ, will not be an age that will constantly threaten mankind, but an age that will gently lead men toward the divine Jesus of Nazareth.

In days when men cannot whip their children, in days when men are arrested for cruelty to dumb beasts, in days when we teach our children beautiful hymns and when we reward them for any act of goodness, in days when there are homes for the friendless and for the fallen, and millions are poured out for colleges where anybody can learn any science or art without charge, in days when a child need not be a beggar, in days in which Russia and America are fresh in the glory wreaths of having set free 60,000,000 of slaves, it can hardly be expected that the pulpit, ignoring this grand uprising of tenderness, will daily point the horrors of perdition while the very street is being enchanted by this vision of love. Oh what a betrayal this would be of the pulpit's trust!

It must be confessed that the motive of virtue found in the word punishment exists. It will always exist; but if there comes along an era that is blinded to this argument by having its eyes fixed upon the love of God and the Saviour, then let the public heart enjoy to the full, this new and powerful passion.

The terrors of the law have had whole periods allotted to themselves and they produced the middle ages, and before them, the Mosaic age. It is possible that an era that shall study the positive side of religion and shall fly to Christ, not because there is a Satan, but because there is a Christ, may work out for the human race better things than came from the age of monastic scourgings or from the penalties of Moses. A book loved under the name of "The new Testament" declares that "ye are not come unto a mount that might be touched and that burned with fire, nor unto blackness and darkness and tempest * * * * so terrible that Moses said "I exceedingly quake and fear, but ye are come unto Mount Sion and unto the city of the living God." The words spoken indeed to Christians do nevertheless announce to all mankind the ruling passion of the Gospel. Its great spectacle is not a Sinai but a Mount Sion, not a fiend devouring men, but a Saviour and a heavenly Father reaching out the open arms of infinite love to gather in us children.

If we have come to an age that seems to take up this dominant impulse of Christianity and to depress other motives, we cannot but bless God that He postponed all our cradles and graves for this era of faith and love and peace. We are, I trust, all more than willing to give our hearts to the spirit of our own times, and would not for any gold go back to the age of terrorism in politics, in domestic life and in Christianity. Confessing punishment to exist as a potential idea, confessing prisons to exist for criminals, and death to threaten all traitors, and divine justice to hang like a cloud over sin, yet we must rejoice in all tendencies of ages and of men to base their moral life upon the attractiveness of the good.

A French writer living in the time of Louis XIV says: "Bourdaloue in his sermons astounds me." This was enough for one tongue. "Massilon frightens me." That also was well. "Bossuet makes me believe." "Fenelon makes me to hope and love." Oh beautiful power of each of this matchless group! If individuals thus have a channel in which their souls must run all their life if it would go with any power or any happiness, so a whole generation may have its path, not as wide as all truth, but very beautiful to it and leading straight to paradise.

The preaching of religion from the standpoint of fear is the shortest mode, is the easiest method, if quantity of thought is considered, for it is only necessary to breathe familiar anathemes over all the sinful race of men. It is a longer and more difficult work to trace out the application of the Gospel to all the details of human life—to politics, to home, to childhood, middle life and old age. To gather up the rationalism of Christianity, its spiritualism—and its humanity, to unfold its Jesus Christ—its Holy Spirit, its faith, hope and charity—to develop in infinite riches of thought and feeling, is a hard, long task compared with the authoritative announcement of infinite sorrow to almost the whole human race. But let us all rejoice that the age demands of us all, pulpit and pew, the longer and more thoughtful method of proclaiming the manifold·riches of Christianity.

The love of Christ that constrains us is not only a passion of that divine heart, but it is a wisdom and kindness penetrating a philosophy. This love of man flows and reflows through all the doctrines and precepts of the Gospel. In the golden rule, in the blessing of children, in the law of liberty and equality, in the doctrines of salvation, faith, penitence and purity, in the vision of God as a Father, in the delineation of immortal life, the love of Christ is perceived—like a beautiful soul inhabiting a beautiful body. It constrains us. It is not a simple passion of Christ for man, but it is a wisdom, an adaptation so kind that men call it love, —it being too full of warmth and tears to be called a philosophy.

OLD TESTAMENT INSPIRATION.

Psalms xxiii and cix.

The Mosaic age presents to the Christian and general student a topic of uncommon interest. The interest is rendered uncommon by the questions of inspiration and policy, and by the entanglement of the Mosaic writings with the questions of geology, and other sciences, on the one hand, and with questions of morals on the other.

Approaching any other old writings, we are permitted to read, and accept or reject, because they are confessedly human; but the contents of the Hebrew books are spread upon a back-ground of inspiration, and this claim excites a clamor and debate.

In our remarks this morning we shall speak of the Mosaic writings only as related to morals, leaving the geological question to future times when that science shall have become more exact. In order properly to estimate the morals of the Hebrew Scriptures, it is necessary to define inspiration, for upon that definition will depend the answer to the inquiry whether the Old Testament is inspired.

If, by inspiration, one is to understand a perfect invasion of the human heart and mind by the Infinite Spirit, so that the human is borne away from itself, and thinks only in the words and thoughts of God, then we should have no hesitation in saying that there was no such inspiration in the souls of the writers of the Mosaic age. God is perfection. Hence a human mind penetrated by the Deity would deal only in perfect ideas and actions. But, if by inspiration we may understand Divine assistance given to man, such that he became enabled to think wise thoughts and better, and devise useful things above the ordinary thought and utility of the times, then, the Old Testament affords abundant evidence of inspiration.

God never at once thoroughly equips man. Minerva is fabled to have leaped forth full-armed from the brain of Jupiter, but aside from fable there is no record of any such event. The Divine Spirit never creates a perfect man, but sets him going with the permission to become perfect. The plan of God is that of perpetual assistance. He fills the earth with ores, with coals, with the power to produce harvests of grass, fruits and grains, and then endows man with an expansive faculty, such that he can develop the world and himself. The world, as God gave it to His Children, is one of opportunities and outfits, and not of completed things.

Inspiration would therefore assume the form of a help rather than of a full occupation of the human intellect and feelings, and would no more be a perfect unfolding of God's whole character than the wild Indian is an expression of God's perfect ideal of the creature man.

Eternity being the time, and immensity the arena of Deity, there would seem demanded a graduated method, such, that to-morrow might always promise something better than yesterday, to-night or to-day brings. In harmony with such a presumption, nature is full of simple beginnings and grand openings. Coming to inquire about revelation, we should expect the phenomenon of imperfection, but of great help, also, and great progress. A revelation that should wholly relieve man from further effort and inquiry along the path of truth, would be in discord with the economy of earth, for man's success comes from the perpetual struggle into which he is cast by the world's method. The Creator would no more grant man a perfect revelation than He would furnish man with ready made furniture, or houses, or clothing.

In the Mosaic economy, therefore, we must expect the human element to predominate, and to be still engaged in the common struggle after more and better truth. It would be unwise to suppose the Old Testament a perfect image of God —the ideal Infinite. There is no emblazonment of God anywhere. Do you imagine that when you find man in the state of nature—man as seen in the islands of the South Sea, or as seen in the wilds of our America—the red man, you have found an emblazonment of the Deity? By no means. You have found only the place where God has made a beginning; the place, not where God has finished a palace, but where the earth has been broken for a foundation, and where a stake has been driven. Upon earth, when men are about to build a marble structure destined to be full of elegance of finish, and full, perhaps, of works of art, they first build a wide fence about the area, and then descend into the wet earth and work in rough rock. Thus the Creator proceeds in His universe, and there is no perfect manifestation anywhere of His full glory or wisdom.

The Mosaic economy was nothing else than a progress. Earth had come to Polytheism, to Pantheism, to Feticism. The idea of a Superior Force was universal, but it had not been gathered up into a great central point and perceived to be God. Each thing that had power, such as the sun and moon and sea—each object that was far away, stars and sky—each creature that was terrible, such as serpents and crocodiles—each animal that was very useful, as the cow and the horse, became deities, and were worshipped as such. The air was full of superhuman powers. Disease was a bad spirit. Thus the idea of a superhuman being was broken up into fragments, and was found in a serpent or stone, or in the fire or wind. Under such a discordant belief, morals were discordant, and customs horrible. With a serpent or a crocodile for a deity, man became cruel. He could slay his children, or eat his fellow, for his Fetich was a bloody devourer, and the worship must become such. The slaughter of children became common. Even Rome could crowd her vast amphitheatres in order to see captives eaten by beasts, or slain by each other in contest.

It is necessary for the superhuman power in the air to be called away from the *many* into the *one*. It is necessary to dismiss the sun with its flame, the lightning with its tongue of fire, the serpent with its poison, the crocodile with its sharp teeth. It is necessary to dismiss the iron-hearted Jupiter, and the Apollo with rattling arrows, and Juno full of resentment, and come to a Being, called God, infinite and unchangeable in His being, power, holiness, justice, goodness and truth.

With such a sublime centre, life moves afresh. The serpent becomes only a rude form of brute life. Things thought to be gods sink to the level of the dust, and no longer influence human hearts, passions and hopes and fears, but, instead of these, there is one vast influence, pure and unchanging, drawing all men up to it. The greatest single idea possible to mankind is the idea of God as a Being, only one all-wise, all-good, all-powerful. Looking up to this, nations cast away their barbarism, and the individuals, Elijah-like, ascend in a beautiful chariot.

The Mosaic age was the bearer of this idea. How far it may have known the truth as to geology, I know not, and care not. There may be men that know, and men that care, but, amid these indeterminate questions, one thing is clear, that the Hebrew age was the perfect filtration and purification of the idea of God. Perfect as compared with all before it and about it. There is the source of our Christianity and civilization. It was the Hebrew philosophy and its immediate result, Christianity, that swept away the iron Jupiter, and bloody Mars, and revengeful Juno, and all bonds and stakes and stones of the terrible past—swept them away, and gave us the uniform morals and humanity of the nineteenth century.

But, while the Jews were cherishing and developing this idea, they did not cease at once to be men, and become the perfect image of God. From the method of the world thus far, it is probable it will require ten thousand years for humanity to produce a perfect civilization. Six thousand years having already passed, it is perfectly safe to say that four thousand years more will be needed. Such being, in part at least, the fact, the Jews in their brief life could only have moved over part of this vast circle, and must necessarily reveal the ordinary attributes of mankind in the details of their career. Whatever was human custom, would be their custom. If wars of extermination were the rule of that age, and were necessary in order to advance the Hebrew Theocracy, then they would appear with Moses and Aaron as leaders, just as naturally, as though Hannibal or Cæsar were leading the Israelites. The age was not one in which the Deity has displaced man, but one in which man was blessed with one or two new truths.

For example, let it be granted that Watt was inspired to invent the steam engine. Mankind needed a new motive power. Unaided, man had failed to reach any thing better than the horse, the ox, or man-power, on land, and than sails on the sea. Watt is at this crisis divinely aided to the discovery of steam. But this would not imply that his engine was perfect, or that anything about it should cease to be human. The machine was rude. A boy stood by to work the valves. Its motion was only in a straight line. It worked a pump, but could not turn a wheel. Here it was in the mines, powerful but imperfect; inspired but incomplete. The inspiration began and ended in a single idea—a simple beginning. The engine was developed until the instrument has reached a beauty and perfection undreamed of by the originator himself. The first instrument is set aside by the new development, and yet, the first one was inspired, and the second one human. Again, the inspiration of Watt's engine not only was imperfect as to the engine, but it did not extend beyond it. The men who worked it were common men. They were profane, they stole, they told falsehoods, they fought, they were more or less indolent, they abused their children and their wives after the fashion of all the colliers and all ignorant classes of that age. And this, too, with the inspired machine in the centre of their daily life.

This illustrates the only intelligible theory of the Mosaic age. It was carrying forward an inspired idea—an idea that was to outlive all Polytheism, and transform the face of society. But the inspiration hung around the idea and did not wander from it. The instant you left the idea, you touched humanity. The people fought, and cheated, and held and sold slaves, just as the Greeks and Romans did, and acquired land after the fashion of the barbaric period. But this is no objection to the inspiration of their idea of God. It might as well be objected to the inspiration of Watt's engine that the coal-heavers fought and lived dishonorably. Regardless of the customs of men, the idea of the steam engine was grand on the outset. And so the Mosaic age, regardless of its particulars, was sublime in its crystalization of the ideas of God.

The character of individuals is often a thing distinct from the character of their work. The men that discovered America, or that settled Virginia, may have been freebooters, as some claim, and yet, their vessels may have sailed by a divine inspiration. The inspiration would not include their character, but would look to the future—far off—of America. God is always suffering the individual to fall away, and disappear, leaving behind him something about to become divine.

Thus Moses and all his compeers walked in a human world having one divine element in it. Holding to a true idea of God as a single spirit, eternal and indivisible, they stole land like men at large. Separating Deity from a Fetich, they sold slaves like the old Persians. Appointed to bear religion a few steps onward, they still claimed a plurality of wives like the Philistines, and falsified like the heathen world. But, as on the freebooter's ship there may have sailed once the civilization of England from the shores of old Rome, or as on the gold-seeking ships of Spain there was borne the coming grandeur of America, an invisible passenger sleeping in the festoons on the vessel's bow, so, in the great Hebrew vessel sailing across the dark flood rolling between the Amalekites and the nineteenth century, there was an invisible passenger of divine spirit and purpose, but the men who worked the sails, and handled the cargo, and cast and heaved the anchor, were tumultuous, sinful seamen, after the fashion of the times.

These thoughts bring me now to the structure of the psalms of David. Many of them being deeply religious, and suitable to all religious hearts everywhere, there are others that belonged only to the days when they were sung. If it was permitted the Israelites to destroy their enemies, and thus establish the better their Monotheism, it was necessary they should sing battle-songs, and that much of their hymnology should be military. In days of an American struggle with England, the song of "The Star-spangled Banner" might be useful and truthful. It might impel men along the best path of the period. In France a few years the "Marseillaise" was rising with power, for it was necessary for the people to check the reckless ambition of Louis Napoleon. These hymns might be confessed to possess a temporary inspiration. That is, their good is unmistakable. But let the world and civilization advance, let war become a crime and a barbarism, let peace become not only an article of religion but a policy of all nations, let all disputes be settled by arbitration and payment of damages, and in that golden age the war songs of America and France become a poor dead letter, and no heart remains so warlike as to sing them.

Thus with such psalms as the one hundred and ninth. They had a temporary significance depending altogether upon the kind of work the Hebrews had to perform. If it was necessary for them to go to battle, it was desirable they should have a battle song, a Marseillaise. If their hands must do bloody work they were entitled to sing a terrific psalm. But the moment the Hebrew method of life passed away, the moment their war for national existence ceased, that moment the one hundred and ninth psalm lost its value. For if the bloody Hebrew war is over, so is its battle-song. There is no logic in perpetuating a war-cry after the war itself has passed away.

But when you read the twenty-third psalm, or a majority of the whole collection, you have not the war-cry of a generation, but the yearnings and feelings of all humanity. Hence I would say that the one hundred and ninth psalm was the good of an hour, the twenty-third psalm is the good of all human life this side the grave.

There is, it seems to me, no other conceivable method of treating the Old Testament than that found in the word *eclecticism.* We must seek out its permanent truths, follow its central ideas, and love them the more because they were eliminated from the barbaric ages with so much sorrow and bloodshed. He that can give the Mosaic age and the old Jewish people only a contemptuous sneer, is a person of little reflection and gratitude. Much as our feelings all rise up against the severity of those ages, yet, in those very times there was being wrought out for us a religion that should introduce Christianity, and thus our morals and our liberty.

Looking back, we preceive not only Washington, and then Luther, and then the old Saxons, and old Romans, and Greeks, but we perceive David and Solomon, and all their grand associates, living, and toiling, and dying for you and me—standing with stout hearts and bleeding hands between the low idolatry of primitive man and the civilization of the nineteenth century. David and Solomon were preludes to the blessed Saviour. Faltering in some of their accents, with imperfect music, indeed, they sang a hymn that carried the world sweetly along toward the grand melody that was soon to appear in the Sermon on the Mount, and in the divine chants of the children of Jesus Christ.

SALVATION AND MORALITY.

Blessed are they which do hunger and thirst after righteousness; for they shall be filled. *Matthew v : 6.*

The Sermon upon the Mount may be offered as the text and warrant of the discourse this morning, and from the text you may easily conclude that the subject of remark will be Salvation and Morality.

It is so difficult to make the discriminations demanded by professional theologians, descended often from dark and narrow periods, that we often feel like abandoning forever, not the truth of the Bible, but the hope of saying words that shall please or profit minds that belong to the exact and exacting class in theology. In our own denomination there are so many always ready to complain that "he preaches a religion of morality, he ignores the work of Christ," that one may well hesitate between an utterance that brings complaint and a silence that secures peace. We all love peace. It is the natural wish of most hearts that their life shall be made up of halcyon days, days when no wind ruffles the waters, and when the sun pours upon them in full beauty and warmth. To gratify this wish, there is constant temptation to speak only such words as will blend with the past, and not jar its peaceful sleep. In face of this temptation, we must confess that it does seem high time something were said about a religion of morality, or if the terms be better — salvation and good works.

We must premise by saying that, in our opinion, exactness is impossible in theology. It seems wholly beyond human skill to define faith and charity and salvation with a material exactness. There are instruments by which a measurement of one millionth of an inch may be readily made, but the moment you get away from material world, this instrument is powerless, and there seems none to take its place. In this poverty of instrumentation, it appears we shall never be able to tell the world just what faith is, just what salvation is, just what the office of the Saviour is, and just what that of man's will and of the Divine Spirit is.

Outside of theology, men have never been able to determine just what literature is, what poetry is, what eloquence is, what the motive of virtue may be, what is the exact value of democracy, or pleasure, or wealth, or education. Paley contends that the greatest happiness is the foundation of morals. Victor Cousin says, "Morals is its own foundation. We do a right thing because it is right."

It would be wonderful if thinking men, by simply passing over into the field of theology, should find a realm full of exactness, and offering the most perfect definitions to any one in the least partial to such pursuits. How is it that the words, literature, eloquence, poetry, civilization, right, are so reluctant to accept of rigid analysis, and that theology is so willing to lie down under the knife of the demonstrators of moral anatomy? How comes it to pass that the question "What is liberty?" or "What is civilization?" will always refuse the world a precise answer, and the question "What is salvation?" may be answered in a moment by the nearest professor in the schools of the church? We recall now the anecdote of science, by which some savan attempted to entrap Franklin, or Columbus, or Pythagoras. "How comes it to pass," inquired Science, "that if a cup be filled to the brim, and then many fishes be put gently into the cup, the water shall not overflow? Instead of explaining the phenomenon, the ideal Franklin or Pythagoras tried the experiment, and the water did overflow.

Thus is our theological world. The question "How comes it to pass that salvation may be so exactly defined?" is to be answered, "It does not come to pass at all. The glass does overflow." The definition, when exact, is so far false; for in order perfectly to define a saved soul, it would be necessary for man to read the judgment of God, and to perceive all that in the last day will be counted in or counted out in the solemn estimate. As it will be the office of God only to assign places to the spirits called away from this life, with Him must rest the detailed facts upon which the sphere of the soul shall be prescribed for the vast hereafter. Hence, the Infinite One only knows the full import of the word salvation. Knows its essentials, its limitations; He only knows exactly what hearts will ascend from the scenes of earth up to a supreme bliss.

One of our hymns says with truth.

> There is a time, we know not when,
> A point, we know not where,
> That marks the destiny of men
> For glory or despair.

It is a true thought, but I would not limit the mystery by the idea of time and place only, but also by the quantity and quality of religion in the heart. There is no measurement by which man can determine just the soul that shall receive the smile seen in the words, "Well done, good and faithful servant," just the soul that shall tremble at the sentence, "Depart from me ye accursed."

Thus interpreting the hymn, it becomes to my heart powerful and thrilling —

> There is a line, by us unseen,
> That crosses every path,
> The hidden boundary between
> God's patience and His wrath.
>
> Oh, where is this mysterious bourn
> By which our path is crossed;
> Beyond which God himself hath sworn
> That he who goes is lost?

In this shadow realm we would not wish to throw down the exact response that "he that believes" shall safely pass the mysterious bourn; for faith is such a broad, indefinable word that to substitute it for the term salvation, would be to leave us still in the air obscure. "Faith in Christ," would be a phrase still indefinite, for not only has faith many forms, but many forms also attach to the person of Christ. He was a sacrifice, but sacrifice has many significations. He was an example. He was a mediator. He was an unfolding of the divine image. Faith in Christ is a phrase which is at once seen to be made of words that are like the bits of colored glass in the kaleidoscope, forming many pictures and all very beautiful.

The faith of a little child in Christ, would differ essentially from the faith in Jesus of a person come to education and deeper thought. In the child's estimate there could enter no analysis of the Saviour in the theological sense of the term. His offices of atoning lamb, of example, of image of God, would all be crowded out of the young heart by the enthusiastic reception of Christ as a loving, glorified, heavenly friend. If to such a child what is called salvation could come, then must we confess that salvation must elude scholastic definition, and make of itself new pictures according to the hand that turns the magical glass. The words must possess an elasticity greater than will be admitted by the schools founded to promulge an exact idea.

Now, this refusal of salvation to be defined in language rigidly exact and sharp, ought to make us all very unwilling to separate it in any way from good works. There is such a growing together of these two ideas in the whole New Testament that any separation of them seems an act of ignorance or vandalism toward the life and history of Christ. The entire Sermon upon the Mount is a union of morals and salvation. It is the most careful unfolding of a religion of morality that was ever uttered or read upon earth. From its outburst, in which heaven is assigned to the poor in spirit and pure in heart, to its last verse, where doing good works is the foundation of rock, upon which every man's hope should be built, the divine discourse marches along to the key-note of morality.

There is no evading the significance of the fact that in all the days and hours of Christ's life upon the earth, the doctrine of good works was the cardinal idea in every speech, and even in the most solemn prayer of Gethsemane. Into the brief, model prayer, into which we may suppose this divine intelligence gathered up the most useful petitions, he taught mankind, that to forgive and be forgiven, to be delivered from temptation and evil, were the blessings needed by the soul, and hence, the essence of its salvation.

Between us and a salvation, the teachings of Christ about an upright life, stand with such a broad depth and sublime height, that it would seem like presumption and egotism in man to announce for the soul a safety in which good works should perform no prominent part. If what is called in exact theology, "faith," is the sum and substance of salvation, it is almost wonderful that the great Captain of our salvation, instead of setting forth this idea in His earthly discourses, in almost every case gave the impulse and sanction of His career to the doctrine of an upright, religious life. With the words of Jesus before us, far be it from us ever to utter a word that would seem to give hope of heaven to a soul not building up a personal righteousness.

The alarm expressed by many pulpits, that many are relying too much upon a life of morality, seems to jar at once with all the words of the Saviour, and with the events of the sad times in which our country lives.

In this Credit Mobilier phenomenon, I see no tendency on the part of public men to base their soul's salvation on good works. That list of names that is at the same time associated with the church and with the acceptance of bribes, does not seem in the least injured by any reliance upon good works for salvation. Their hope of heaven must be based upon faith alone. The righteousness they dream of must be wholly an imputed righteousness. In presence of Sin, bursting forth in high and low places, like as plague issuing from the plains of India; Sin, with one hand full of bribes, the other dripping in blood, we should tremble, as a servant of Christ, to utter one word that would warn mankind against placing too high an estimate upon the value of a sinless life. Upon all the horizon we cannot behold any encroachment of this evil. The only persons visibly wedded to the moral life, are certain followers of William Penn, and in the group of bribe-holders, between Kansas and the Atlantic, no one of these "mere moralists" seems visible. Caution against salvation by good works would, therefore, seem premature. With the Catholics buying righteousness with a price, so many pardons for a sinful soul, and with many Protestants, warned against placing confidence in anything but faith, the time for being alarmed at any over-development of Quaker morality, appears not yet to have come.

Standing amid the scenes that surround us all to-day, if there be any connection spoken of in the Bible as existing between a man's morals and his destiny, this would seem like the year and our country the place, in which all such relationships should be brought out in all the theological schools and rostrums in the land. There has never been a time when the morality of the Quakers could be so well endured. Would that there might be, in all the schools of the land, a Quaker professorship of honesty endowed along with the chair of saving faith. Unable as we all may be to see what influence upon heaven a salvation by help of good works might exert, whether it would leave that blessed realm to be a solitude, it must be confessed that actual human righteousness would be very valuable to this star and this generation.

If Christ by His death wrought out a salvation for man, man's heart must be the prize bought with the sacred life and death. There is no salvation for a sinful soul except a pure life. Hence, if Christ effectually assists man to this pure soul, He is man's Saviour, and the pure soul is the salvation. If good works are the salvation, Christ is still the Saviour. Hence, salvation by good works and salvation by Jesus the Redeemer are so inseparably blended that any effort to separate, must result in an insult to the Cross in the one hand, and to the Sermon on the Mount on the other. It cannot be that Christ would save a race in their sins, but from their sins, and hence, the flight from sin is always a flight to the bosom of God. This is therefore the essence and soul of Christianity, this upward flight.

If to us, lost in a wilderness, without a sun, nor a star, nor a path to guide, there comes a benevolent hermit, a dear Mentor, and leads us to the right path, and sets our faces homeward, he is at once our saviour; but no perfect salvation will come from to our going that path. Our "going", and the Mentor combine in the escape, and yet he lives in memory as the kind saviour of our bewildered hearts.

Thus Christ may be the Saviour of mankind, and yet leave our morality as the final embodiment of His salvation. All the work of Christ contained in the word Calvary, or atonement, is only the objective part of the soul's rescue, whereas, man's own personal righteousness is the subjective salvation, the thing for which the other exists. Good works are the explanation of Calvary.

The words and life of Christ show that what He most desired, was the spiritual perfection of His children. "Be ye perfect, even as your Father in heaven is perfect," was the ruling wish of His heart. All His eloquence was aimed at, not simply acts of sin, but even sinful thought. In the transcendent light of His morals, the Ten Commandments faded like a snow-drop upon the bosom of ocean. The heaven of Jesus was both a purity and a place, and hence, the final analysis of salvation will show us a sinless soul, at one with Christ, as He and the Father are one.

There is no conflict, perhaps, between Paul and the Saviour. I use the word "perhaps" only as a further confession of the impossibility of determining with scientific exactness the whole of Paul's thought on the one hand, and the whole of the Saviour's thought on the other. Assuming inspiration, there of course is no conflict. But not thus begging the question and appealing only to rationalism, there seems no discord in the two strains of music. Paul unfolds salvation from without. He tells what is necessary outside of man. Hence Calvary and law and imputation and satisfaction come upon his horizon at all hours. There the Jewish altar is transformed into a cross. The first Adam and second Adam meet. The past sins of humanity are gathered up mountain high, and a price is to be paid for them, paid in blood and death. While these scenes of objective salvation are pictured in intense colors upon the sky of the saint, the scenes of the subjective salvation are passing along through the mind of the Saviour — souls full of virtue, full of brotherly love, souls from which even evil thoughts have been banished forever. Paul is busy with the paths to a destiny; Christ with the beautiful destiny itself. There is no necessary conflict, but Christ remains as always everywhere the greater. He never halts in any vestibule, or sits down upon a confine. He passes into the holy places of the soul and utters the final wisdom and prayer and destiny of the poor mortals waiting for His words.

In this salvation which hath two parts, the way and the going in that way, the hand is rash indeed that would separate the human character from the salvation. In order to do this it is not only necessary to abandon all the Gospels of Christ, but it is necessary also to misunderstand Paul and torture him upon the rack of a system. In a world where the absence of integrity, the absence of a righteousness is so remarkable as to fill society with alarm by day and by night, and in an era, too, where what is called salvation by faith alone has been crowded forward with wonderful ability and success, as to acceptance, it seems high time the scholastic meaning of salvation where made to expand until it should receive into its polluted heart the Sermon on the Mount and the morals of Jesus. The faith demanded by this sinful race is one that will not simply look upon a price for its sins, but upon a career of individual virtue, a faith that believes in Christ, not only upon Calvary, but in the Gospels, Christ not only in Mosaic types, but Christ in the spotless purity recorded by Matthew and St. John. A religion is needed that will not dare tell mankind that works are of no significance, that will not cast contempt upon any righteousness except an imputed one, a religion that will not dare spurn the entire life and words of Him who spake as never man spake. This is not a salvation without Christ. The difficulty will be found to be that it has too much of Christ in it. To the teachings of Calvin and Luther it adds the teachings of the Saviour as an important supplement.

The divine Jesus with His morality, with His curse upon one who even called his brother Raca, with this prayer "Be ye perfect," with His benediction for him who did the last commandment and taught men so, with His whole career full of man's subjective salvation, is an object too vast to be swept from the Christian sky by the besom of any school, past or to come. Be you anywhere, my friend, in the journey of life; in youth, or middle life, or old age, do not suffer any voice to confuse your heart as to the need of a personal obedience rendered the teachings of the Saviour. The precise meaning of salvation may elude your power of definition. You may not be able to find that line that crosses every path—

> "The hidden boundary between
> God's patience and His wrath,"

but whatever darkness may gather around you, admit the obscure definitions of men, there will always be in the imitation of Jesus Christ a place where no shadow can come. A religion that will make the Sermon on the Mount play a second part in your earthly career, comes it under any name, Calvinist, Methodist, Baptist or Catholic, that religion decline, or abandon so far, and draw nearer to Him who knew better than all the schools, wherein lies the best destiny of the soul.

All through the life of Christ the music of heavens sounded to the pure in heart, and an awful thunder rolled in all the sky, over the spirit that sinned in deed and in thought; and when a generation after the Saviour's death, the heavens opened to the vision of St. John, and this divine Being stood a radiant star on the border of earth, there came the same music again for the virtuous, the same thunder in the futurity of the wicked. "Blessed are they that do His commandments, that they may have right to the tree of life, and may enter in through the gates of the city; for without are dogs and sorcerers and murderers and idolators and whosoever loveth and maketh a lie." Here the morals of Jesus return to us in awful significance. Let us not add to nor take away from the words of the prophecy of this book.

We have come to evil days—days when public men who stand forth as members of the Christian church, even of the churches called orthodox, hesitate not to carry in the same heart a salvation by faith and a willingness to receive bribes. Among the public men now charged with glaring dishonor there may be some who can establish innocence, but the awful fact is even here confessed, that there are thousands of Christians who are getting their salvation by faith and their fortunes by rascality. If the parties could be found who have in the past brought about this divorcement between salvation and good works, they should be urged to come forward and confess their sin before the nineteenth century, so injured in all the sacred places of its soul. In the name of injured virtue, in the name of public calamity, come and coming, they should read and preach, not only the grand philosophy of Paul, but the still grander morals of Jesus Christ.

There is a Christianity that will save the world. It has not only a faith, but it has a morality as essential as its faith. It not only says "Believe and be saved," but it assigns damnation to him who leads a wicked life. There is a Christianity that will not only fill heaven with saints, but earth with good citizens. In it Paul and Christ are not rudely separated, and the human placed above the divine, but the morals of the Gospels come back to mankind, and the anxiety for faith is no greater than the hungering after righteousness.

In the pictures and images of the Cross seen in all homes in this era of tenderer sentiment, there is often to be seen a garland of flowers, surrounding the cruel wood in their loving imbrace. Emblems of life and death indeed! but may they be to us always, emblems of the Sermon upon the Mount, inwreathing the atonement, forming a part of the indefinable salvation—inseparable. The Christ that gave the world the Cross, wove also the garland of morality that completes its adaption to the wants of man.

THE JOYFUL SUNDAY.

"For My yoke is easy and My burden is light."—*Matthew* xi, 30.

Three facts combine to place this Sunday beyond the reach of the pulpit's prose. We would do well to surrender the occasion to song and flowers and the full heart's meditation. It is a Sunday in springtime; it is Sunday of the holy communion, and it is Easter Sunday. May your hearts all find in their own depths a measurement of the occasion which words cannot express. What help you may not gather from the pulpit's formal words to-day, you may find in the flowers that wreathe the altar and in the spiritual associations of the hour. What remarks you are invited to hear shall be in some way suggested by the presence and character of the Easter day.

It is only conjecture that has located this sacred anniversary upon the border of spring. Many of those details which are carefully reported in an age of printing, and in an age of such restless inquiry as the art of printing has developed, wholly escaped record and remembrance in the far-off times of the Testament. The history of modern events is gathered by hundreds of busy hands, and hundreds of presses multiply the exact report, so that the day that witnesses the end of a war, or the death of a great individual, places in the hand of every citizen a history of the great war or the great life. History, worthy in a high sense of the name, begins with the art of printing. All history, up to the coming of that "art preservative of all arts," is only a poor outline of a world, instead of a full-faced picture of the great subject. It is comforting to the Christian, however, to feel that the life of his Master is full beyond the custom of profane biography, and in detail of the life and thoughts and deeds and death, surpasses the chronicles the world possesses as to any great character of the far past, not excepting such a philosopher as Plato, or such an emperor as Cæsar. The life of Christ is remarkable for the number of its witnesses, and for the credibility they merit by their honesty and opportunity. But they gave us no birthday nor deathday of their Master, and after the old, half-civilized generations in the third century had absolutely fought battles over different opinions about the time of the resurrection, the council of Nice established a day by decree, and since that date the Christian Church has, so far as it has regarded the event at all, celebrated the morning which our generation is learning to love more and more deeply.

Aside from the exact day, it is quite probable that this event of sorrow and joy occurred in the spring months, for as the Christian Church followed closely with its life the event of the cross, it is hardly probable that the oldest persons in the first century should have possessed incorrect data regarding the season of the year when their Lord was crucified, and that they should have located in the spring an event so significant that occurred in the late harvest or midwinter. It seems quite certain that the Lord thus died and arose in the spring time, and thus by design, for there is not much of accident in the world, associated His life and His religion with the realm of flowers and beauty and hope. Spring is the peculiar property of hope. We all, from the young child to the most venerable father of three score and ten years, feel that when the long winter relents and the wind has begun to blow softly upon the cheek, a new world is about to come, and each morning bird song seems a herald declaring a new joy and new existence to the heart. There are many wonderful harmonies between the God of nature and the God of the soul. They are so numerous that the spirit of man can express all its varying conditions by asking us to look upon the world of material. If unhappy, it declares its sky to be clouded; if happy, its sky to be bright; if young, it appeals to springtime as its emblem; if beyond manhood and forsaken, it cries,

> "My name is in the yellow leaf,
> The flowers and fruits of love are gone;
> The worm, the canker, and the grief
> Are mine alone."

Thus there are no shadings in human experience which may not behold their image in the great temple of nature in which man lives and dies. The majority of mortals come upon death in the night hours, as though the great evening shadow which wraps in its gloom wood and field, and even the loved home where the sick one lies, were designed of God to be an accompaniment to the shadow about to come to the spirit. If, therefore, the God of nature and the God of the heart are seen to move along in such parallel lines, why may we not suppose that if a Savior was to come and rise from the tomb in presence of a world, that the infinite wisdom would ask the great springtime to open her flower beds for that tomb of new life and hope. It is only one of a thousand harmonies if that season which casts its best sunshine and happiness upon the shores of earth, is that one which was asked to cast the Son of Man upon the shores of immortality.

When the Easter Sunday became established it was called *dominica gaudii*—"the joyful Sunday,"—and thus for fifteen hundred years this day has journeyed along to receive not the offerings of dust and ashes, not the worship of sighing and despair, but the offerings of the sweetest bloom and the worship of gratitude and hope. A large part of the Protestant world has faithfully closed its eyes to the reality and value of this anniversary in Christian history, and thus has robbed religion of one of its beautiful robes, leaving it more and more dependent upon a costume of nothing but sackcloth. The reason of this past neglect is manifold. Protestantism in its puritan and dissenting divisions was a reaction against a service of an extremely material character. The spiritual seemed forgotten, and the outward symbols to have taken the place of an "inner life." The pulpit that had been set up in early years as a teacher of truth, had been crowded almost out of existence by a great stage filled with bishops, priests, and acolytes, where eloquence seemed deposed by pageantry. Against a religion which seemed an extravagant development of the spectacular, Presbyterianism, and Methodism, and Congregationalism, and Quakerism, were a form of revolt, for it cannot be denied that the creed of these new sects was not such a full departure from Episcopacy or Romanism as was the genius of their new worship, its spirituality and simplicity. Having set forth in a full dislike of the state Churches, and particularly of the Roman Church, these independent sects feared and despised everything Roman, and hence saw the hand of Satan not only in the "confessional" and in the "infallibility," but also in a Church organ and in Easter happiness.

A second reason for this neglect may be found in the fact that these dissenting sects arose further north than Palestine and Italy and France, and amid hardships of government, of sky, of race, and hence amid severity of thought; hence religion omitted much that was beautiful and gentle, and dealt greatly in the logical and the most practical; and if any further reflection is needed to account for the neglect which this day receives in many puritan branches of the Church, we may remember that the Free sects have been compelled to fight their whole way along through history, and hence could not accomplish much with a sword in one hand and Easter flowers in the other. The poetry of religion died in the long conflict.

In the joy and gratitude of this day, our hearts should not fail to be thankful that the world has so advanced in the enlightenment which destroys prejudice, and in the deeper study of religion, and in the development of a Christian brotherhood, that now at last this day comes back to our sanctuary and excites no ill will, no past bitter memory of pope or bishop, but only remembrance of the open tomb of Arimathea. The Christian heart universal is so emptied of old animosity and narrowness that the Protestant Churches rejoice, I believe, to join this day with the Catholic world in confessing the religious worth and beauty of this occasion, and in joining with them, though at separate altars, in this worship of joyfulness.

In coming up to such a day as this, we have not encountered a kind of accident of the religion of Jesus, but have come to its inmost and permanent spirit. When the Divine Author of religion declares that "His yoke is easy and His burden light," we may accept of the words as covering all the days of this pilgrimage. When looked at from the stand-point of old Jewish law, full of imperfections, full of wrath, and too narrow either for life or death, whose confines were a single nation, and whose religion was an external offering of flocks, and whose great emblem was a Sinai covered with thunderings and vivid lightnings, Christ's yoke, with its perfection of reason in its new law, and with its redemption on the cross, and with its forgiveness, and its brotherhood of man and loving presence of God, became easy and His burden light.

When the Testament in many places assures us that whoever would follow Christ must deny himself and take up the cross, it would seem that Christianity was sent forth on a mission of sorrow, but much of that language was directed to those immediate times when to follow Christ was to place the foot in a path which led to martyrdom. It was necessary for a St. Paul and for tens of thousands around his grave to turn away from the paths of earthly happiness, and bidding farewell to friends, to look death calmly in the face as the fate of the morrow not far away. The prayer of Milton over the martyr of Piedmont passes beyond his horizon and becomes full of awful solemnity when breathed over the first four centuries after our Lord:

"Forget not: in Thy book record their groans
Who were Thy sheep, and in their ancient fold
Slain by the bloody Piedmontese that rolled
Mother with infant down the rocks. Their moans
The vales redoubled to the hills and they to heaven,
Their martyr'd blood and ashes sow
O'er all the Italian fields."

In view of these dark ages, whose fury it seems was not wholly to die away for a thousand years, Christ handed down to His children the form of His own cross to go with them, the emblem of many a sorrow and many a martyrdom. Thus I feel that many of the half-melancholy words of Christ were spoken as against the persecutions that would follow and did exhaust themselves upon that special shore, leaving His broadest and everlasting declaration to be that of our text: "My yoke is easy and My burden is light." Sorrows may come here and there, to this or that period, or to this or that heart, but as a general truth embracing all lands and all humanity. Christianity is the most abundant fountain of happiness of whose waters the human family may ever drink. If there is any happiness in this world it ought to be found in the obedience of such morals as are found in the Sermon upon the Mount, and in such a life of broad love and charitable action as are seen in the life of Christ, and in that refuge for the soul found beneath His Cross, and in that hope which there bursts upon the vision beyond the open tomb.

If I should declare that apart from the fear of persecution and martyrdom there is no cross to be borne, I should overlook a certain self-denial which does indeed belong to this religion. But it is almost worthy of contempt, for it is not a denial of a *good self* but a *wicked self.* We are not asked to deny self of anything that belongs to the broadest and highest development of mind and heart, but if there is anything low and satanic in our nature, we are invited to cut off that form of human energy. Self-denial seems to be a denying the heart the privilege of its own self-disgrace. If not to steal, not to envy, not to bear false witness, not to despise the poor, nor be insensible to the wants of one's fellow-men, are a self-denial, then Christianity is full of it; but if we pass by a depraved or unworthy nature as being something whose gratifications is a simple disgrace, and if we think of only a lofty soul and the highest form of character, Christianity is not a self-denial, but a self-love and self-gratification. Much of the asceticism which lingers in the Christian philosophy and practice has been gathered up from half-civilized ages, all through which religion advanced mingled with the horrid ideas of paganism. As the Hindoos try to please their gods by hook-swinging and by thrusting hot irons through the flesh, so the semi-Christian times, lingering on the borders of this pagan darkness, have had their saints of pillar and cave; and as the children of Bengal have for thousands of years run forth to see the fakirs coming into the village, cutting their own bodies with knives, so have the Christian villagers in Europe followed in wonder and reverence a procession of flagelants marching to a chorus of whips, and with feet sprinkled with blood. Both these scenes, one in India under Vishnu, the other in Europe under Christ, are pictures of the same human heart living in a native ignorance which was still bringing to bear upon the new Gospel a folly of logic and of soul that had long been producing the deformities of religion along the Tiber and Nile and Ganges. Wherever a Christian has starved himself, wherever a Christian has worn a girdle of thorns, wherever a Christian mother has tried to love her children less, that she might love her God more, wherever a saint has withdrawn from the bright sunlight that he might dwell only in the light of God, wherever any heart anywhere has felt that by self-imposed suffering it might gratify God the more, there all these well-meaning ones have revealed not the import of Christianity, but the dark shadow of that realm beyond Christ, where the mother drowns her infant for God's sake, and where strong men have in the name of God held up their right arm till it withered, or have gazed at the sun till they became blind forever. Many an age has groaned under what they called the "Cross," which instead of being a cross was only a *folly.* When Mme. Guyon resolved that she would not feel sad when her children should die, but would lay them in the grave as she had put them in the cradle at night, and when we perceive that this she actually did, and shed no tear, but smiled on them dead as she had smiled on them living, we must not be betrayed even by her rank and culture or fortune into the belief that she was unveiling any of the mysteries of our religion, but must confess that her great mind and heart were touched by that shadow of infirmity which has thrown its dark line in some form across all the intellects which have ever lived, however great or humble. Every soul born into the world is born into mistakes. Be the intellect lofty as that of a Demosthenes or a Matthew Hale, be the genius as divine as that of Dante or Shakespeare, be the heart as sweet as that of Fenelon or Cowper, across it somewhere will fall a dark line, the shadow of man's frailty, reminding us that there is none good but God. Escaping from this influence of innate infirmity and of surrounding barbarism, and coming up face to face before the actual religion of Christ, we are bound to confess that its yoke is easy and its burden light. The escape from a low life to a higher one, the refuge from sin found in the Rifted Rock and in forgiveness, the new love toward all mankind and toward God, the better reading of life's significance, and the perpetual looking to heaven from amid all the sorrows of this shore, should not be confessed a cross for bowed-down shoulders, but rather a joyful crown for the temples.

There is one consideration which tends to rob Christianity of that lightness of heart which belongs to the innocence of childhood and to the absolute pleasure-seekers of mature years. It has not so loud a laugh, nor so many sunshiny days. But the reason of this is so vast and so noble that one might well accept of its sacrifice of merriment, to gain instead the soberness that comes from so honorable a cause. Let the human mind and heart espouse any truth that leads to a deeper study of man, a philosophy that studies the wants of the human family in all its races and ages and conditions, a philosophy which must go along with all these years, and then look over into eternity, a philosophy issuing from an infinite sympathy and which must go where the orphan is weeping and the sick dying, and this philosophy will be one which, in what we call merriment, can be surpassed always by the childhood which knows nothing, or by the empty years of sin and fashion which nothing cares. As the statesmen who, like Cobden, or Bright, or Lincoln, espouse the destinies of the multitude, are borne away from the butterfly joy which they knew in childhood, and which they can still behold along the fashionable avenues, so Christianity, fully accepted by the soul, brings with it often a study of mankind and a longing for the world's welfare which sobers the waking hours and even invades with its anxiety the once peaceful and sweet world of dream.

Compared, however, with a childish life or a sinful life or an empty life, Christianity is not in our century, escaped as it has from much pagan abnegation, and centering as it does upon an era of love and happiness, any longer a bondage, but its yoke is easy and its burden light. Its cross was borne by its Christ that it might not be borne by His children. The cross weighed down His body and spirit to the tomb, but to His children it is worn on the bosom, an ornament of beauty and hope. Once stained with blood, it is now wreathed with flowers.

Two Sundays in the year are now dedicated to the spirit of happiness. The Protestant Church has now for the most part admitted these two oases into a broad desert, and all that remains is for us to read the Gospel of our Lord that we shall seek to make these two "Sundays of joy," these islands in the sandy plain widen out till the vision of waving palm trees shall always lie before every traveler in this lonely march. When modern art and modern ambition had traced a canal from the Nile to the Suez station, verdure followed the waters through the desert, and now trees wave in blessing where for ages the burning sand blistered the foot and filled the travelers heart with only a sense of desolation. It is coming to pass, and it will come to be confessed more fully in future times, that Christianity is a stream flowing through a desert world, only that more palm trees may rise up and flowers bloom for the joy of the multitude that move to and fro in these wide plains of life.

Such are our thoughts for the day when the cross of death is wreathed with the flowers of eternal life. In presence of this wreath all others of earth fade. The bride wreathes her forehead in the name of a long friendship, but her beauty and joy, her home, would all become dust after a few years, as perishable as the wreath of her forehead, were it not for the hope of immortal life which wafts her and all she loves forward to a world of unending bliss. So the wreathes of statesmen and philanthropists, of all love and friendship, look to the great resurrection beyond these narrow confines as fulfillment of their hopes and reward of their toils. Hence we have come to-day to the wreath of all wreathes, to the bloom that causes all blossoming. Oh, blessed Easter flowers! the scattered roses of every field cast their color and perfume down before your more sacred import. As the sheaves of his brethren all bowed before the sheaf of Joseph, in the old, beautiful dream, because they saw that his hands would feed the hungry in far-off years, when their own grains had perished, so before the Easter immortelles all the lilies and roses of a wide world may come to worship, because, gifted with prophecy, they may well see in these emblems of immortality a beauty which shall reappear in eternity long after their own leaves shall have been scattered and their perfume all breathed away into the silent night.

THE GRADUAL DECLINE OF VICE.

"It shall be more tolerable for the land of Sodom and Gomorrah." *Matt. x : 15.*

The names of these two cities, over whose ruins the Dead sea is supposed to roll its bitter waves, are read before you this morning as words that may remind you that the present is not the only age of vice, but that great sins lie back of our times. I announce as my theme "The Decline of Vice." The discourse before you last Sunday closed with an appeal to you to gird up your strength against the evils of the age; but that we may all possess some general, truthful view of the work on hand, of its magnitude and despair or hope, it seems desirable that an hour should be given to inquiry as to the present attitude of human depravity compared with the long yesterday. This inquiry may lead us along two paths, the one leading through the *a priori* question, What should be the result of the increase of knowledge? The other leading through the actual facts with the question, What has been the history of sin? The relation between knowledge and virtue is, as a general truth, the relation between a cause and an effect. While no one will contend that knowledge will fully regenerate the heart and make a saint out of a sinner, yet the tendency of information is to raise the individual to a higher plane of morality. Our penitentiaries, and also our observation, teach us that ignorance is the mother of vice. Says an old Greek, "Better to be unborn than untaught, for ignorance is the root of misfortune." The great Robert Hall said, "Ignorance gives an eternity to prejudice; a perpetuity to error." The majority of convicts in the dungeon or upon the scaffold cannot write, but use that fatal emblem called "his mark." All through the Scriptures virtue is represented as a light, and sin as a darkness, and in obedience to this distinction, Satan is the prince of darkness and Christ the light of the world. Every motion man makes is along the line of his information, it being the great pathmaker for him in the wilderness, his pillar of fire and cloud in all his long journeying.

If you find an Indian planting a few seeds in wild Oregon, or setting forth with his spear to kill fish, or with his treacherous arrow to attack his enemy, he is moving along the lines of his information, and he will use all his light about planting his maize or spearing the fish or waylaying the white man. Over his dead enemy he will shed no tears, for he knows nothing of a golden rule, and nothing of the rights of man or the sacredness of life. All moralists or casuists so feel the causal relation between ignorance and crime that they hold the heathen world to be responsible for not having sought such light as might have improved their virtue, thus confessing that the order of nature is "light" and then "virtue." When a mind like that of William Penn or Richard Cobden has made a study of man, and has looked into the rights of life, liberty, and the pursuit of happiness, it becomes incapable of the atrocities which give actual pleasure to the untutored Modoc of the West. Penn and Cobden are rays of light upon the heart, emblems of that softening of soul which God's great truth always brings.

God's moral world and His physical world being covered all over with a network of laws as numerous and delicate as the tenderest threads in the spider's web, the first equipment for living in this world is a wide information as to these laws of body and mind and society and religion. A knowledge of these is the sun which must turn night into day and sleep into life.

It is now seen that under the increase of knowledge in the medical art, the average of human life has risen and is now ascending. The relation of air and exercise and food and sleep to health has been so studied from the standpoint of science and experiment, that this new light pouring around the body lengthens its years and makes them not only longer but happier. But God's world being all founded upon the same fundamental law, information will play the same part in morals that it performs in the medical art, and will tend to add to the quantity of virtue as truly as the study of pathology has extended the human lease of life. In such vast empires as India and China, where murder, and theft, and infanticide are customs allied to those of religion in a wonderful, but senseless partnership, the entrance of light alone, omitting any religious principle, has gone as far toward checking the bad customs as the new steam plow in Turkey has gone towards supplanting the old crooked stick that was once dragged through the fields. It is a great mistake to suppose that all the ills of mankind come from their not being religious or conscientious, and that all the human family needs is a sudden conversion to our Christianity. Conversion will only check those actions which the mind knows to be wrong, but will only add fuel to a line of bad conduct, which the mind supposses to be right. Religious conversion brings only an increased desire to follow the right, but it does not designate a new right for the mind. Hence, in the dark ages, a religious revival among the Catholics was always attended by a new slaughter of Protestants, because the new zeal in the heart did not bring any new information to the intellect, but only fanned the existing ideas into flame. What is demanded along with a well-disposed heart is a well-informed intellect. However good a man may be, it will be perfectly impossible for him to escape a vice unless he knows it to be such, and hence information or knowledge is an absolute condition of morality or manhood. The opium-eaters among the lowest classes in China, and the dirt eaters and whisky drinkers among the Indian tribes, do not descend from an origin of sin only, but from an ancestry of ignorance. Their noble life will come not simply from a study of religion, but also from a study of physiology and all the laws of health and refinement. Men are bad enough through sin, but they are wretched beyond this through ignorance. In India the most devout fakirs, who live for nothing but God and the soul, will once a day roll in the mud, or in the foulest gutter, in order to show their contempt for the sinful thing called the body. Now what those fakirs need is not an increase of religion, but an increase of sense. They need to learn that sin is not in the body but in the soul, and that the true God is not a being worshiped by a beastly conduct, by a wallowing in the mire, but by a noble, perfect soul in a pure, perfect body. When Christ forgave His murderers, on the ground, that they *knew not what they did*, He reaffirms for us the proposition that much of the world's sin and evil comes from an ignorance that thinks in the midst of awful actions that it is doing God's service. It serves Satan under the supposition that he is God. The evils of the world are wider than the direct desire of mankind to commit sin, for millions do wrong supposing it to be right, hence, in order to find some foundation as broad as this dreadful superstructure, we must combine ignorance and wickedness, and then we have the base adequate for the fabric.

Having thus found that ignorance is a vast cause of the world's great evils, we infer from the gradual spread of intelligence that the great vices are on the gradual decline. If the cause is declining we need no *a posteriori* inquiry to show us that the effect must be so far on the wane. If the supply of food has failed in India, we need not wait ninety days in order to learn the effect from the actual dying beds of mothers and children; and if a rich harvest soon comes, we need not wait to learn the result from the strong men in the streets next summer, and from the ringing laughter of children. God's world is so unbending in its relation of cause and effect that the moment a cause is abated one jot you may assume an equal abatement in the result. Now, much of the evil of society coming from ignorance, we may, so far as ignorance is being dispelled, congratulate the world upon a decline of its moral sorrows.

Having thus allnded to the influence of increased knowledge, the question that remains is, Has human knowledge increased? Has ignorance been modified? Has this plague been somewhat abated? We think that no one will deny that knowledge has gradually increased in those nations which have in twenty-five hundred years spread out from the Mediterranean. Light steadily advanced in the Hebrew nation, from Abraham to Daniel; and from the Greek and Roman starting points down through the great nations of Europe and America, information in all departments has been steadily amassed and handed down from one era to the next. Especially in the last three centuries has all truth become an object of pursuit and love, and hence, every science, from politics to chemistry, every inquiry, from the rights of the throne to the most practical physiology, every theory of health, from a study of health to a study of exercise, has been unfolded in new breadth and new affection. The sciences of chemistry and physiology and hygiene have marshaled their startling truths in front of the great vices of the social evil, and intemperance of drink and of food, and have battled them for a hundred years, and the attack increases in fierceness each generation. Hence, if there be some relation between ignorance and vice, that ought to be abating the vice which is confessedly so abating the ignorance.

But we behold another great light shining down from the Mediterranean shore, a light better than the stars that shone from the sky of Greece and the sky of Italy. While all information in Christianity or politics or philosophy has its secret influence in favor of virtue, yet it must be confessed that a knowledge of all the high duties of man, man as related to self and to friends and to society and to God, is of all the best, and if any truth will check sin, that relating to duty and soul and God must be that powerful knowledge. Looking back we see a star that makes all others fade. Its light, radiating out from nothing but a manger in the outset, and from a rude cross at last, has for eighteen hundred years diffused itself all over the Western hemisphere, embracing Russia, Germany, France, England, America, all as a mother throws her arms around the children who were lost but are found. Christianity set forth, not as a conversion alone, but also as a light for the mind. Pontius Pilate may have been sincere, but he was ignorant of duty, and weak in his moral attributes. Christianity moved upon the world not as a simple zeal, but as a light, and hence, if to know what the body is, and what the soul is, and what earth is, and what death is, what heaven and what hell may be; if to have some just conception of God, if to hold some correct view about our neighbor and all the reciprocal duties of life, if to know the golden rule and that the pure in heart shall see God, are truths of any value, then Christianity comes as the profoundest information which has ever burst through the clouds and shone down upon the world of man. Looking upon Christ as a moral light, and looking as far as a feeble intellect can grasp such an effulgence, we ought to conclude that vice has suffered a shock in that so much of its foundation of ignorance has been swept away. But we reminded you that evil had two elements in its foundation, the one ignorance, the other hostility to the truth, even when well known. Christianity attacks both these foundations of evil, and works equally with the intellect and the heart, revealing duty and making the soul love duty.

Seeing, therefore, a gradual increase of knowledge from the great Eastern sources, Greece, Rome, and Palestine, and seeing this knowledge spreading out Westward in all that varied magnificence of science and Gospel, of crucible and cross, of body and soul, of human liberty and divine love, and then remembering the invention of printing which has poured this varied wisdom into every house as sunlight pours into the window, I must reach the conclusion that the vices of the civilized world ought to be on the decline. There are agencies abroad in the world which appear adequate to a reduction of the quantity of wickedness.

Our second inquiry was designated as being a survey of the actual facts in the case. Having seen what the spread of light ought to accomplish, we inquire whether there has been any such moral achievement. First, let me warn you against supposing that the loud outcry now raised on all sides against every form of vice and dishonor, indicates that evil is on the advance and goodness on the decline, for the present turmoil proves only that the public sense has progressed so far that it will no longer submit silently to great wrongs and follies. The judgment and the moral and prudential senses have been so developed in the past, especially in the recent past, that silence is no longer possible. What former ages endured easily because of the feeble public light and public conscience, raises now a vast uproar when seen in the new light and morals of the passing century. The great emancipation war which raged in our land from 1830 to 1860 did not arise from the new barbarism of slavery, for, as a fact, bondage had not grown more inhuman, but arose from the fact that an old evil had encountered a new intellectual and moral development, and hence came the great conflict. It is with such reflections we look upon the present conflict over intemperance and the social evil. These monsters have not absolutely gained in vice and ferocity, but the public conscience has grown until it has not the indifference to vice which marked the world when kings lived for glory and pleasure and nobles for banquets and the fox-chase. These monsters, which we call by the general name of vice, have been dragging their foul lengths along over hundreds of years, and much of battle is located in our time, because it has so gathered light from reason and Christianity that it can no longer endure such great wrongs. The sin has been stationary, but the public impatience has advanced.

Leaving these suggestions to the judgment of each of you, it remains to allude only in a brief manner to the historical facts in the case. Whoever would deduce any conclusions regarding the moral progress of society, must deal only in long periods, for earth is a star whose physical days are indeed composed of twenty-four hours, but whose moral days are each as a thousand years. Coming up out of God's eternity, where ages sink like snow-drops in the ocean, our earth brought with it this awful disregard of time, and makes little count of the days of you and me, looks upon a summer and a winter as only grains of sand upon its mighty shore; and all our three-score years sink into its mighty life as autumn leaves fall upon the mountain side and are only received tenderly into its mold, but create no jar in the wide and deep foundations of adamant. To estimate the morals of the human family, to mark an increase or decrease of sin, you must look away from this day, this year, this generation, and so far as possible behold all the impressive spectacle that reaches from the old Eden to the newest America.

What was the past? The words Sodom and Gomorrah recall at once some of the early forms of the world's corruption. The vices of that period, as revealed in the history and conduct of Lot, were not the incidental vices of a savage tribe, but the vices of the most civilized nations, for the Hebrew commonwealth, as far as the age of David and Solomon, repeated the sins of Sodom, only upon a diminishing scale, and thus was a mirror, not of barbarism, but of the best type of old civilization. The history of Egypt is a history of mingled science and splendor and sin. The Egyptians actually worshiped gods of vice, and in all respects equaled the reputation of Sodom and Gomorrah for indescribable depravity. The exhuming of Herculaneum and Pompeii has lifted a veil from the customs of the Greek and Roman worlds, for those two civilizations were combined there, and there at that mountain's base those two cities sat while nature suddenly embalmed them for far-off generations. The excavations there reveal equally old wealth and old vice, art and dishonor, a cultivated intellect and a darkened conscience, a light upon canvass and marble, but little light upon the soul.

Passing by the notorious immorality or impurity of the Greek and Roman and Egyptian lands, look upon some features of those ages not so commonly alluded to in these surveys of antiquity. Slavery was universal. The rights of man as man were unknown. The Greeks knew the rights of Greeks; the Romans the rights of Romans; but neither knew the rights of man. Hence, no citizen did anything which a slave might do. If pecuniarily possible, the literary man lay upon a lounge while slaves wrote down his thoughts, or brought and took away a volume, or prepared a glass of fragrant wine. Marriage was a frail partnership, and the courtesan often more honored by statesmen than the more refined, home-loving wife. The amphitheatres were a full blossoming of the ignorance of the rights of man, and of the absence of mercy from the heart. In days when ten thousand innocent men were dying in one reign, in presence of eighty thousand spectators, composed of the best citizen of Rome, Cicero was justifying the bloody spectacle; and in one instance when no exhibitions had been given for a time, a petition was sent to the district governor, or prefect, that he would order a show at the amphitheatre, and he graciously said "that not to grant their request would be cruelty."

All through this Roman splendor parents held the power of life and death over their children, and infanticide was very common; and next in cruelty to that was the exposing of infants, under the law that whoever found the exposed child could claim it as his slave forever. Its chance was for death or bondage. Mothers who did not choose either of these barbarous resorts, could sell their infants into bondage in open market.

Lecky says the classic religion exerted no influence upon public morals, for when it taught any valuable truth there was no religious zeal that would nourish the truth into life. At your leisure, my friends, look into the picture of Roman and Greek life, and you will rise from the study thankful that you live in even this wicked city, and that between your home and antiquity the light of a new knowledge and a new religion has fallen in heavenly beauty. As to the great special vices, intemperance and the social evil, which so injure our land, it ought to cheer the heart that these powerful foes are only two out of a large host which once attacked society, and that these two are feebler than they were a hundred years ago. The social evil was almost universal in Europe from Cæsar to Napoleon. Montaigne says there were no virtuous men in his day, and, indeed, we all know that the social vice has swept over the old world as no pestilence or war ever desolated its cities and homes. As to the use of drinks, it may be said that abstinence was almost undreamed of before our generation, and an intemperate use of liquors, from ale to distilled drinks, is as old as the genius that invented the villainies.

We need not descend into particulars. You can recall them. Called upon as you are to contend to-day against the vices of our land, you all seem fully authorized to feel that knowledge and religion do gradually wear away these hard rocks, and give the world a better soil for the moral growth of this generation and its children and the myriads to come. God is no more in the law of gravitation than He is in the laws of reform, and hence as the Niagara has cut its deep ravine back from Queenstown, so the moral power of education and religion are as surely carving a channel through the mass of wickedness on earth. God's word, His truth, will not return unto Him void. As the sun's heat always melts the snow of our fields, and always will while sun and snow continue, so the word of truth spoken by anyone anywhere always will add something to the progress of mankind. God is not only immutable in the law of chemistry and all physics, but in the laws of His love, and if His children assail ignorance with truth and sin with conscience, every movement of the humblest Christian will record itself for good in the bosoms of those that come after the record. Let us look at these great facts and always be of good heart, for although viewed by itself alone, the present looks dark in its sinfulness, and although the efforts of Church and press seem powerless, yet looking away from our few years and reading the changes of society as recorded upon the centuries, we plainly perceive that every good word and deed of each day is embalmed in the great brain and bosom of mankind. As each tree helps make the green of the distant forest and does its part in the impenetrable shade, so the truth of all lips to-day and the prayer of each heart are, in some manner unseen to us but seen of God, handed down to those who shall come when your lips and heart are dust. To a child looking upon the cold sky of March it seems impossible that spring and summer are coming, or can come, but the older mind looks beyond the single morning, looks beyond April and May, and beholds in June a continent covered with waving grasses and trees, and in soft morning air dripping with dew-drops from Maine to Oregon. Thus gradually mankind advances toward an era when the banner of knowledge and the banner of the cross shall wave over every city, and light and love and virtue shall be in every soul. Such a destiny is read in the nature of man and in the character of God.

A MISSIONARY RELIGION.

"Go ye therefore and teach all nations."—*Matthew* xxviii, 19.

This being the missionary day of this congregation, it would be a great neglect of duty and of a great theme of inquiry should we simply make our annual offering of gifts. Once a year at least we may well look at the cause in its forms of fact and philosophy, and thus enable ourselves to base our contributions upon some knowledge of their destination and value. The Christian religion is nothing but a great mission scheme, of which the world is the field and Christ the first and the chief of a missionary host. The religious systems up to the Savior's day were systems only for the porch or closet. Most of the moralists were only men of seclusion, men of the grove or the porch, who, pacing to and fro a few steps, spoke as they walked, and thus were dreamers in a secluded spot, rather than messengers to the world. It was necessary for the few who knew of the existence and haunts of these wise men to make long journeys to their presence, and there encamp for a time to drink in the sweet waters of these rare springs. In all those days of Roman and Greek and Indian wisdom, moral systems were a curiosity more than a public cultus, and were studied as a kind of mental exercise, rather than as a mode of daily life.

Whenever a moral system assumed the form of a worship, and attempted to spread itself, as in the Hebrew and Mohammedan states, it spread as a government rather than as a religion. It sought not so much a universal salvation as a universal empire. It will, it seems, be sufficiently true if we affirm that the New Testament religion is the only one that deliberately announced the idea of a world-wide religious crusade, having for its object the spiritual enlightenment and transformation of mankind. It cut religion away from state duties and temptations as from a deadly hindrance, and sent it forth upon a purely spiritual mission. Separating itself from government, the world became its field, and man universal became its object of prayer, and love and pursuit. Hence Christ used with wonderful significance the word "world." He Himself was the light of the "world," and He sent His disciples into the "world," and the "world" was to be preached to by His messengers, and the end of the "world" was to follow this wide evangelization. If you will read carefully the Testament for this purpose, you will perceive that Christianity announced itself not as a world-wide state, but as a world-wide religion. We seem to hear those sacred pages saying, "Long enough have there been local forms held in some Jerusalem available only after long journeyings, long enough have there been wise men of the temple and the porch who have stood afar from the people, muttering their for the most part obscure soliloquy, long enough have the sibyls sung their ambiguous words from hidden caves whither none but kings or warriors could come; full time is it for a word that shall go forth to the people, be they of empire or republic, rich or poor, and upon any shore." Such seems the announcement upon the face of the New Testament, and in grand harmony with this professed idea Christ moved from place to place the friend of all; and the apostle to the Gentiles sailed from island to island and land to land, the ambassador to the world. It is said that Paul even crossed Spain, and at the atlantic coast found, as he supposed, the limits of the world. That broad wave turned him back.

The fact that the Christian Church was first named an *ecclesia* points out not obscurely its ideal scope, for that word had for hundreds of years indicated a convention of the people. The Ecclesia was the Greek house of representatives—a house which stood as a check upon archons and senates, a mediator between the multitude and the ambition of orators and generals. As the public throng was called by heralds who passed along from street to street, the meeting was so named, "the called out," or the "ecclesia," and from such associations it has descended to us. Thus all the parts of Christianity, its Christ, its apostles, its avowed object, its ignoring states, its simplicity of doctrine and its very Church name, confess it to be a religion for the whole people, and hence nothing but a holy crusade against the sins of the wide world.

Such being the avowed design of the founder of this religion, we who profess to believe it are in the path of duty only when we are in sympathy with this large design, and are shaping our thoughts and feelings and actions to this immense scope of the Gospel. We as a Christian nation and as private Christians are here to-day in what religious truth we have, only because the religion of Palestine assumed the form of a mission rather than of a local faith. Palestine had held its Hebrew ideas for two thousand years without having sent outward one single chapter from Isaiah or one single psalm from David. Wonderful and divine as was the Deism of the old Testament compared with the polytheism of the classic states, and sacred as were the hymns of the temple compared with any religious songs of the surrounding lands, yet none of the theology of the Hebrews seems to have broken out of its national confines into the classic world, and not a psalm of David seems ever to have sent its music over to where Homer held a harp, or to where Virgil was devoting his life to a chaste and an elevated poetry. Palestine lay beside Greece for hundreds of years with only a fragment of the Mediterranean between, and yet between Athens in her glory and Jerusalem in her almost equal splendor, no exchange of creed, or prayer, or hymn seems ever to have taken place. What thoughts these two cities had of each other must have been in the line of wondering, when the armies of one might thunder at the gates of the other. The active idea with both was, not how they might spread their poetry, or their psalms, and their worship, but how they might advance and support their thrones.

Born into such a spirit, Christianity would have remained in Palestine, just as Hebraism had remained there. But Christ reversed the genius of religion. He separated it from state, and attached it to man as a citizen of the world; and moved it from its narrow borders, and from that hour the psalms of David, and the songs of the new Church began to cross the sea by every wind that wafted the merchant's ship. It must have been a thrilling passage of eloquence when one of the Roman orators, in perhaps the second century, arose in the public assembly and said, "Your altars and temples are all becoming vacant, your laws are passing away before the temple and laws of this Christ."

The violent deaths suffered by the early apostles and disciples prove that this religion did not confine itself to the home of its birth or attach itself to the existing temporal powers, but did so cast itself forward as into a wider destiny, that each petty governor feared it as being the embodiment of a most unbridled ambition. Paul so waked up the world by his eloquence that he was put to death at Rome, as though like Cæsar he was reaching forth for a crown; John was banished to Patmos, after having been put to torture; James was hurled from a battlement in Jerusalem, and thus crushed to death; Matthew was put to death in Abyssinia; Simon Zelotes received his crown of martyrdom in Persia; and in Persia, also, Jude was slain by a cruel death; the death of Thomas took place on the coast of Coromandel; Philip was hanged to a pillar in Hierapolis; Andrew was crucified at Patræa in Achaia, and James of Zebede in Asia the Less. Thus in this bloody death-page, where every land is seen to have opened its bosom to receive the mangled form of a disciple, we read in these crimson letters that Christianity is the religion of all which may claim the glory of having taken the whole world into its heart. All these widely separated tombs tell us that from the cross itself the testament religion began at once a march which was to pay no more regard to geographical and national lines than Christ paid when He died for humanity.

How much the Christian philosophy differed from either the Mosaic or the Indian you may infer from the two facts, first that no Hebrew hymn passed over to Greece or Rome in 500 years, though the lands lay upon one small sea and under one sky, and yet in fifty years after Christ his form of religion had penetrated to the British islands. Bishop Stillingfleet says "there is good evidence that the Christian Church was planted in these islands in the first century:" perhaps alluding to the evidence of Eusebius, who says the apostles passed over the ocean and preached in the British isles, and to Theodoret, who says "the Britons embraced the religion of the fishermen and publicans and tent-makers." In the former part of the second century the Gospel had reached Germany, Scythia, Spain, Gaul, and Briton, and in view of this wonderful contagion an orator by the name of Arnobius said: "Is it not a powerful argument that in so short a time the sacraments of Christ are diffused over the world? That orators and rhetoricians, lawyers and philosophers now love this religion and despise what they formerly trusted?"

It would seem from these facts that the religion we cherish was in the very outset a world-religion, not confessing any distinctions of place and people such as have marked all other forms of human worship. The Hebrews looked over their geographical lines with only covetousness or anger; the Chinese built a wall that they might have no intercourse with the multitudes beyond, and calling their own land the "Celestial empire," they despised all other climes; and so all through India it was the effort of thousands of years to build up such a law of caste as would include certain persons in favor and exclude certain others forever. In the very face of all this habit of society, both in its social and political and religious practice, Christianity came as a world-wide creed and worship, the most universal, the most democratic, the most generous, the most God-like of all religions in which the knee has ever bent in prayer.

This missionary spirit, which is bound up in the words of the text and which sent the apostles in all directions spreading out from the tomb of Christ like radiating light from a sun, and which scattered their tombs over all the known world, approached our Canadas and Floridas when the natives were worshiping a devil and pouring out the blood of innocent children each new moon to appease his wrath. When the Spaniards founded their New Spain on the Florida coast, they found the natives offering human sacrifices, and were actually drowning children in the lake to please their horrid deity. Though the Spaniards were seeking only wealth, yet they had with them the Catholic religion, and that

Gospel they planted and began at once to overthrow the inhuman customs of the new world.

It was the painful degradation of America and of several lands which travel was bringing into notice, which called to the front such heroes as Xavier in the sixteenth century. You have heard, once before at least, the noble response Xavier made when his friends attempted to alarm him and dissuade him when he was about to sail upon his great mission:

"Hush you! close your dismal story,
What to me are tempests wild?
Heroes on their way to glory,
Mind not pastimes for a child.
'Tis for souls of men I'm sailing,
Blow ye winds north, south, east, west;
Though the storm be round me wailing
There'll be calm within my breast."

It was the advent of a few such heroes that won for the eighteenth century the name of the "Missionary Century," but our century has come now to rob the past one of its special fame. The era laid great foundations and our century builds upon its solid rock, thus dividing the honor of the world's evangelization.

Thus stands that great religious work toward which you are asked to contribute your mites to-day, gifts which will perhaps express not your pecuniary ability so much as your thought or care about this vast benevolence among your fellow-men. A gift does not always express one's power but often only the amount of his information and his sympathy. Thousands give little because they know and care so little about the matter in whose name the offering is made. It ought to be enough of information, the single remembrance, that our religion is all a missionary action and a missionary result. The condition of this land compared with the old centuries of cruelty is to be credited to the outgoing religion of Jesus that cuts the cables that bound their ships, and sent our fathers hither when the land was a wilderness and the very sky full of wintry storm. It was not the richness of the soil, not the flowing rivers, not the chains of lakes, not the timber of the forests, not the ores in the earth, which have given our country its happiness and varied excellence, for the Indian roamed all over this grand continent, but remained a savage still; it was not civil liberty alone that made us a great people, for the Indians enjoyed the most perfect civil liberty all over this broad prairie and mountain world; it was rather the religious and ethical ideas which were sent over in the Christian ships that marked out a future nobler than the career of the savage. Money was gathered just as we ask for it to-day, and brave hearts sailed away from home and country, just as now the missionary sails, and that gave us America, just as your gifts and a hundred years will give the world a Christian India or a Christian Chinese Empire.

"Now as the conquerer comes,
They, the true-hearted, came
Not with the roll of stirring drums
And the trumpet that sings of fame.

"Not as the flying come
In silence and in fear;
They shook the depths of the deserts gloom,
With their hymns of lofty cheer."

This poem recalls the cause of American greatness, and the deep foundations of her destiny, but this hymn is nothing else than a repetition of the sentiment that moved Francis Xavier, and Paul, and the divine Master of all.

In our country all this form of benevolence merits a special respect, inasmuch as the Protestant Churches have ignored the distinctions of sects which prevail at home, and for almost a hundred years, dating from the London society, have gone to the benighted lands in the name of great leading truths of Christianity instead of in the name of a multitude of sectarian ideas. Although recently certain fields have been assigned to certain great denominations, yet this has been done in the name of efficiency and economy rather than in the name of sectarianism. After the hundred-year experiment, there is no probability that any missionary gold will be exhausted upon any indoctrination of the heathen world in denominational ideas, for the tendency of the present is to abandon sectarian ideas at home; hence there will be little disposition to inculate abroad doctrines which are rapidly dying by our own firesides. The Church of England joins with the dissenting Churches in India as a fact, and cares little for the apostolic succession in a land where the Brahmin can so far outdo it in the quantity and absurdity of holy touchings and holy pedigrees. And there the Calvinist conceals his five points, for the crowd of Indian philosophers can always propose ten points far more obscure, and thus all the Protestant sects approach the whole pagan world with the Gospel reduced to its simplest expression. Blessed era it will be when we shall be as fully ashamed in America of the things that divide us as we are when our feet touch India or Japan. Can it be possible that it requires home training, that is, local and youthful prejudice, to enable us to see the immense worth of our dogmas, and that approaching foreigners not fully drilled in the sectarian method and tactics we fear their smile of unbelief or derision? It is ominous if, having a score or so of peculiar ideas, we should all get together and agree to say little about them to this Chinaman and that Brahmin. Such a condition of things would seem to indicate one more step along this path, an agreement to say little about these differences to persons not pagans and not upon foreign shores.

We have come to-day to a survey of Christianity in its truest significance, and hence in its wanderings about from race to race, from island to continent, from river to sea, we may learn what are its essential parts. A student shutting himself up in his room may, from the Bible, elaborate a perfect system which shall omit nothing regarding to human will or the mode of quality of everything, but the world in actual experiment may not need, nor even faintly appreciate, one-tenth part of this closet-made system. But when the Gospel is observed out among men in India and America, there in the faces and life of its votaries one may make out such a true biblical theology as no closet can ever produce The whole mission work at home and abroad is the best interpretation of Jesus Christ that we can anywhere find, for it determines for us what truths on the sacred page are most valuable for the vast stream of life that is pouring along across earth to eternity. If this spectacle is not badly read it indicates that what the world needs is a perfect combination of Christ as an example and Christ as a mediator, a full confession of man's power and God's power, a full conversion and a high enlightenment. The world reveals three great wants — pardon through Christ, light through Christ, a new heart through the Spirit. Give a soul these, release from its guilt, a new heart for new deeds, new light that its deeds may be right, and it has found the inmost heart of Christianity. Not only does the great mission movement at home and abroad reveal the valuable part of theology, but it declares to us what Christianity is in its essence. It is only a perpetual crusade. It is not a life-long encampment in the midst of luxury and ease, but is a march in search of the happiness and holiness of society. Hence, the great awakenings of the past have come from Christians who were almost homeless and Churchless, who were light-armed and unencumbered, fully out in the world for a campaign. Mankind does not run to a new life from an instinct. Men make long journeyings to fields where diamonds are sown, and to where gold sparkles in the sand, but they do not seek a spiritual religion thus. It makes the journeyings and bears the cross, the hymn and prayer, to Greenland's icy mountains and India's coral strand.

It is the glory of these missionary centuries that they have inaugurated a religion which does not withdraw into a little circle marked out by wealth, or ease, or selfishness, and there wait for a wicked world, and a neglected and unwelcome world, to come and beg to be let into the mercies of Christ hidden by the cruelty of man, but a religion which issues forth from the disgraceful repose of past ages and sings its hymn and offers a loving invitation out in the wide world by every shore, under every sky. The world has seen enough of a religion which wraps itself up in indifference and knows and cares nothing of the human family. Greece had such a type of morals, Rome had such a form of spiritual death; and enough has the world had of religion that was bound to state and had no destiny but that of empire; and ready now is society for a Christlike faith that goes forth like the perfume of roses free to child and king alike, a fragrance which climbs over walls and out of palace windows, and mounting into the chariot of the summer wind crosses the field of the poor laborer and the highway of the traveler, a breath from heaven, an emblem of God's grace.

CHRISTIANITY A LIFE.

"For the law of the spirit of life in Christ hath made me free from the law of sin and death." —*Rom. 8, 2.*

In the verses adjoining our text, Paul clothes the sinful nature of man with the attributes of a person or spirit, and thus while in man's intellect there is a spirit of good, there is in his body at large a sprit of evil. Instead of teaching the Manichæan idea of two souls, he seems only using the varied forms of illustration admissible in rhetoric, and in this liberty speaks of a good in the mind and an evil in the flesh. From this figure he passes to that of two laws, one that is spiritual, and one that is material, of the flesh, and when he would do good at the command of the former, he suddenly does bad at the command of the latter. As in a dream one often in his whole mind wishes to fly from danger but finds his feet unable to run or his voice to sound the alarm, and thus is wholly baffled by the conflict between his wishes and his feet, so Paul stood still, his life being neutralized between the conception of a noble life which lay in his reason and the instinct of a wicked life that lay in his flesh. He delighted in the law of God, but he saw another law in the members warring against the law of his mind, and bringing him into a captivity, and thus, oh wretched man that he was, with no one to deliver him from a body full of death, from a flesh that warred with the spirit. Thus might a dreamer, whose feet would not move in the moment of peril, pray to be set free from such a body of death that the released soul might escape. Commentators inform us that prisoners were often fastened to a dead body as part of their punishment; but evidently here Paul would love to be delivered from his own flesh, which carried in it such perpetual discord as to the spirit's highest ideal. He had a dead body of his own. While Paul was thus dragged in two ways by two equally balanced forces, there came to him a new force, even Christ, who turns the tide of battle, and soon the triumphant apostle said that the spirit of life in Christ had made him free from the law of sin and death. The influence of a life in Christ was so spiritual that the law of the humble, depraved flesh had retired from the strife, and had left the law of the mind free.

From these seventh and eighth chapters springs up much of the "holiness" idea of some of the Methodists, and from them sprang the German mysticism of the fourteenth century; but to us living in a less impassioned age comes the plain lesson that Christianity is a Life. That spirit of life which was in Christ, that spirit of being, so far above the sins and weaknesses of common humanity, developed also those who were "in Christ," and they walked no more after the flesh, but after the spirit. By common consent, if not by actual demonstration, it is affirmed of material things that they will perish. From the great gardens of Babylon to the hut of the peasant, from the splendor of marble palaces to the blooming roses, all, all, the cheek of youth, the eye of beauty, will fade and become dust. So perfect is this desolation, that even the heavens must pass away as a scroll and the elements all melt with fervent heat. Along with this perishable organic world will go all the mental actions and emotions that were based wholly upon it. Appetite, passion, ambition, all states of mind that grew up from the material of earth, point downward toward that dust whence they came, and as the poet says,

"Here the sword and sceptre rust,"

along with them will perish the passion that drew the sword or the tyranny that swayed the sceptre.

On the other hand, by common consent, the world accepts of a spiritual realm which is the antithesis of the great dust-seeking kingdom, a world where all the ideas and sentiments and actions are tending away from the grave, and are reaching up toward where God dwells, to the land of immortal life. Love, charity, friendship, righteousness, benevolence, belong to a certain upper life called the life of the spirit.

Passing by the inquiry how the humble, dust-loving soul may be transformed into such a spiritual character as that one which came to Paul at Damascus, we come to the simple idea of the text that Christianity is a spiritual life as compared with a material or fleshly life; that it is a life regulated by a law of the spiritual world, the opposite of a life regulated by the law of sin and death.

When some of the former centuries came up to these two lives, the one of spirit and the other of flesh, they came to a great truth, but they ruined the great principle by their false definition of both the lives. They made the whole circle of human joy and industry and pleasure to be the life of sin and death, and they made a life of retirement and self-denial to be the ideal of spiritual existence. Hence came all that development of human sorrow seen in the old monastic, ascetic system. When we remember Pascal, who tried to eat his food without being conscious of its pleasant taste, and who would not permit his sister to address him kindly, lest he might experience the weakness of a human friendship; and when we read that a'-Kempis did not look upon the glory of springtime, because such material beauty might make him forget the moral beauty of God, we perceive the doctrine of a sinful and a higher life all ruined by the false definitions of the two shapes of being. They grasped the truth that religion is a life, but failed to know what life is in its truest significance. They thought the whole outer world a sin and a dungeon, the only arena of virtue. Our century having reached a new measurement of life, having defined the word "flesh" to mean only sinful pursuits, and having enlarged the spiritual life until it embraces all the pleasures and honors, all the faculties of body and soul, having reversed the past by declaring all God's world to be the arena of virtue, and a monk's cell to be the soul's eclipse, it should now come up afresh to the proposition that Christianity is a Life and by its new wisdom restore a truth which the past has already ruined by its folly. Before mankind will consent that Christianity is to be their life, they will need to know what you mean by "life," for if you indicate by that term the ascetism of Pascal, or the narrowness and severity of the Puritans, they will reject the religion as rapidly as all the pulpits can offer it. Only in the current year has a pamphlet been issued by a clergyman, calling the attention of this synod to the alarming fact, that there are Churches all through the land which have built a kitchen department, and do in many ways thus dare to combine the temporal and the eternal. And last week we read a printed letter from some religionist, who was arguing with great zeal against the common household games of every kind, as being only stepping stones to the great games played for a stake. With such intellects ("if shape that can be called which shape hath none") to throw down before a community not naturally partial to the Gospel a definition of life, is to cast before the pulpit not only the common obstacle of original sin, but the additional stumbling-block of fresh, monkish absurdity. But for generations the Gospel has had to contend, not only against the "total depravity" of the world, but against the almost "total infirmity" of the Christian intellect, for, with the New Testament declaring Christ to be a life, the Church has almost drowned the voice by so defining "life," that educated persons could, with great difficulty, be persuaded to seek or even to admire it. With life defined as a solemnity, as a sorrow, with home transformed into a prison, of which the father was the jailer, with the Church conducted as a penance, with all the pleasures of life identified with sin, laughter being a form of evil spirit in the young, with Sunday weighed down by austerities, the Church, instead of making men free from the law of sin and death, rather perfected the bondage, and brought, if not sin at least a death of the intellect and the heart.

Before we can preach Christ as a "new life," a life of the spirit, it is necessary that we declare before all the world that the spiritual life is wide and deep and beautiful. It is not the life of Pascal nor St. Bernard. It is not the life of the early Calvinist. It is not the life of the later Puritan, nor of the Quaker who despises music and literature, nor of the pietists who have discarded reason, and who wait for the Holy Spirit to tell them when to sleep and when to wake, when to read and when to walk! No! Life must be defined with the map of earth before us, and into its pleasures must enter all the landscapes and all the seasons, all the fruits and flowers, all its forests, plains, and mountains; must be defined with the map of the mind before us, with all its faculties of conscience and reason and imagination and sentiment; must be defined with the map of society before us, with all the obligations and duties which spring from the presence of our fellow-men in all their conditions and destinies, and above all must be defined with the outlook of the soul before us, with its wonderful, almost divine, relations to God and the Savior, and to worship here and eternity hereafter. That it has called the infinite career of man as to this world by the name of "flesh," and has frowned upon it as being subject to the law of sin and death, is a calamity out of which our generation is struggling hard to escape, that it may find a religion which the young may accept without chilling their hearts, and which the educated may accept without exchanging a broad world of study for the narrowness and complainings of a monk.

Our century perceives that under all the pursuits and pleasures of this existence the law of a spiritual nature may lie, and that a naturalist, or a statesman, or a queen, or a musician, or a judge on the bench, or a young heart in the open fields, may be wholly within the spiritual life introduced to our gaze by the Savior. The law of the spirit of life in Christ is nothing more than a grand, broad human life all pervaded by righteousness, and a certain elevated sentiment toward God and man. A spiritual life is only a life purified and elevated. It is not an existence *narrowed* as our ancestors thought, but a life sweetened by holier impulses. Compare the politics of Charles Sumner and the politics of Henry VIII. Under that of the American lay a spiritual law, lifting all his words up into the higher air of God; under that of the English king lay the law of the flesh, dragging the throne down toward the infernal world. Thus all through human being spirituality is not a shrinkage of the heart into the limits of a cell, but a purification of its vast natural breadth and depth. The middle age Christianity was a destruction of man, but the true Christianity is an expansion of the whole human intellect and sentiment. As the philosophy of Guizot or Cousin was only expanded by their spirituality above the philosophy of Epicurus, who said, "Let us eat, drink and be merry, for to-morrow we die," so all human life, from its love of nature and love of friends and love of truth, to all its powers of progress and enjoyment, is only enlarged by the spirituality which Christianity casts into these many streams of its action and being.

It is with such an definition of life before us that we gladly announce the proposition that Christianity is not a group of doctrines, not a long, hard creed, but is a life. A creed is much like the architect's plan of a house. If competent workmen should follow those plans a house would be the result, so when any one possesses an orthodox creed in his mind as being true, he is in the situation of a man who has plans for a palace or a ship or a home. He has all except the palace or the ship or the home. When any one comes to us boasting over his perfect creed, we should remind him that if he will only live that creed he will become a Christian.

We all remember when the Hungarian patriot journeyed all over our country carrying with him a written constitution of a free state. He even issued bonds in the name of the new republic of Hungary. That parchment was the creed, but inasmuch as a state is not a creed, but a life, the great Hungarian must sit down in sorrow and wait for death to remove him from a world of blighted hope. The creed of the church is just such a written constitution. It has been read long and loud at all crossroads, but I will leave it for you all to answer whether we have the house or only the plans of the architect, whether we have the state or only a good constitution for one in some far off futurity.

It is a most singular fact that in this great temperance reform there is one special multitude of intemperate men, and a large multitude it is too, which sustains full membership in an orthodox Church, in a Church that surpasses all others in asserting the divinity of Christ and the expiatory atonement. No Church can equal it in delineating the pains of hell and the joys of heaven, and yet with all these cardinal doctrines flaunted upon its silk banners and intoned by all its priests, this most profoundly orthodox Church sends forth from its bosom, especially from its Emerald Isle, a swarm of human beings almost wholly ruined by poverty, ignorance, and vice. They land upon our shores by the thousands every week, and against their coming we do not object, for all Christian hearts ought to welcome them from a land of famine and bondage to one of plenty and liberty; but coming, they prove that an orthodox creed no more indicates actual Christianity than poor Kossuth's constitution was equivalent to an enlightened state. The sorrows of Ireland all come from the fact that no Christianity has ever been given them, except that of a complex series of articles; the spirit of life which was in Christ has not been busy these hundreds of years, freeing them from the law of sin and death, but instead of this spirit of Christ's life being preached and acted before them, a hundred articles have been repeated over their darkened minds and enslaved hearts, with the accompaniment, "Believe and go to heaven, or disbelieve and be lost."

In this awful treatment of human souls the Catholic Church did not alone approach Ireland, but accompanied by a vast Protestant Chnrch which, repeating the same creed, did not exact even that fragment of piety to be found in an intellectual assent, but only so much of the "spirit of life in Christ" as is found in heavy taxes imposed upon the poor to support an idle royalty. Between the Roman Church, which carried nothing to Ireland but words, and the English Church, which sent them nothing but an armed posse to drain rents, the poor island has groaned for hundreds of years under Paul's law of sin and death. But I often think that God at times selects some spot of earth to be an example, and there permits some of man's errors to culminate, that other lands may see the awful outcome of their own religious and social philosophy. What would Ireland not have been to-day, with its rich soil, its perpetual spring, its ocean roads connecting it with all nations, with its great race of Celts and Gauls, which race is the best of all history, if only the Roman and English Churches had gone with a Christianity that was a life, instead of with one which was only forms and taxation? There can be no Christianity without a new spiritual life. Its first move is to rise above intemperance, above all bad passions, above ignorance, above idleness, above barbarism, which is only a general name for sin, and to this end it is a light to enlighten and a spirit to transform, and under these forces the soul becomes freed from the law of sin and death, and rises like Paul up toward the higher being. But instead of going to the green isle with this spiritual regeneration, two of the largest Churches in Christendom, the Roman and the English, repaired thither, the former with nothing but a poor belief, the latter with taxes and with the same belief, only modified far enough to become unwelcome. Between both these good Samaritans money and education and virtue and self-respect and industry and hope disappeared; and now all the poor Irish at home and abroad can do is to celebrate each year, in March, the memory of one Christian saint who once touched that island, a thousand years ago. It is to be hoped the story is true, for so few Christians have touched those shores since, that we would better as long as possible cherish this lonely legend.

I have dwelt thus long over Ireland, because, as I said, it is only a spot where a philosophy that exalts a creed and depresses a life has come to full maturity, and thus points out the destiny that awaits our land so sure as we fail to make our religion aim at the education and morals of men.

The danger of being misunderstood when one thus speaks about creeds, or of being misinterpreted by those who do not wish to understand, is fully appreciated; but the fact in the case is so true and so alarming, that the danger of my being misunderstood is nothing compared with the danger of the public morals, if Christ should not be more fully presented as a life. He must lift upward the whole mental nature until all intemperance, all dishonesty, all uncharitableness, shall be loathed as a deep dishonor. Christ must be an education, a refinement, a purity of heart; not a history attested by four evangelists and confirmed by Josephus and Tacitus, and hence believed, but a spirit entering the heart and sweeping away the law of sin and death. An intemperate Christian, or a dishonest Christion, must be confessed to be the real infidel, for whatever his lips may say, his soul is against Christ. There are islands in the Pacific which it is said had no vices until Christians went there; and that awful scourge under which one nation groans, and by which our city is deeply injured, is said to be the peculiar invention and favorite of Christian lands. It will remain so until the whole Church moves from an external history of religion to an internal spiritual state, and makes the spirit of Christ the true test of discipleship, and the sole object of all preaching and of all houses of worship. In this chapter from which our text is taken it is affirmed that "if a man have not the spirit of Christ he is none of His," but the Church has never believed it, but has offered heaven to misers and drunkards, when once a year they have shown some zeal for an external creed. The difficulty in Christianizing India lies in the pitiable characters revealed there by the British officers and subjects, all of whom have sworn to the thirty-nine articles. The German pietist Tauler was right when he said Christianity is an experience within, and one thought of God is beyond the worth of the external world.

The world has tried external doctrine to the most extreme limit. It has taken the ideas of the Testament, and has stated them in a thousand ways, and has called them everything from Arianism to Calvinism; from Lutherism to Wesleyism; from Romanism to Protestantism; from Mysticism to Quakerism, until the creeds of the Church would form a large volume; and yet not a soul from the atmosphere of any of these creeds has ever been anything except so far as he cast himself simply upon the spirit of Christ's life, and suffered that vast spirituality to separate him from his body of death, to crush the law, that when he would do good evil was present with him; and whenever any soul has done this, he has risen up in the same spiritual beauty, whether he was a Catholic like Fenelon, or a Methodist like Wesley, or a Calvinist like Chalmers; risen the same, because there is no rising at all for a Christian except right up out of the spirit of Christ. Christianity is in man a "well for water springing up," and hence no one can distinguish between the Catholic Massilion, and the Protestant Robert Hall, because they came not from an external, changing creed, but from the life of the Lord. Let our sun sink where it may, the same gold gathers about the West in Oregon that hangs out its banners in England or on the mountains of Asia, because the atmosphere is the same and the sun is the same, and the clouds are the same everywhere; and thus true Christians are all one, because they come not from manifold doctrines, but they are the same soul colored by the same Christ, whether he is seen in old Judea or new America.

My friends, we are living in an era of great vices. The fact that there are such vices so sweeping, vices which seek the sanction of law, and which already laugh at the puny arm of religion, should make us doubt whether the ages of simple doctrines do not, by their failure, invite us to a Christianity of life which shall plead for all reforms, and shall by education and a love of the dissolute multitude which shall lead us to espouse whatever will tend to lift them above ignorance and wickedness, help them not to our long theology, but to such a life of spirituality and purity and moral grandeur, as is spread out before them in that golden page of Bethlehem. To built up this "higher life," in the multitude let us omit nothing; from school house to Church, from entreaty to prayer, from reason to divine spirit, from the intercession of man to the intercession of the cross, use all not in the name of an external history, but in the name of a most radical reform:

Our course is onward, onward *into light*,
What though the darkness gathereth amain!
Yet to return or tarry both are vain.
How full of stars, when round us dark the night;
Whither return? What flower yet ever might,
In days of gloom and cold and stormy rain,
Enclose itself in its green bud again,
And hide itself from tempest out of sight?"

A RELIGION OF WORDS.

"Not every one that saith unto me Lord, Lord, shall enter into the kingdom of heaven, but he that doeth the will of my Father which is in heaven."—*Matthew vii: 21.*

Spirituality is one of the highest stages of civilization, and therefore comes latest in the course of human development. Material associations are the first, hence man first makes up his language and his pantheon of gods out of the solid substances that surround him. The first man was of the earth, earthy; the second man was the Lord from heaven. That is first which is natural, and afterward that which is spiritual. And as man has borne the image of the earthy, so shall he bear the image of the heavenly. The first Adam was made a living soul, the second Adam a quickening spirit.

In this great transition from the material to the spiritual, years are consumed in the life of the most earnest individual, and in the advance of society in this path a thousand years count only a little. The most sincere heart escapes from materialism so slowly, and so slowly resolves itself and its God into a quickening spirit, that an infinitely long existence would seem to be foreshadowed in this leisurely evolution. To that which grows slowly we attribute long time. The glacier and the accumulating shore of the sea, and the vast oaks of the Pacific slope ask us to allow them long periods in which to have developed their peculiar plan. So the slowness of human unfolding asks us to grant to the individual and to society a vast field called immortality. Instead of drawing only sadness from this tedious march we also find in it an assurance that there are many years beyond.

But our theme for the hour is that a spiritual religion comes last in human experience, and before it comes a religion of things and of words. To offer things to God was earth's first form of being religious. The old temples were full of bows, arrows, shields, helmets and jewels put away from human use by a solemn gift-making to the gods. Horace reveals the fact in one of his poems that the sailor rescued from drowning, hung up in the temple what he wore on his body when the divinity rescued him from the grave. A gift was the only known acknowledgment. Different cities vied with each other in making their gods rich. What gold! what garments, what jewels, what armor in the temple of Juno, and what luxuries there were in the temple of Jupiter!

The Athenians, upon the eve of a battle, vowed to Apollo that if he would grant them success they would offer to him as many kids as there were slain of the enemy on the field of battle, and so bloody was their success that the classic nation did not possess flocks enough to meet the vow of the worshippers, and the state funded, as it were, the promise, and offered five hundred a year through successive generations.

Worship was thus conducted by offerings. From baskets of fruits and flowers to thousands of valuable sheep and oxen, gifts were heaped upon the altars. At the dedication of his temple which was itself a costly present to Jehovah, Solomon sacrificed twenty-two thousand oxen and one hundred and twenty thousand sheep as an offering to Him who had brought them out of the land of Egypt and out of the house of bondage. All the earth was covered with this religion of gifts. Hindoo and African, Jew and Gentile, Indian and Roman, Parthian and Greek, accomplished the life of religion by offering some things to their favorite deity.

Good came from the custom, for, that spiritual worship is the highest form of religion, does not make useless or harmful a form full of material things and ideas. The gift-making worship only takes a second position, inferior, but not useless nor absurd. In Solomon's days not to offer a lamb to Jehovah was to be an infidel, for the religious thought and feeling of the times flowing in that channel, the heart that made no offering was an infidel heart. Each age has its own atheist and infidel fashioned out of its own shape of life. Solomon's vast offerings, aside from any relation to a coming Calvary, were, in the current hour, an act of religion, just as an imperfect song is music to those who love it, or as a rude log-hut is a sweet home to those, perhaps half-starved and half-clothed children, who have lived only by its door-sill and its hearth. To laugh at what others possess and to base that laugh upon the superiority of what is our own, is often a mild form of ignorance and self-conceit. Each age has drawn honey out of its own flowers, even if the flowers were wild and of pale single leaf. A gift was a surrender of self, a confession of dependence and a first leaf of charity.

The gift-worship at last passed away. Christ long borne in such an earthly casket outgrew the narrow confines and appeared in fullness and broad liberty. In Palestine, the religion of gifts terminated virtually in the Sermon upon the Mount, and in the marvellous spiritual life of Jesus. The gift of himself ended the whole gift idea by divine appointment, and by its excessive grandeur, and the purely spiritual philosophy of Christ and His apostles flying on the wings of the Roman language, and Roman fame and power, passed over the world in a circling, rapid flight. All the ends of the earth had felt the Roman power of arms, of letters, of law, of genius, of energy, so that Christianity, climbing into the chariot of Rome, was rapidly borne to all human hearts within the civilized empires of that era. Gifts disappeared from all the temples, lambs and oxen from all the altars, and religion began to resolve itself into a prayer, and penitential tear, and a faith and a hope.

While property measured the value of man and of his god, the surrender of it by man was the most obvious form of service, and the favor of heaven was bought not by a change of human character, but by a bestowal of human goods.

With the uprising af Christ, religion began to withdraw from presents to the Deity and betake itself to the heart. "Blessed are the pure in heart." "Blessed are they that hunger and thirst after righteousness." "The hour cometh and now is when the true worshipper shall worship the Father in spirit and in truth for the Father seeketh such to worship Him." "The hour cometh when ye shall neither in this mountain nor yet in Jerusalem worship the Father."

In this second state of religion a new heart became the chief object to be reached, and rewards from God were promised, not to him who would bring richest presents, but to him who would bring the purest life. But mankind was not ready for this cardinal idea. At least mankind will do nothing hastily. It will not pass to perfection in a day. It will not suffer itself to be hurried, but, like the glacier, must have its own rate of speed — the inseparable trait of its character. No voice has ever found instantaneous obedience. A spiritual religion announced and a spiritual religion accepted are different matters. A divine being and a few followers may announce one, but the world is always far below the leading divine souls, and hence after heavenly words are announced it will continue for a time in paths much like those of yesterday. A resemblance is demanded.

From a religion of gifts the world soon hastened to a Christianity of words. Words were the outward sign and in that the heart paused. There were a few generations of simple piety such as St. John revealed, but the measurement of Christianity was soon found in the proposition to which one was willing to subscribe.

Words are the forerunners only of deeds. They are heralds that announce a coming king, but the king's chariot it slow. Hence when you find in the times of Cæsar or Louis XIV., or Calvin, the finest statements about purity and charity, that is no sign that there was any public purity or charity. They had simply been announced, just as a vessel has been signaled when it is yet far out at sea, and perhaps falling back before storms. Words precede actions often by a thousand years. And thus the Sermon on the Mount is not so much man's law as man's prophecy. The world is grand, not when a prophecy is uttered, but when the fulfillment comes.

Millions were finally put to death in the long Christian centuries when they would not repeat the words of the party in power. Honesty of life, religious devotion, prayer, kindness at home, purity of deed and thought, counted nothing if the regular words of the ruling power were not pronounced. The most exemplary men, the tenderest mothers, the most gentle daughters, fathers whose families were dear to them beyond language, were hurried to the flames or rack because they could not say the words fixed upon by the pope or the tyrant in power. It was words, words, words, and death everywhere. No estimate was placed upon the inward life. Myriads died singing or praying to the spiritual God and their lives had been full of purity.

Elizabeth imprisoned for life all who conducted religious service without using her Prayer Book. Persons not believing in bishops were branded with an iron. Anabaptists and Arians were tortured and then hung. As internal piety was little dreamed of as being a religious test, it was as absent from man as from God. God was a being partial to a prayer-book or to a bishop. Forms were everything. Knox declared that one mass was more fearful to him than ten thousand armed enemies landed in any part of the realm, never harboring, for an instant, the idea that beneath the service of the mass there might be a pious heart. There was no weighing of soul; it was all a listening to words, and a crowding to the fagot those whose words deviated a hair's breadth from the model held in the hand of some bloated ruler or licentious priest. In this awful reign of iron sentences little girls of childhood innocence, and mothers whose love is an emblem to earth of love infinite, went down to early tombs in the double agony of flesh and heart; but the heart of a dove counted nothing in an age of vowels and consonants. Catholic words killed thousands of Protestants, and Protestant words killed thousands of Catholics.

All imaginable doctrines have, in the long, bloody period, been made a ground of life or death. Words about baptism, words about the Trinity, words about the pope, words about transubstantiation, words about the Virgin Mary, words about the Eucharist, words about the doctrine of purgatory, about astronomy have exposed the body to the stake and the soul to perdition. The holiness of Galileo were of no avail if he taught that the earth turned round each day. It was not an inner belief that was demanded, but an outward unity of dogmas Hence life was offered to heretics if they would only repeat the rejected dogma. What he really believed was not a matter of importance, if he uttered the conventional creed. No change of heart was expected or thought of, for the soul was not so much thought of as church unity. The outward orthodoxy was the grand consideration. Hence when Galileo consented to the idea that the earth does not turn and that the sun does go around it, he descended from the public penitential platform saying in a whisper, "The earth moves." No one cared for his inner thought if he only stood by the public words on the subject.

This zeal for dogma resulted from two causes. First cause, the fact that man comes slowly to a spiritual religion. That is the perfection of worship, and hence like all perfection must come slowly and come last. To get away from the outward and to throw one's whole being into the idea that what God demands is a pure heart, is a condition of mind to which only Christ and the angels have yet come.

A second cause of the enthronement of dogmas lay in the union of church and government. A new dogma might build up a new party, a new party might displace the party or power. The class believing the earth to turn around might become so powerful as to overthrow the party that plainly heard the Bible declare the sun to rise and set, and that saw the sun set every day. The inner life of a man was nothing, the silent belief of a philosopher was of no moment, but the perpetuity of the party in power, the long continuance of power and incomes was very desirable, and hence the dogmas held by the party on the throne must be spoken to the crowd by all, and by all constantly and everywhere. Certain assemblages of words stood for the pope. Other words might exalt an astronomer or a Pantheist and his followers. Thus forgiveness was always offered a victim even on the pile of fagots if he would repeat the pet ideas of the church, because the church meant not salvation, so much as power and regular incomes!

In our own country it has been the sorrow of us all to see a doctrine regarding slavery made more conspicuous, for a half century, than the doctrine of a pure life, rendered a test of orthodoxy not because of any heaven or hell, but because of Congress and patronage and high and low caste. Thus in these two causes—the difficulty in the way of a spiritual religion and the identity of church and state one may find the influences that gave mankind a religion not of the soul, but of many and intricate, and often contemptible doctrines.

That there are great doctrines, the obedience of which is life, the disobedience of which is death, is very evident. Truth is the food of life, the stuff that life is made of; but these truths are few compared with that assemblage of ideas that can be seen on the bloody field of history. Each aspirant had a discrimination of idea upon which to base hope, not of heaven so much as of earth. Certain ideas stood not for a virtue, but for a party in the church or state. They were not paths of spiritual salvation, but the emblems of authority. Like the secret words of masonry, they were not words that converted a soul, but words that stood for an empire. Morgan was put to death not because the ideas he uttered were valuable, but because they had been agreed upon and stood for a masonic order. So heretics were burned, not because what they said interfered with virtue, but because it interfered with some mitre or crown. A new idea was treason. This was all done in the name of sincerity, for it was easy for the Deity, who had once been a Deity of gifts, to become one of dogmas. God became a Being to be worshipped with dogmas. A man not baptized was so offensive to God that hell was only too good a place for that soul! An infant not baptized died hopeless, God was so partial to baptism! If this baptism were not administered by the proper church, it was still worse than no baptism, God was so partial to a particular church! And thus onward, until the blessed God was wholly occupied in the protection of a hundred forms of speech, and the human soul was occupied, not with purity of heart, but with repeating the terms pleasing to the ideal Deity and the pope. This pope was not always Catholic; sometimes he was Protestant.

Now salvation is a term whose meaning depends upon that which is lost. If one has lost property, his salvation will be the recovery of that property or its equivalent. If one has lost his good name by false accusation, his salvation will be found in the emblazonment of the falsehood, and on the return of public good will. This man does not need much dogma, but rather he needs acquittal and a better fame. If the soul has lost virtue and piety, then salvation will be found in a return to piety and purity, and the truths of salvation will be those that lead him to that one result. This is the destiny of Christ's mediation. Hence the essence of religion is found in the one event or phenomenon, a righteous heart. Gifts to the Deity were the infant creepings of religion, the shadow of a coming reality, the manifestations of an incipient love that did not know how to express itself. Not knowing that what God most wished was a pure heart in His children, they loaded His temples with their jewels and raiment, and His altars with their lambs.

Then came the days that brought God an offering of words. Imagining Him to be a God of articles and forms, they repeated thousands of words and baptized their guilty foreheads in much or little water as an act of salvation.

And now the world awaits the last transfiguration of human worship, into a spiritual condition, into a soul lifted above sin, and exulting in a nearness to the image of God. The nations await with tears of past sorrow, a religion that shall indeed baptize men and children, either or both, but counting this as only a beautiful form, shall take the souls of men into the atmosphere of Jesus, and into the all-pervading presence of God, and detain them there, until sin shall have become a hated monster, and perfection of spirit the heaven of this life, and that to come. Terms must give place to righteousness and communion with God.

In our day the empire of words still lingers. The churches are still wedded to quantity more than to quality, but wedded by bonds that are growing weaker under the uprising of the "inner life" philosophy. The churches still eagerly keep count of their membership, and publish the members that joined their bodies last year, but keep no record of the number of Christians that lived dishonorable lives in the last decade, quantity rather than quality still being a ruling passion in our half-civilized world. But Jesus Christ was not gifts, nor words, nor quantity, but quality; and surely as the world shall last, mankind, under His leadership shall march nearer and nearer to the world of spirit, where quantity and words shall all be overwhelmed by the sweet music, "Blessed are the pure in heart."

If Christ was anything, He was spiritual perfection. He was not a voice saying "Lord, Lord," but He was a spotless soul. Hence the world coming up to His religion, at last, will find itself in an atmosphere not full of the tenets of

Elizabeth, or Mary, or Calvin, but full of that transcendent whiteness that indicates that sin has been washed away and that the righteousness of Heaven has come to the heart, like a joyous morning in paradise.

In this coming era upon whose margin I do feel that the world is standing now, like Florida upon the border of flowery spring, our citizens, our fathers, our brothers, our friends, our children, will remove before us, not with conventional words upon their lips, but with faces radiant with the consciousness of a nobler life. The good deeds of yesterday, the good deeds of to-day, the perfected goodness of the morrow, a deep love for man, a consciousness of the presence of God will fill the whole face with a nobleness and happiness to which earth has thus far been willingly a stranger. This will be a salvation, and Christ will be a Saviour.

And as for those dear ones, who in the long past have died because of words, the Covenanter children, whose parents were burned before their eyes in fires of agony and orphanage; the Quakers, flying before the vengeance of outraged dogmas; the Catholics murdered because they looked toward Jesus through some symbol, will all come back to a spirit-shore, where Christ will know His children by the golden thread of love in their hearts and where no fallible human judgment can ever come to separate a Christian soul from the realm of perfect liberty, perfect justice, and perfect happiness. Man as a ruler, as a tyrant, has perished. He lives only as a brother. The dominion and power have returned to the Infinite One—infinite in tenderness.

CHARGES AND SPECIFICATIONS

IN THE CASE OF

PROF. F. L. PATTON vs. PROF. DAVID SWING.

CHARGE FIRST.

Rev. David Swing being a minister of the Presbyterian Church in the United States of America, and a member of the Presbytery of Chicago, has not been zealous and faithful in maintaining the truths of the gospel; and has not been faithful and diligent in the exercise of the public duties of his office as such minister.

SPECIFICATION FIRST.

He is in the habit of using equivocal language in respect to fundamental doctrines, to the manifest injury of his reputation as a Christian minister, and to the injury of the cause of Christ; that is to say, in sundry sermons printed in the Chicago Pulpit, and in sundry other sermons printed in the Alliance newspaper, and also in sundry other sermons printed in a volume entitled "Truths for To-day," said sermons all purporting to have been preached by him, the references to one or more of the following doctrines, to wit: the person of our Lord, regeneration, salvation by Christ, eternal punishment, the personality of the Spirit, the Trinity, and the fall of man; are expressed in vague and ambiguous language; that said references admit easily of construction in accordance with the theology of the Unitarian denomination; that they contain no distinct and unequivocal affirmations of these doctrines as they are held by all evangelical churches.

SPECIFICATION SECOND.

That the effect of these vague and ambiguous statements has been to cause grave doubts to be entertained by some of Mr. Swing's ministerial brethren, respecting his position in relation to the aforesaid doctrines, that leading Unitarian ministers, to wit: Rev. R. Laird Collier, and Rev. J. Minot Savage, have affirmed that his preaching is substantially Unitarian; that Mr. Swing, knowing that he is claimed by Unitarians as in substantial accord with them, and of the doubts existing as aforesaid, and moreover, having his attention called in private interviews to the ambiguity and vagueness of his phraseology has neglected to preach the doctrine of our Lord's Deity, the doctrine of the Trinity, of Justification by Faith alone, and of the eternal punishment of the wicked.

SPECIFICATION THIRD.

He has manifested a culpable disregard of the essential doctrines of Christianity by giving the weight of his influence to the Unitarian denomination, and by the unworthy and extravagant laudation in the pulpit, and through the press, of John

Stuart Mill, a man who was known not to have believed in the Christian religion; that is to say, that some time in the past winter, and during successive days he was advertized to lecture in the city of Chicago, in aid of a Unitarian chapel, and that he did lecture in aid of said chapel, and in doing so aided in the promulgation of the heresy which denies the Deity of our blessed Lord; that in an article written by him, and published over his name in the periodical called the Lakeside Monthly, bearing date, October, 1873, and entitled "The Chicago of the Christian," a passage occurs, which, taken in its plain and obvious sense, teaches that Robert Collyer, a Unitarian minister, and Robert Patterson, a Presbyterian minister, preach substantially the same gospel, that the gospel, meaning the Christian religion, is mutable, and may be modified by circumstances of time and place, that the "local gospel," meaning the gospel of Chicago, is a "mode of virtue" rather than a "jumble of doctrines," and moreover, that on the Sabbath following the death of John Stuart Mill, a well-known Atheist, Mr. Swing preached a sermon in reference to Mr. Mill, the natural effect of which would be to mislead and injure his hearers by producing in them a false charity for fundamental error.

SPECIFICATION FOURTH.

In the sermons aforesaid, language is employed which is derogatory to the standards of the Presbyterian Church, or to one or more of the doctrines of said Church, and which is calculated to foster indifference to truth, and to produce contempt for the doctrines of our Church: that is to say, that he has at sundry times spoken disparagingly of the doctrine of the Trinity, Predestination, the Person of Christ, Baptism, the Christian Ministry, and Vicarious Sacrifice. That by insinuation, ridicule, irony, and misrepresentation, he has referred to the doctrines of our Church in such a way as to show that he does not value them; and that by placing in juxtaposition true doctrines and false minor points in theology and cardinal doctrines of evangelical religion, he has treated some of the most precious doctrines of our religion with contempt. The reference is particularly to sermons entitled "Soul Culture," "St. Paul and the Golden Age," "Salvation and Morality," "Value of Yesterday," "Influence of Democracy on Christian Doctrine," "Variation of Moral Motive," "A Religion of Words," all published in the Chicago Pulpit, and to "Religious Toleration," "Christianity and Dogma," "Faith," "The Great Debate," "Christianity as a Civilization," published in "Truths for To-Day," and in the sermons entitled "The Decline of Vice," "Christianity a Life," and a "Missionary Religion," published in the Alliance newspaper. The following passage illustrates the allegation: "Over the idea that two and two make four no blood has been shed; but over the insinuation that three may be one, or one three, there has often been a demand for external influence to brace up for the work the frail logical faculty. It is probable that no man has ever been put to death for heresy regarding the Sermon on the Mount. Its declarations demand no tortures to aid human faith; but when a church comes along with its 'legitimacy,' or with its Five Points, or with its Prayer Book, or its Infant Baptism, or Eternal Procession of the Holy Ghost, then comes the demand for the rack and the stake to make up in terrorism what is wanting in evidence."

SPECIFICATION FIFTH.

Being a minister of the Presbyterian Church, and preaching regularly to the Fourth Presbyterian Church of this city, he has omitted to preach in his sermons the doctrines commonly known as evangelical—that is to say, in particular, he omits to preach or teach one or more of the doctrines indicated in the following statements of Scripture, namely: that Christ is a "propitiation for our sins," that we have "redemption through His blood," that we are "justified by faith," that "there is no other name under heaven given among men whereby we may be saved." That Jesus is "equal with God," and is "God manifest in the flesh," that "all Scripture is given by inspiration of God," and that "the wicked shall go away into everlasting punishment."

SPECIFICATION SIXTH.

He declares that the value of a doctrine is measured by the ability of men to verify it in their experience; in illustrating this statement, he has spoken lightly of important doctrines of the Bible: that is to say, that in a sermon entitled "Christianity and Dogma," printed in the volume called "Truths for To-Day," the following and similar language is used: "The doctrines of Christianity are those which may be tried by the human heart." "The doctrine of the Trinity as formally stated cannot be experienced. Man has not the power to taste the oneness of three, nor the threeness of one, and see that it is 'good.'" "If you, my friend, are giving your daily thought to the facts of Christianity, and are standing bewildered to-day amid the statements of science and Genesis about earth, or its swarms of life, recall the truth that your soul cannot taste any theory of man's origin—cannot experience the origin of man, whatever that origin may have been."

SPECIFICATION SEVENTH.

In the sermons entitled, respectively, "Old Testament Inspiration" and "The Value of Yesterday," published in the Chicago Pulpit, and in sermons entitled "Righteousness," "Faith," "The Great Debate," printed in "Truths for To-day;" also in the "Decline of Vice," printed in the Alliance, he has used language which, taken in its plain and obvious sense, inculcates a phase of the doctrine commonly known as "Evolution" or "Development:" that is to say, he uses the following and similar language: "Low idolatry of primitive man," meaning Adam. "The Bible has not made religion, but religion and righteousness have made the Bible. Christianity is not forced upon us; our own nature has forced it up out of the spirit's rich depths." "The Mosaic Economy was nothing else but a progress; earth had come to Polytheism, to Pantheism, to Feticism. It was the Hebrew philosophy and its immediate result Christianity, which swept away the iron Jupiter." "This multitude measures a great revelation of God above that day when earth possessed but one man or family, and that one without language and without learning and without virtue." "In the first human being God could no more display His perfections, than a musician like Mozart could unfold his genius to an infant, or to a South Sea Islander." These passages conflict with the Confession of Faith, chap. viii. § 1; chap. vii. § 3, 4, 5; chap. iv. § 2.

SPECIFICATION EIGHTH.

In a sermon entitled "Influence of Democracy on Christian Doctrine," published in the "Chicago Pulpit," and preached April 20, 1873, he has made false and dangerous statements regarding the standards of faith and practice: that is to say: he uses the following and similar language: "When we come to moral ideas, we are compelled to do without any standards:" "You may, my friends, at your leisure, seek and find further instances of this modification of Christian belief by the new surroundings of government. Christian customs will also be modified along with the creed." "In this casting off of old garments, it no more cheerfully throws away the inconceivable of Christianity than the inconceivable of Kant and

Spinoza." "In this abandonment there is no charge of falsehood cast upon the old mysteries; they may or may not be true; there is only a passing them by as not being in the line of the current wish or taste; raiment for a past age, perhaps for a future, but not acceptable for the present."

SPECIFICATION NINTH.

He has given his approval, in the pulpit, to the doctrine commonly known as Sabellianism, or a Modal Trinity: and has spoken slightingly of the doctrine of the Trinity, as taught in the standards of the Presbyterian Church: (Confession of Faith, chapter 2, §3): that is to say: in the volume "Truths for To-day," he uses the following and similar language: "But the moment he (Jesus) has uttered our text,—that "Those which man can subject to experience, are the doctrines that be of God," reason rises up and unites its voice with that of simple authority. The doctrines of Christianity are those which may be tried by the human heart." "The doctrine of the Trinity, as formally stated, cannot be experienced. Man has not the power to taste the threeness of one, nor the oneness of three, and see that it is "good." "Hence, Christianity bears readily the idea of three offices, and permits the one God to appear in Father, or in Son, or in Spirit.

SPECIFICATION TENTH.

In the sermons entitled, respectively, "The Great Debate," and "Positive Religion," printed in the volume called "Truths for To-day," false and dangerous statements are made respecting our knowledge regarding the Being and attributes of God: that is to say, that the following and similar language is used: "When Logic informs you and me that God is a law, or a wide-spread blind agency, let us not be deceived, for all it has done is to take away *our* God." "Perfect assurance is just as impossible to a free religionist or atheist, as it is to the Christian. Remembering, therefore, that there is no moral idea of beauty or love or soul that may not be denied, and remembering, too, that the assurance that there is a God is always logically equal to the oppo-belief." "We know not what nor where is our God, our heaven." (Confession of Faith, chap. ii. §1 and chap. ii.)

SPECIFICATION ELEVENTH.

In a sermon entitled "A Religion of Words," published in the Chicago Pulpit, and in the sermon entitled Religious Toleration, he uses language in regard to the Sacrament of Baptism inconsistent with the doctrinal standards of the Presbyterian Church (see Confession of Faith, chap. xxvii. §1, 2, 3, 4, and chap. xxviii. §1, 5); that is to say, he speaks flippantly of infant baptism, and, in the sermon above mentioned, uses the following words: "The nations await, with tears of past sorrow, a religion, that shall, indeed baptize men and children, either or both, but counting this as only a beautiful form, shall take the souls of men into the atmosphere of Jesus," etc.

SPECIFICATION TWELFTH.

He has used language in respect to Penelope and Socrates, which is unwarrantable and contrary to the teachings of the Confession of Faith, chap. x. §4, that is to say, that in his sermon, entitled "Soul Culture," the following passage occurs: "There is no doubt the notorious Catherine II. held more truth and better truth than was known to all classic Greece—held to a belief in a Saviour, of whose glory that gifted knew nought; yet, such the grandeur of soul above mind that I doubt not that Queen Penelope of the dark land and the doubting Socrates have received at Heaven's gate a sweeter welcome than greeted the ear of Russia's brilliant but false lived queen."

SPECIFICATION THIRTEENTH.

In a sermon printed on or about 15th September, 1872, from 11 Peter iii. 9, he made use of loose and unguarded language, respecting the Providence of God.

SPECIFICATION FOURTEENTH.

In a sermon preached at installation of Rev. Arthur Swazey, D. D., as pastor of the Ashland Avenue Presbyterian Church, Chicago, and previously preached about January, 1872, in Standard Hall, Chicago, he repudiated the idea of a call to the ministry, and taught that an office of the ministry like the profession of law and medicine, is the natural outgrowth of circumstances; that is to say, he said in substance, that the merchant is called to his business, the lawyer to his profession, just as much as the minister to the duties of his office, and other statements contradicted the teaching of the Confession of Faith in chap. xxv. §3, and Form of Government, chap. i. §3. Confession of Faith, chap. xxx. §1 and 2. Confession of Faith, chap. xxvii. §4: chap. vii. §4.. chap. xxix. §3.

SPECIFICATION FIFTEENTH.

He has made false and misleading statements respecting the Old Testament sacrifices; that is to say, that in the sermon, entitled "A Religion of Words," he speaks of the aforesaid sacrifices, as "gift worship," and uses the following and similar language: "Gifts to the Deity were the infant creepings of religion; the shadow of a coming reality, the manifesting of an incipient love that did not know how to express itself. Not knowing that what God most wished, was a pure heart in His children, they loaded His temples with their jewels and raiment, and His altars with their lambs." See Confession of Faith: chap. vii. §5: chap. viii. §4: chap. xiv. §3. Larger Catechism, art. 34.

SPECIFICATION SIXTEENTH.

In the sermons aforesaid, religion is represented in the form of a mysticism, which undervalues the evidences of revealed religion, and is indifferent to the distinguishing doctrines of Christianity; that is to say, that in the sermon preached on the occasion of the death of John Stuart Mill, above referred to, and in the sermon called "Positive Religion," printed in "Truths for To-day;" also in the sermon, entitled "The Decline of Vice," printed in the Alliance newspaper; and in the volume, called "Truths for To-day," the following and similar language occurs: "That Mr. Mill did not accept the orthodox creed is not what a liberal world need regret the most, but that he revealed little of the religious sentiment and hope, is what we must confess to be a shadow upon his memory." "Victor Cousin of France was the rival of Stuart Mill in wisdom, in genius, in intellect; and so Guizot. These three were similar and strikingly great. But the two latter possessed the power of sentiment. That golden atmosphere of love and hope, that hangs around religion, enveloped Victor Cousin in its life-giving folds. Setting out from the same points of thought, Cousin always came up to God and heaven, and Mr. Mill to the practical of this life; to the happiness of man here and then paused."

SPECIFICATION SEVENTEENTH.

In the sermons aforesaid, he employs the words used to indicate the doctrines of the Bible in an unscriptural sense, and in a sense different from that in which they are used by the evangelical churches in general, and the Presbyterian Church in particular; that is to say, that he so uses such words as "regeneration," "conversion," "repentance," "Divine," "justification," "new hearl," "salvation," "Saviour."

SPECIFICATION EIGHTEENTH.

He, in effect, denies the judicial nature of the condemnation of the lost, as taught in the Confession of Faith, chap. iv. §4, chap. xxxiii. Shorter Catechism, chap. xix. art. 84; that is to say, in the sermons, entitled "Faith and Christianity and Dogma," printed in the volume, called "Truths for To-Day," he uses the following and similar language: "The least trace of infidelity lessens the activity; unbelief brings all to a halt, and damns the soul, not by arbitrary decree, but by actually arresting the best flow of its life. Unbelief is not an arbitrary but a natural damnation."

SPECIFICATION NINETEENTH.

He teaches that faith saves, because it leads to holy life; that salvation by faith is not peculiar to Christianity; that salvation is a matter of degree, and that the supremacy of faith in salvation arises out of the fact that it goes further than other Christian graces towards making men holy, that is to say, in the sermons entitled, "Faith," printed in the volume called "Truths for to-day," the following and similar language occurs: "Faith in Christ is a rich soil, out of which Righteousness is a gorgeous bloom." "If there were enough truth—truth of morals and redemption in the Mohammedan or Buddhist system to save the soul—faith would be the law of salvation within these systems." "Salvation by faith is not a creation or invention of the New Testament, but is a law that has pushed its way up into the New Testament from the realm without." "No other grace could so save the soul. Charity may do much. It softens the heart, and drags along a train of virtues; but it is limited by the horizon of this life. Voltaire and Paine were both beautiful in charity toward the poor, but that virtue seems inadequate; and, of the highest form of charity, a religious faith is the best cause, and hence charity must take the place, not of a leader, but of one that is led. Even penitence is a poor 'saving grace,' compared with faith." See Confession of Faith, chaps. xi. xvi.

SPECIFICATION TWENTIETH.

He teaches that men are saved by works; that is to say, in the sermons entitled "Good Works," "The Value of Yesterday," "A Religion of Words," the following and similar language occurs: "There is nothing society so much needs to-day as not Divine righteousness but human righteousness." Heaven is a height to which men climb on the deeds of this life." "Coming to the grave, he only can look forward with joy who can sweetly look back." "The good deeds of yesterday, the good deeds of to-day, the perfected goodness of to-morrow, a deep love for man, a consciousness of the presence of God, will fill the whole place with a nobleness and happiness to which earth has thus far been willingly a stranger. This will be a salvation, and Christ will be a Saviour. (Confession of Faith, chap. xi. §14.)

SPECIFICATION TWENTY-FIRST.

He denies the doctrine of Justification by Faith, as held by the Reformed Churches, and taught in the Westminster confession of Faith; Chapter xi., that is to say, in the sermon entitled "Good Works," he uses the following and similar language: "Works, that is, result—a new life—are the destiny of faith, the reason of its wonderful play of light on the religious horizon. Faith, as a belief and a friendship, is good, so far as it bears the soul to this moral perfection."

SPECIFICATION TWENTY-SECOND.

In the sermon aforesaid misrepresents the doctrinal views of those who believe in Justification by Faith alone, by using language which is calculated to produce the impression that those who hold the doctrine aforesaid, divorce faith from morals, and believe that man may be saved by an intellectual assent to a creed without regard to personal character.

SPECIFICATION TWENTY-THIRD.

He has spoken of the Bible, or portions thereof, in terms which involve a denial of its plenary inspiration as held in the Presbyterian Church and taught in in the Confession of Faith, Chapter I, and also in the following passages of Scripture, (2 Tim. iii. 16. Acts i. 16–20,) that is to say, in a sermon entitled "Old Testament Inspiration," and in sundry articles written by him and printed in The Interior newspaper, he refers to the 109th Psalm as a "battle song," as the "good of an hour," "a revenge"; and in an article printed in The Interior, September 18, 1873, he uses the following and similar language: "The prominence given to the 109th Psalm in my remarks arises only from the fact that it has long been a public test of the value of any given theory of inspiration. This is one of the places at which the rational world asks us to pause and apply our abundant and boastful words. Most of the young men, even in the Presbyterian church, know what the historian Froude said of this Psalm a few years since: 'Those who accept the 109th Psalm as the word of God, are already far on their way toward *auto-da-fes* and massacre of the St. Bartholomew,' and while they may, for a time, reject these words, they will soon demand a theory of inspiration very different from the indefinite admiration of the past.

SPECIFICATION TWENTY-FOURTH.

He has spoken of the Bible, or portions thereof in terms which involve a denial of its infallibility, and which tend to shake the confidence of men in its divine authority—as taught in Confession of Faith, Chapter I, that is to say, in the sermon on "Old Testament Inspiration," the following passage occurs: "There is, it seems to me, no other conceivable method of treating the Old Testament than that found in the word *eclecticism.* We must seek out its permanent truths, follow its central idea, and love them the more because they were eliminated from the barbaric ages with so much sorrow and bloodshed." Moreover, in the article in The Interior above mentioned, he says that "Christ declared the Ten Commandments defective;" also, in an article written by him and printed in The Interior, September 4, 1873, he speaks of "battles"—meaning the battles of the Israelites—engaged in with the approval and by the command of Jehovah, "that surpassed in cruelty those of Julius Cæsar." He also teaches that the Mosaic legislation was cruel and unjust, and uses the following and similar language: "If David's personal character had been preceded by generations which dripped in blood, by generations which punished over thirty forms of offences with death, by generations which slew women and children, by generations which punished impurity by a fine of one animal from the flock; and, if reared in such an atmosphere, David sent Uriah to the front and thus secured Uriah's beauteous wife, one certainly should not attribute this immorality to any lack of revelation, indeed, but rather to an absence of that quality of revelation found afterwards in the morals of Jesus." Moreover, in an article written by him and printed in the periodical known as the "Sunday School Teacher," and bearing date July, 1873, he uses the following and similar language. And moreover, in a sermon entitled "St. John," printed in the volume called "Truths for To-day," he uses the following and similar language: "There are no prophecies of literal events in the Apocalypse any more than there is in Tasso, or Tennyson, or Whittier." * * * "For us to inquire the meaning of the seven seals, and to enquire whether Rome be not the 'Babylon,' would be for us to seek the 'Deserted Village' of Goldsmith or the 'Beulah Land' of John Bunyan."

The foregoing charge with its specifications may be proved by the printed sermons and articles of Mr. Swing as above mentioned, and by the testimony of the following witnesses:

Oliver H. Lee, Horace A. Hurlburt, William C. Gray, Charles M. Howe, Leonard Swett, Wm. C. Ewing, Mr. McClurg, (of Jansen, McClurg & Co.,) Messrs. "Carpenter and Sheldon," Rev. W. C. Young, Rev. J. B. McClure, Rev. R. K. Wharton, Rev. C. L. Thompson, Rev. R. Laird Collier, Rev. J. Minot Savage, C. O. Waters, Rev. Arthur Swazey, D. D., F. A. Riddle, Rev. R. W. Patterson, D. D., A. D. Pence, John McLandburg, Rev. Robert Collyer, Henry G. Miller, William C. Goudy, Rev. J. H. Trowbridge.

CHARGE SECOND.

Rev. David Swing, being a minister of the Presbyterian Church in the United States of America, and a member of the Presbytery of Chicago, does not sincerely receive and adopt the Confession of Faith of this Church as containing the system of doctrine taught in the Holy Scriptures.

SPECIFICATION FIRST.

Since he began to minister to the Fourth Presbyterian Church he has declared to the Rev. Robert Laird Collier, a Unitarian minister in charge of the Church of the Messiah, in Chicago, in substance, that he agreed with him, Collier, in his theological views, but thought it best to remain as he was for the time, as he could thereby accomplish more good for the cause.

SPECIFICATION SECOND.

He does not accept and believe doctrines contained in the Confession of Faith, viz.: the doctrines commonly known as Predestination, the Perseverance of the Saints, and Depravity, as appears from the sermons above referred to, and the testimony of Geo. A. Shufeldt, Esq.

SPECIFICATION THIRD.

He has declared, in a letter to George A. Shufeldt, Esq., since he began his ministry in Chicago, that he had long before that time abandoned three of the five points of Calvinism affirmed by the Synod of Dort, naming the three, meaning three of the doctrines adopted and taught in the Confession of Faith.

SPECIFICATION FOURTH.

In a sermon delivered in the Fourth Presbyterian Church, April 12, 1874, he made statements which, by fair implication, involve a disbelief in one or more of the leading doctrines of the Confession of Faith, to wit: Of Election, Perseverance, Original Sin, the Vicarious Sacrifice of Christ, the Trinity, and the Deity of Christ, that is to say he uses the following and similar language:

"After the hundred-year experiment, there is no probability that any missionary gold will be exhausted upon any indoctrination of the heathen world in denominational ideas, for the tendency of the present is to abandon sectarian ideas at home; hence there will be little disposition to inculcate abroad doctrines which are rapidly dying by our own firesides."

"The Church of England joins with the dissenting churches in India as a fact, and cares little for the apostolic succession in a land where the Brahmin can so far outdo it in the quantity and absurdity of holy touchings and holy pedigrees. And there the Calvinist conceals his five points, for the crowd of Indian philosophers can always propose ten points far more obscure, and thus all the Protestant sects approach the whole pagan world with the gospel reduced to its simplest expression. Blessed era it will be when we shall be as fully ashamed in America of the things that divide us as we are when our feet touch India or Japan."

"Can it be possible that it requires home training, that is, local and youthful prejudice, to enable us to see the immense worth of our dogmas, and that approaching foreigners not fully drilled in the sectarian method and tacties, we fear their smile of unbelief or derision? It is ominous if, having a score or so of peculiar ideas, we should all get together and agree to say little about them to this Chinaman and that Brahmin. Such a condition of things would seem to indicate one more step along this path, an agreement to say little about these differences to persons not pagans and not upon foreign shores."

"We have come to-day to a survey of Christianity in its truest significance, and hence in its wanderings about from race to race, from island to continent, from river to sea, we may learn what are its most essential parts. A student shutting himself up in his room may, from the Bible, elaborate a perfect system which shall omit nothing regarding the human will or the mode and quality of everything, but the world in actual experiment may not need, nor even faintly appreciate, one-tenth part of this closet-made system."

The Specifications contained under Charge I are relied on as contained under and in support of Charge II, the same as if repeated, excepting the 6th, 10th, and 16th.

The foregoing charge with its specifications may be proved by the printed writings of Mr. Swing, as above referred to, and by the testimony of the following witnesses: Robert Laird Collier, George A. Shufeldt, and also of the witnesses named in Charge I.

Respectfully submitted,

FRANCIS L. PATTON.

CHICAGO, April 13, 1874.

PROF. SWING'S DECLARATION.

To the Members of the Chicago Presbytery:

Called upon in the outset of these proceedings to enter my plea to the charges and specifications presented by Francis L. Patton, I beg permission to submit the following: I object to the charges as too vague and as embracing no important offense, yet, not wishing to raise any technical objections, I enter the plea of "Not guilty." I admit the extracts from sermons and writings, but I would ask the Presbytery to consider the entire essays or whole discourses from which the extracts are made. I avow myself to be what, before the late union, was styled a New School Presbyterian, and deny myself to have come into conflict with any of the Evangelical Calvinistic doctrines of the denomination with which I am connected, and I beg permission to enter as a part of my plea the following statements: 1. Regarding my relations to the Liberal Churches. 2. Regarding my relation to the Presbyterian Church. Of these I shall speak in their order.

By way of explaining the quantity of the public offence, I will state that of fifteen lectures delivered in this city for benevolent purposes, all but two were on behalf of the Evangelical Churches, and, in all cases but one, remuneration was declined. Hence the spirit that prompted such lectures must have been not any marked partiality for the so-called liberal societies. This much as to the quantity of the alleged offense. Upon the quality of the conduct I would submit the following observations:

1. There is no valuable theory of life except that of good will toward all men. It is only upon the basis of a wide friendship any one can live well the few years of this existence, and hence to decline to lecture on behalf of a Unitarian chapel would do more harm to the mutual good will upon which society is founded, than it would do good to an orthodox theology, or harm to a liberal creed.

2. If the object of the Evangelical pulpit is to promulge its better truth, it can do so only as far as its ministry reveal a deep friendship toward all mankind, and so far as they unfurl the banner of their own love, while they are presuming to speak of the impartial love of their Divine Master. There remains no longer any power of authority in the pulpit. The time when the civil police drove a halting sinner into the true Church has disappeared, and the modern pulpit must communicate its ideas along the chords of friendship, and he will persuade the most men whose heart can gather up the largest and most diverse multitude into the grasp of his pure affections.

3. But let us come now to the grandest reason why a Presbyterian may express in many ways a kind regard for these so-called Liberal sects. The sin of the "lecture," as charged, must be based upon the assumption that the Unitarian sects are outcast from God, having no hope in the life to come. The names of Channing, and Elliot, and Huntington, and Peabody, in the pulpits of that sect, and the Christ-like lives of thousands in the congregations of that denomination, utterly exclude from my mind and my heart the most remote idea that in showing that

brotherhood any kindness I am offering indirect approval to persons outside the pale of the Christian religion and hope. The idea that these brethren are doomed to wrath beyond the tomb I wholly repudiate. It is, indeed, my conviction that they do not hold as correct a version of the Gospel as that announced by the Evangelical Alliance a few years ago, yet I am just as certain that the Blessed Lord does not bestow His forgiveness and grace upon the mind that possesses the most accurate information, but upon the heart that loves and trusts Him. It is possible that the venerable Dr. Hodge, of Princeton, holds a more truthful view of Jesus than may be held by the distinguished Peabody, who has just lectured from his Unitarian standpoint before the Calvinists in the Union Theological Seminary; but we can point to nothing in the Bible that would indicate that heaven is to be given to only the one of these two giants who may possess the clearer apprehension of a truth. It may be assumed that God grants the world salvation only on account of the expiatory atonement made by a Redeemer; but that God will grant this salvation to only those who fully apprehend this fact, is an idea not to be entertained for an instant, for this would give heaven only to philosophers, and indeed only to those of this small class who shall have made no intellectual mistake. Looking upon the multitudes who need this salvation, and seeing that they are composed of common men, women, and children who know nothing of the distinctions of formal theology, we cannot but conclude that paradise is not to be a reward of scholarship, but of a loving, obedient faith in Jesus Christ.

When we remember these things, and recall that Dr. Isaac Watts was accused of being a Unitarian, so difficult often is it to perceive the dividing line, we cannot for a moment place these persons called Unitarians outside the great and generous love of the Saviour. I stand ready, therefore, at all times to express toward these sects a friendship not only human, and wise, and social, but also Christian.

The harmony existing between all these brethren and myself is not a harmony of views in the mind, but a harmony of love in the soul. They each and all know that I differ widely from them, but this they and I know: that only the most gentlemanly treatment in public and private will we all receive always from each other. Much as I love Presbyterianism, a love inherited from all my ancestors, if on account of it, it were necessary for me to abate in the least my good will toward all sects, I should refuse to purchase the Presbyterian name at so dear a price.

The second point to be alluded to was my relations to Presbyterianism. A distinction evidently exists between Presbyterianism as formulated in past times and Presbyterianism *actual*. A creed is only the highest wisdom of a particular time and place. Hence, as in State, there is always a quiet slipping away from old laws without any waiting for a formal repeal, as some of the old statutes of Connecticut are lying dead, not by any legal death, but by long emaciation and final neglect of friend and foe; so in all formulated creeds, Catholic or Protestant, there is a gradual, but constant decay of some article or word which was once promulged amid great pomp and circumstance. And yet no Church is willing to confess its past folly and repeal the injurious or untrue. All, Catholic and Protestant, simply agree to remain silent.

In the Presbyterian Confession of Faith there are about 200 formulas of truth, or supposed truth. It is a wonderful argument in favor of this compendium that not one-tenth of these have been found false to the Bible or false to the welfare of society. To designate these 200 as Calvinism is a gross injustice, for they are almost all only valuable truths, common to all Churches, and gathered up from the sacred page.

But from a few statements out of this large number the *actual* Presbyterian Church has quietly passed away. Conventions cannot be called every few years to amend or repeal some one article. It would entail endless debate and expense, and perhaps promote wide discord, thus to call from time to time a new Westminster Assembly. As the Christian world avoid a revision of the translation of the Bible because of the tumult such a new version would probably create among the sects, so each particular Church postpones as long as possible any formal modification of its historic statements of doctrine. But meanwhile individual minds cannot be slaves; they cannot suspend the use of their judgment and best common sense. Hence, unable to revoke any dangerous idea by law, the Presbyterian Church permits its clergy to distinguish the *actual* from the Church *historic.* To the Presbyterian Church actual I have thus far devoted my life, giving it what I possess of mind and heart.

Chief among the doctrines which our Church has passed by as being incorrect, or else on overdevelopment of Scriptural ideas, are all those formulas which looked toward a dark fatalism, or which destroy the human will, or indicate the damnation of some infant, or that God, for His own glory, foreordained a vast majority of the race to everlasting death. It has been my good or bad fortune to speak in public and in private to a large number of persons hostile to our Church, and in nearly all cases I have found their hostility based upon the doctrines indicated above, and in all ways I have declared to them that the Presbyterian Church had left behind those doctrines, and that her religion was simply evangelical, and not, *par excellence,* the religion of despair. In my peculiar ministry a simple silence has not been sufficient. I have, therefore, at many times, declared our denomination to be simply a Church of the common evangelical doctrines.

Besides the formulas of its books, our Church has suffered more than pen can record from the wild utterances of some of its great names, and from these it has been my frequent duty to try to separate her fair and sweeter present. There were ages when mothers wailed in awful agony over a dead infant, because they had been taught that children "not a span long" were suffering on the hot floor of hell, and each new-born infant was only a "lump of perdition;" and, under the awful lashing of these thoughts, mothers used to baptize their *dead-born* little ones, piteously beseeching God to ante-date the sacred rite. In the midst of this wail of infants damned, Luther himself says, "God pleaseth you when He crowns the unworthy; He ought not to displease you when He damns the innocent."

Against the doctrine of fatalism, as implied in the perfect independence of God's decree as to all human conduct, against the ultra form of human inability, it has been my constant duty, as it seemed, to protest, and thus defend our Church from the influence of ideas so repudiated by modern thought. An eminent churchman, perhaps Luther, said, "All things take place by the eternal and invariable will of God, who blasts and shatters in pieces the freedom of the will."

Next to the baneful Calvinistic estimate of the will, comes the overstatement of the idea of salvation by faith all along through the Presbyterian history. Said Luther, "You see how rich is the Christian. Even if he would, he could not destroy his salvation by any sins, however grievous, unless he refuse to believe." "Be thou a sinner and sin boldly, still more *boldly believe.* From Christ no sin shall separate, though a thousand thousand times a day we should commit fornication and murder." In my ministry I have toiled the harder to unite faith and holiness, because of this dreadful page of history written down against the Calvinistic branches of the Protestant Church.

Next to the injury the Presbyterian Church has sustained from its errors as above mentioned, it has become a source of actual infidelity by its terrific doctrine of hell. Even to the day of Edwards, and since, the pictures of perdition have been such as at first, indeed, to frighten the multitude, but such as afterward to destroy the idea of God. Look where men might, it was perdition to all but his sect, and to look upon other sects in the pains of hell, was to form a part of the happiness of the blessed. The fagot, the rack, and the boiling oil were a resort of potentates, for, if God was so glorying in the torment of heretics just beyond, it was a small matter if the Church tormented them slightly on this side the tomb. We need not disguise the fact, my brethren, that the dark side of Calvinism gave birth to infidelity in that age when the Church was narrow in its love, broad only in its damnation. But permit me to quote from one who has not been arraigned for bad teaching, but whose words have just been published by the American Tract Society, — Theodore Christlieb. He says: "It was the former century which prepared the way among ourselves for the prevalence of rationalism. Was it not the petrifaction of evangelical faith into dry forms of a dead orthodoxy? The sermons of that period were for the most part * * * about Crypto Calvinists, Syncredists, Synergists, Majorists, Antinomians, Osiandrians, Weigelians, and Arminians. * * * * * * At such a time, when a cold orthodoxy was almost everywhere substituted for living faith, when a slavish adherence to the Church's standards was put in place of a free inquiry into the sense of Scripture, and a fresh bondage to the letter was introduced, it became a simple necessity for energetic minds like Lessing to come to an open breach with traditional Protestantism. * * * Rationalism was right in contending for simple morality in opposition to a theoretic orthodoxy." "It must be confessed that the Church theology of the last century was chiefly to blame for the general apostasy from the ancient faith which then began. From the middle of the eighteenth century to the end of the first third of the nineteenth, the chief authorities in pulpits and institutions of learning were promoters of rationalism. * * * * For this spirit we theologians have only ourselves to thank. We are now reaping what we ourselves have sown."

Such are the words of a profound thinker, who, to his fame as a thinker, adds a parallel fame of piety. Amid some of the unparalleled doctrines of our Church arose the intellectual revolt of the present times, and we can only check the progress of the evil by withdrawing the cause. It is an ominous fact that the liberal creed which the charges in this case so attack has sprung chiefly from that land which once lay wholly subject to the severe tenets of the Puritans.

It seems to me the world is now fully ready for an orthodoxy that shall firmly, yet tenderly, preach all of the creed, except its plain errors of dark views of God and man. Not one of you, my brethren, has preached the dark theology of Jonathan Edwards in your whole life. Nothing could induce you to preach it, and yet it is written down in your creed in dreadful plainness. Confess, with me, that our beloved Church has slipped away from the religion of despair, and has come unto Mount Sion, into the atmosphere of Jesus, as He was in life and in death, full of love and forgiveness. And yet it is only in the narrow field just pointed out that I have in any way departed from the doctrines of the Presbyterian Church.

One of the most distinguished of our theological teachers in the East has just written: "There is not enough in that indictment to convict one of heresy. All these commotions only point to a time when sectarianism will disappears, and all Christians will meet on the platform of a common faith in one Christ and one

Saviour, and, fastening all their faith upon Him as a Redeemer, will cast off many of the forms which now perplex them."

Beloved brethren, holding the general creed as rendered by the former New School Theologians, I will, in addition to such a general statement, repeat to you articles of belief, upon which I am willing to meet the educated world, and the skeptical world, and the sinful world, using my words in the evangelical sense: The inspiration of the Holy Scriptures, the Trinity, the divinity of Christ, the office of Christ as a mediator when grasped by an obedient faith, conversion by God's Spirit, man's natural sinfulness, and the final separation of the righteous and wicked.

I have now read before you an outline of my public method and of my Christian creed. It is for you to decide whether there is in me orthodox belief sufficient to retain me in your brotherhood. Having confessed everywhere that the value of a single life does not depend upon sectarian relations, but upon evangelical or Christian relations, I am perfectly willing to cross a boundary which I have often shown to be narrow; but, going from you, if such be your order at last, it is the evangelical Gospel I shall still preach, unless my mind should pass through undreamed of changes in the future.

From the prosecutor of this case I would not withhold my conviction that he has acted from a sense of duty; therefore, to him and to you all, brethren, I extend good-will, and hope that in a wisdom religious and fraternal you will be enabled to do what is right in the sight of God

Yours, with love,

David Swing.

Arguments for the Prosecution and Defense.

Presbytery opened at 10 o'clock yesterday morning in the chapel of the First Presbyterian Church. The attendance was very full. Professor Swing was not present. After roll call and reading the minutes, the Stated Clerk, the Rev. Mr. Johnson, read the following report from the committee in whose charge was given

DR. SWAZEY'S PROTEST

against the charges:

"The committee appointed to prepare a statement of reasons for the Presbytery's action in relation to the testimony of H. F. Waite, Esq., submit the following:

"1. The judicial action of an Ecclesiastical Court, often, as in the present case, pertains to matters of religious opinion, and even to the impressions made by public services. It is, therefore, not possible to confine the testimony on either side strictly within the technical rules of evidence that are enforced in the jurisdiction of civil courts. But especially in this trial, on the part of the accused, who is permitted to produce any testimony that has a direct or indirect bearing upon his exculpation. The judicatories of our church, so far as we are aware, have always, in such cases, arrived at substantial equity without much regard to technicalities, and this Presbytery, in adjudicating the present question, has permitted the prosecutor to make charges and to introduce testimony that would not for a moment be admitted in a civil tribunal. The charges, and many of the specifications, take a very wide range, and the rebutting testimony could not be fairly restricted, except by the limit already indicated and already accorded to the prosecutor. No rule of our church has been produced to require more than this.

"2. No rules of evidence applicable in civil courts which could have any proper bearing upon the procedure of this judicatory would exclude any of Mr. Waite's testimony. Under these rules the accused is accorded many rights that are not granted to the prosecutor. At this point the committee quoted Greenleaf and other authorities.

"3. The several motions of the prosecutor were denied in the application of the foregoing principles as follows:

"1. The first motion was denied because the testimony of the defense was not confined to specification 5, and if it had been evidence to the language spoken at other times was admissible on that issue, the burden of proof resting on the prosecution, against whose evidence any presumption might be raised by proving the previous evangelical character of the respondent's teachings. Besides, the charges and specifications are general and carry the court back to the year A. D. 1867, especially specifications 2 and 3, charge 2.

"2. The second motion was denied because written sermons are not necessarily the only primary evidence. Such documents are not in the nature of written contracts duly executed. They are merely the speaker's memoranda, from which he may depart more or less in the delivery. Lectures are also public teachings, and specification five refers expressly to preaching or teaching. In this case the written expositions of Scripture, which are in fact sermons, offered the best evidence, because Professor Swing, under the extraordinary circumstances of the society, when they had no house of worship of their own, preached to very miscellaneous congregations, a large portion of whom might, in his judgment, be specially benefited by general discourses adapted to their state of mind as partial unbelievers. He may, therefore, have reserved most of his more strictly doctrinal teachings for the benefit of his own people to his Wednesday evening lectures. Besides the entire impressions of regular hearers are in some respects better evidence as to the evangelical character even of written sermons than the sermons themselves would be if read before this body in a critical spirit, and under the charge of radical defects or error. Moreover, it would be impracticable to read to this body all the sermons of Professor Swing, delivered during a period of two years and a half, in order to determine the point at issue. The defendant may produce by condensed evidence available in such a case, the burden of proof of course being upon the accuser.

"3. The third motion was denied for the reasons already given.

"4. The fourth motion was denied for the reasons stated under the second motion.

"5. The fifth motion was denied for all the reasons aforesaid.

"Respectfully submitted.

"D. S. JOHNSON,
R. W. PATTERSON,
FRANCIS A. RIDDLE."

This was accepted and approved.

The Rev. Mr. Noyes called attention to a rule which allowed members of Presbytery, after testimony and arguments were all in, to rise and state their views of the case, "to a reasonable extent." He wished to have Presbytery settle what would be "a reasonable extent." The request was temporarily past over.

The Rev. Mr. Blackburn read this resolution, being the one he gave notice of on Friday last:

Resolved, That the Presbytery of Chicago overture the General Assembly to institute measures at its session in St. Louis, 1874, for the revision of the Book of Discipline. Presbytery does not deem it necessary to refer to any other reasons than the necessity evident on the face of the book for such a revision and the experience of the church.

Which was temporarily laid upon the table after the Rev. Mr. Trowbridge had moved as an amendment that the confession of faith be included in the revision.

Dr. Patterson offered this:

Resolved, that in the judgment of the judicatory it is due to the interests of impartial justice and to the dignity of an ecclesiastical court that the members of this body, and especially the parties, or either of them, engaged in the case now pending, should obtain from the publication and circulation of criticism upon the action of the court, and from public discussions of the merits of the case, outside of the judicatory, before the final issue is reached.

As a very strong disposition to discuss this point at length instantly manifested itself, the resolution was laid on the table, like its predecessors.

Dr. Patterson then recurred to the limitation of time suggested by Mr. Noyes. The Rev. Mr Young moved that both prosecution and defense be allowed as much time as they might deem necessary. Laid upon the table.

Whereupon the Moderator admonished Presbytery of the solemnity of its duties as a court of Jesus Christ; and observed that the time had come (the testimony being finished) for comment by members of Presbytery; "first of all, from the prosecutor," at which Professor Patton, calm and bloodless as the spirit of Hamlet's father, arose and began:

MR. MODERATOR AND BRETHREN OF THE PRESBYTERY: Grave charges are proposed against a popular minister. He is beloved by his congregation, and he has the sympathies of the city. To many of you he stands in the relation of a warm personal friend. You and he have been in the habit of taking sweet counsel together. It is as if the children of a family were impaneled at the bar to listen to charges preferred against one of their number at the hands of a stranger. I should not think it strange if your first impulse were to stand by your friend, and out of your convictions as to his faith, to shield him from reproach. I can conceive what questions may be asked at the institution of such a case. To these questions I would answer that when the cause of truth is in issue, we can afford to risk something. The burden of this battle, God has seen fit to cast this burden upon young shoulders. I will go on, sustained by the consciousness that I am pleading the cause of my crucified Lord. Let me ask you, brothers, to lay aside all personal predilections, and act purely for the glory of God and the advancement of His kingdom.

You will notice that one of the first charges brought against Professor Swing is the charge that he has departed from his ordination vows. And that he has not been zealous and faithful in the discharge of his duties—unfaithful in the several forms and specifications set forth. It should rest with the defense to disprove each particular item of these charges and specifications. It seems to be clear, if anything is, that the defense is bound to disprove each of these in precise terms—not to assert other things than are mentioned in them. The specifications are true, or the y are not true. They either sustain or do not sustain the charges. What is the standard by which is to be decided the question whether these charges, if true, constitute offenses? It is an offense to revile the doctrines of predestination and of infant baptism in the Presbyterian Church, whatever it may be in other churches. Then the question follows, What is the Presbyterian Church? The standard of the Presbyterian Church is Confession of Faith and the catechisms of the Westminster Assembly. Even though it so happened, once in the history of the church, that the body of her people saw fit to divide, each wing took the Confession of Faith; and when, in the process of time, it seemed fit for them to reunite, they came together on the basis of the confession. Never has it been dreamed that the church should lose her anchorage and drift away from the Confession of Faith.

The broadest basis ever dreamed of by either Old or New School, was one which contemplated the preservation in its integrity of the Reformed or Calvinistic system. The plan of reunion, as proposed in 1869, was afterward adopted unanimously by both bodies on a rising vote and read with emphasis the declaration that this solemn decision was of binding force. Is the Confession of Faith thus decided upon to be called in question by the Chicago Presbytery? I think it was when Presbytery listened to the accused and gave some indications of approval, not in its corporate capacity, but by the action of individual members, to the plea of Professor Swing, when he admitted that he was not in accord with the Confession of Faith; that he had actually departed from that Confession of Faith so far as one or two of its doctrines were concerned, and what was more, when he actually in the face of this solemn body declared that the Presbyterian Church was a very different thing actually from what it is in its formulated theology. The plea of Professor Swing was an admission that he did not believe the doctrine of the Presbyterian Church, or take that Confession of Faith, as the expression of his belief and as containing the system of doctrine taught in the Word of God. I scout the idea set abroad that this trial is raising the old points of dispute between the Old and New Schools. I know Professor Swing claims to be a New School Presbyterian—I have never charged him with being an Old School Presbyterian. The plea had no reference except to enlist the sympathy of the Presbytery and to revive past divisions. Swing's pleas were an insult to the Presbytery, and if they were loyal Presbyteries they would have resented it on the spot.

Professor Swing's sermons do not contain any distinct and unequivocal statement with reference to the main Presbyterian doctrines.

I do not wish to be understood as saying there is no language in Professor Swing's sermons which to unpracticed ears might sound as though it conveyed a teaching of the divine character of our Saviour. On the contrary, I shall quote from his sermons many just such passages. For instance, in "Truths for To-day," page 64, he says: "The inferences from this dependence of human purity upon God must be these: Christ, in unfolding the character of God, in tearing down old idols, and in filling the universe with one spirit, infinite and blessed, has done a work that should bind Him upon the forehead and heart of man."

And upon pages 78 and 79: "Let us now approach a more warmly-disputed proposition—that the divineness of Christ is something essential in the Christian system."

I quoted that to one of the gentlemen on the stand, and asked him whether he thought that was teaching the divinity of Christ, and he said it was.

"For if Christ be not divine, every impulse of the Christian world falls to a lower octave, and light, and love, and hope alike decline. There is no doctrine into which the heart may so inweave itself and find anchorage and peace as in this divineness of the Lord. Hence, Christianity bears readily the idea of three offices, and permits the one God to appear in Father, or in Son, or in Spirit."

That is Unitarianism. That is the doctrine of James Freeman Clarke, whom I mean to quote before long. On page 263 we read:

"'In the beginning was the Word.' That Greek term which we translate Word had long been upon the tongues of scholars. Its meaning was always somewhat hidden. It seems to have represented the Supreme Being out upon an errand of mercy, or creation, as light flies away from the sun. It is that light before which darkness flees; that life before which death retreats. It is indefinable and inconceivable. Yet John saw this *Logos* entering the human body as light seems to rush into the eye and sound into the ear. It dwelt among us, and we beheld its glory, full of grace and truth."

Many persons would call this a clear statement of Christ's deity, yet any Arian might say as much. Page 266:

"Out of John's soul we see issuing these ideas: Christ, the saviour; Christ, the divine; Christ, the intimate friend. The opening chapter reveals the divinity of John's master, and the office of Saviour is revealed in every page."

Now, in order to make good the proposition that these are not unequivocal statements, let me read to you from Dr. Rider, who does not make any pretensions to belief in the divinity of Christ. In his sermon entitled, "Is Universalism Evangelical?" he says:

"Christ is with us literally the hope of glory. Without Him as the interpreter of God to men and the mediator between Him and us, we are without God and without hope in the world."

Universalists talk about a Saviour, too:

"Man is created innocent—all men are—but by voluntary acts they become sinners, and so need a Saviour to guide and sanctify."

In page 264 on the "atonement," Dr. Clark said:

"In conclusion we may say that orthodoxy is right in maintaining that Jesus has by His suffering and death brought forgiveness to mankind—not by propitiating God or appeasing His anger, not by paying our debt or removing a difficulty in the divine mind, but by helping us to see that the love of God is able to lift us out of our sin, and present us spotless in the presence of his glory with exceeding joy. The way in which His death produces this result is the sympathy with human sinfulness and sorrow, which finds in it its highest expression. Those whom men cannot forgive, and who cannot forgive themselves, see that God, speaking through the sufferings of Jesus, is able to forgive them. So the love of God brings them to repentance, and those who were afar off are made nigh by the blood of Christ.

Pass to page 81:

"Cast yourself into the laws of faith and conversion, and repentance, and love and hope, and of the Divine Lord, and upoh these be carried by a new, recreative experience over to a new world called a new heart love—called heaven hereafter."

What does he mean? I challenge these elders to tell me what that means. Theory can't do it.

Look at page 179:

"Our tears might well mingle with those of the penitent banker, if he be penitent, and we might say, along with him, 'we stand afar off.' This Christ has fulfilled a law which we have broken, and to us, no longer able to flee unto ourselves and find peace, He says, 'Come unto me, all ye that labor and are heavy laden, and I will give you rest.'"

I will venture to say that if the defense quotes anything it will quote that. It is the strongest in the book. We will go next to page 238:

"Salvation of man, therefore, must be man's transformation from a sinful to a holy nature. It is a return of that which was lost. A legal salvation may be a preliminary or a concomitant, but cannot, in morals, be the chief salvation. In the financial department of life, a debtor can be saved by having his debts paid. Condemned to death, a criminal can be saved by a letter of pardon having upon it the seal of the king; but in morals, a salvation is not simply a discharge from debt, or an escape from a penalty, but a change in the spirit, a transition from vice to virtue. The term, therefore, draws its deepest interest from the term *lost*. If a man is lost in wickedness, he is found again in a perfection of moral character. If my calamity is hunger, food is my release; if my soul's calamity is sin, virtue is my only rescue. In law there is such a thing as an inferential danger or technical safety. In the dark Kansas days, there was such a thing as 'constructive treason,' a treason inferred from resemblance to real treason—but there can be no such thing as inferential salvation, a constructive release, a technical escape. The meaning of the term is to be determined by its location. In morals, salvation is spiritual perfection. The forgiveness of past sins, the payment of a moral debt, may be preliminaries, or attendant events, and may, by their importance, aspire to the name of rescue; but these titles are the gift of a gratitude rather than of fact, for after a man's sins are all forgiven or atoned for, he stands forth, still lost, for he retains the low nature that produces sins and made necessary the pardon, or the atonement. If to us, lost in a wilderness, without a sun, or a star, or a path to guide, there comes a benevolent hermit, a dear mentor, and leads us to the right path, and sets our faces homeward, he is at once our saviour; but our perfect salvation will come from our going that path. Our going and the mentor combine in the escape, and yet he lives in memory as the kind saviour of our bewildered hearts."

Pretty clear that he regarded doubt upon that subject as at least pardonable. I will read you from a book entitled "Orthodoxy—its truths and errors." Its author was James Freeman Clarke:

"The gospel of Christ, as we understand it, undertakes to effect an entire change, a radical reformation, in human character. It proposes to reform his life by changing the heart, by giving it new aims, new affections, new aspirations, new objects of love and pursuit. Jesus does not endeavor to alter and improve, a little here and a little there, on the outside of the character, to improve a little our modes of action in this and the other particular; but he alters the character by altering the fundamental ideas and inspiring inward life. This wonderful change, which takes place in the profoundest depth of our nature, under the influence of the gospel—this great event of life, which forms the turning point of our being and history—is called in the New Testament 'the new birth,' 'regeneration,' 'to be born again,' 'to be baptized with the Holy Ghost and with fire,' 'to put off the old man,' 'to have Christ formed within us.'

"I don't think Professor Swing ever said anything more precise than that." See on page 205.

Those, therefore, who could find God nowhere else, found him in Christ. Those who saw *him*, saw their Father. As when through a window we behold the heavens, as when in a mirror we see the image of the sun, we do not speak of the window or the mirror, but say that we see the sun and the heavens. So those who looked at Christ said that they saw God.

"The Apostle said that God was in Christ; and this was wholly true. Christians afterward said that Christ was God; and they thought they were only saying the same thing. They said that Christ had a divine nature as well as a human nature; and in this also there was no essential falsehood, for when we speak of our nature, we intend merely by it those elements of character which are original and permanent, which are not acquired, do not alter, and are never lost. God dwelt in the soul of Christ thus constantly, thus permanently. The word thus became flesh, and dwelt among us. The word of the Lord came to the prophets, but it dwelt in Christ. He and his Father were able to see God manifested in man as a living present reality. 'Here,' they say, 'is God; we have found God. He is in Christ. We can see Him there.'

"'Is it any wonder that men should have called Jesus God? that they should call Him so still? In Him truly 'dwelt the fullness of the Godhead bodily;' and this indwelling spirit expressed itself in what He said and what He did. When Jesus speaks, it is as if God speaks. When Jesus does anything it is as if we saw God do it. It becomes to us an expression of the Divine character. When Jesus says to the sinner, 'Go and sin no more,' we see in this a manifestation not merely of His own compassion, but of God's forgiving love; and when He dies, although God cannot, yet he dies according to the Divine will, and thus expresses God's willingness to suffer the redemption of the world.

"Either Christ was God, united with a human soul, or He was a human soul, united with God. When Christ uses the personal pronoun I, He must mean by that I, either the finite man or the infinite God. I believe the Unitarian is right in saying that this personal pronoun I always refers to the finite being and consciousness, and not to the infinite being."

That is honest. I like a man to come right out and say what he thinks. It is clearer than anything David Swing ever wrote; and Professor Swing never wrote or said a word with regard to the personality of Christ that James Freeman Clarke would not say amen to. I challenge contradiction of the allegation that Professor Swing did not make any statement respecting certain doctrines which could be construed as being Unitarian. The deity of Christ divides the theological world into two hemispheres as distinct as the equator divides the earth. Is the Presbytery going to say a Presbyterian minister was right who allowed himself to be claimed by men who carry on their banner an impeachment of the royalty of Christ, and to be so claimed without contradiction? Every daily newspaper came forward and appealed on his behalf that he "had cast away his old doctrines." Not only were doubts raised in this way as to Swing's orthodoxy, but two years ago a member of that court and friend of the accused wrote to a ministerial brother in which he said, "We are greatly troubled." It is time then for the accused to have set their doubts at rest. The defendant's plea amounts only to a reply to specification 1, charge 1. Swing said there were several doctrines on which he was willing to meet a skeptical world. But is was not a question as to his meeting the skeptical world at all, but is was a question as to what the defendant believed. He affirms that he believes in the divinity of Christ; not the deity of Christ. Then he believes in the inspiration of Scripture. But could it be shown that Professor Swing had made use of the expression, as the Presbyterians regarded it, as necessary to good standing in Church? Chicago Presbytery has committed itself to the plenary inspiration of the Scriptures. We mean that Mr. McKaig and the Ninth Church shall not be condemned and Professor Swing acquitted, because the principles in both cases are the same. Then Professor Swing says he believes in the trinity. The Unitarians believe in a sort of trinity, as did Plato and the Hindoos. Did Professor Swing believe in the three persons in the God-head equal in power and glory? Again, he says he believes in the mediation of Christ. But the Unitarians distinctly affirm the same thing. He says he believes in the final separation of the wicked from the good. So do the Universalists and Unitarians. But does he believe in everlasting punishment, as a judicial act, by God? Taking the Confession of Faith, which the accused sets forward as the platform of the Presbyterian Church, you might go round and obtain the signature thereto of every Universalist and Unitarian. But Professor Swing said he held the doctrines in evangelical sense. The point, however, is as to what "evangelical" religion is. The Unitarian and the Universalists each maintain that their doctrines are evangelical. Professor Patton next read from sermons in the Chicago *Pulpit*, to show the defendant's equivocation. At page 67 he said:

"The good deeds of yesterday, the good deeds of to-day, the perfected goodness of the morrow, a deep love for man, a consciousness of the presence of God, will fill the whole face with a nobleness and happiness to which earth has thus far been willingly a stranger. This will be a salvation, and Christ will be a Saviour."

At page 12 there was the following passage, which has been offered by one of defendant's witnesses to prove that the accused taught eternal punishment:

"But amid all the fluctuations of patriotism, the law of death for treason yet remains written upon the book of nations. And so in Christianity. However any class or any age may rise above the influence of penalty for sin, yet punishment remains a perpetual fact in its economy of our God. Its dark cloud will rise or fall, according to the quality of humanity. Wherever there are hearts that can see no goodness in holiness, none in honesty, and in charity, none in Jesus Christ, none in the worship of God; wherever there are minds incapable of being led by the intrinsic good of religion, then this dark cloud of divine wrath is ready to descend and to envelop with its thunders the soul that cannot and will not be enveloped by love. The result of sin, expressed in all religions by the word hell, is a perpetual influence, liable to go and come as humanity advances or retreats in the path of intelligence and morals—but it must be a perpetual fact in a world of beings capable of being immortal. A world of sin must be a world of punishment." Any Unitarian could say this. The witness stopped there, but I will continue. The next paragraph says: "In days when men cannot whip their children, in days when men are arrested for cruelty to dumb beasts, * * * * days in which Russia and America are fresh in the glory-wreaths of having set free 60,000,000 of slaves, it can hardly be expected that the pulpit, ignoring this grand uprising of tenderness, will daily paint the horrors of perdition while the very street is being enchanted with this vision of love. Oh, what a betrayal this would be of the pulpit's trust!" In a sermon entitled "The value of yesterday," published in the Chicago *Pulpit*, he says:

"Yesterday is full of past usefulness and of its ways and means, full of tears and their causes and cures. In that shadowy domain there stands the cross, and there is the Saviour dying for the vast myriads of a race."

The question whether that is evangelical all depends upon what you mean by the "dying of men." In his next sermon, "Salvation and Morality," page 85, in which he brings out the very idea that the use of words does not necessarily convey an orthodox meaning, since words may convey an ambiguous sense, Professor Swing says:

"In this shadow realm we would not wish to throw down the vast response that 'he that believes' shall safely pass the mysterious bourne; for faith is such a broad, indefinable word that to substitute it for the term salvation would be to leave us still in the air, obscure. Faith in Christ would be a phrase still more indefinite, for not only has faith many forms, but many forms also attach to the person of Christ. He was a sacrifice, but sacrifice has many significations. He was an example. He was a mediator. He was an unfolding of the divine image. Faith in Christ is a phrase which is at once seen to be made of words that are like the bits of colored glass in the kaleidoscope, forming many pictures and all very beautiful."

This shows how he derogates the standard of the Presbyterian Church. The next passage has been quoted by one of the witnesses for the defense to prove that Professor Swing believed in the doctrine of eternal punishment.

(The sentence referred to was one of those read by Elder Lee on Friday last.)

Damnation, according to him, simply means with him the natural consequence of a man's sin—if a man sins, he suffers. In sermon "Soul Culture," page 137, he says: "To live a life amid such surroundings as earth now possesses, must be to live a career of preparation for a world more blessed. To lose one's soul must be to pass through this sublime temple without drinking in its virtue and holy worship, and not only to have rejected the true, but to have suffered the falsehoods of society to rush upon the delicately strung harp of the spirit and break its strings and hush its melodies."

He may believe that "he who refuses to believe may be damned," but it is a very rosewater way of putting it. [Laughter.]

Next we come to the third specification. A great deal has been said about this specification. This specification has reference to three facts. The facts are admitted; the simple question is in reference to their criminality. The first was the delivery of a lecture in Mary Price Collier's Chapel. Second, publishing the sentiments in the *Lake-side Monthly*. Third, his publication of a sermon in eulogy of John Stuart Mill. If any Unitarians were present they would appreciate my zeal for the points of difference which separate me from them as an indication of unkind feeling towards that denomination. After expressing his admiration for the learning of Unitarian ministers, the prosecutor said: "If it was wrong for Professor Swing to give his name and influence to Unitarianism, it was not the less wrong because the society 'in whose behalf' he lectured was about to erect a chapel in memory of a woman whom he admired and whose Christian character has never been in dispute. So that the question reverts to the naked issue, whether it is right for a Presbyterian minister with the vows of a Presbyterian minister upon him, and having promised to be faithful and zealous in maintaining the Confession of Faith and the truths of gospel, and who has his name assailed day after day in the public press, with an enterprise which has for its sole object the erection of a chapel, in which chapel will be a gospel preached deriding the deity of Christ, calling this question "His co-eternity with the faith." Is it right, that is the question? His position, however, is that a Unitarian preaches the gospel, and, having these opinions, he maintains it is right to exchange courtesies with those sects. How would Professor Swing go about the conversion of a Unitarian after what he has here stated? Why, he could not do it.

I will pass to the next charge and read from the *Lake-side Monthly*, page 337.

"Chicago is an attempt at evangelism; all the details of the creeds between Jerusalem and Geneva seem forgotten. It has been driven to what is called a practical gospel—driven by its conviction that in virtue more than theology religion lay, and by the failure of didactic theology elsewhere. All the way from Robert Collyer to Robert Patterson, the preaching is practical, free from sectarianism, full of persuasion, though love. What sect is honored by the membership of Farwell and Moody, few know, because all names are forgotten in the more general title of Christians.

The city being the halting place for a great army of business men, and the public sanctioning a blinking Madonna, the local gospel was compelled to become a mode of virtue rather than a jumble of doctrines."

I don't think Dr. Patterson thinks it any great compliment to be put into the same category with Robert Collyer, because I know his theology is the antipode of Robert Collyer's. What would be the effect of that article upon the mind of an unprejudiced reader? Would you think David Swing was a Presbyterian? With all respect to Robert Collyer, and his denomination, I wish to say that if my gospel is *the* gospel, there is no other.

He is comparing Chicago with other cities. He is comparing Chicago gospel with the gospels of other cities. They differ. Chicago's gospel is a mode of virtue, while the others are a jumble of doctrines. Was this kind to say of the city of Pittsburgh, where there are so many Presbyterians? It means that the gospel says to be good—it says nothing about the deified Christ.

You know that John Stuart Mill grew up without any religious convictions whatever; you know that especial care was taken with his education that he should have no religious convictions. When he grew up he espoused a system of philosophy which was fatal to all religion. From even what we know of him, there is not the slightest ground to doubt that he was an atheist. Yet, upon his death, Professor Swing preached a laudatory sermon upon him, which was published in the morning papers of the 19th of May, 1873, taking for his text the very significant words, "One star differeth from another in glory."

(From this sermon, which has been so many times gone over and raked up that the public is tolerably familiar with it, Professor Patton read at considerable length, and commented.)

It is not difficult to get the sentiment of that sermon. He differed from the doctrines of Christianity, wherefore a shadow was cast over him. This shadow would have been removed if he had cultivated the religious sentiment to the extent that Victor Cousin did!

He knows as well as I do that John Stuart Mill founded the *Westminster Review*, which is atheism; he knows he was a prominent contributor to the *Fortnightly Review*. He knows he led in the van of that philosophic school of thought which carries away with it the very fundamental principles of Christianity and all religion. There never was a greater insult offered to the Presbyterian Church than when David Swing stood up in a Chicago pulpit and preached a sermon that was calculated to produce the notion in the minds of his hearers that it was not so bad a thing to be John Stuart Mill after all! [Applause to the right of the Moderator's stand]

We will pass to the consideration of the next charge. A man comes into the church of his own free will. He is not drawn into it. Has he no right to remain in it when he has ceased to be in accord with it?

Listen to this:

"Over the idea that two and two make four no blood has been shed; but over the insinuation that three may be one, and one three, there has ever been a demand for external influence to brace up for the work the frail logical faculty."

What does that mean? Doesn't it mean that he is using the very objection of the Unitarian, and saying that three are one and one is three?

"It is probable that no man has been put to death for heresy regarding the Sermon on the Mount. But when a church comes along with its legitimacy and its five points, or with the prayer-book or its infant baptism or eternal procession of the Holy Ghost, then comes the demand for the rack and the stake, to make up in terrorism what is wanting in evidence."

Would a man who honestly believed in these doctrines ridicule them thus? Would you, Brother Kittredge, do it? I would like to see Professor Swing go to one of the lady members of his church and ask why her infant was not baptized. Would you blame her if she says she does not believe in infant baptism?

Pass to page 23 of the same book.

"Rubric, surplice, prayer-book, two souls of Christ, the Eastern time, the transfiguration light, *the election*, *the predestination*, the laying on of hands, all count no more with the thoughtful historian seeking for the merits of an age than counted the costumes of those eras or the carriages they drove."

Take predestination out of the Presbyterian Church, and what is left to it? It is the distinctive doctrine of the church.

Go to page 65 of the Chicago *Pulpit:*

"Elizabeth imprisoned for life all who conducted religious service without using her prayer-book. Persons not believing in bishops were branded with an iron. As internal piety was little dreamed of as being a religious test, it was as absurd from man as from God. God was a Being partial to a prayer-book or to a bishop. Forms were everything. Knox declared that one mass was more fearful to him than ten thousand armed enemies landed in any part of the realm, never harboring for an instant the idea that beneath the service of the mass there might be a pious heart. There was no weighing of soul. It was all a listening to words, and a crowding to the fagot those whose words deviated a hair's breadth from the model held in the hand of some bloated ruler or licentious priest. In this awful reign of iron sentences, little girls of childhood innocence, and mothers whose love is an emblem to earth of love infinite, went down to early tombs in the double agony of flesh and heart. But the heart of a dove counted nothing in an age of vowels and consonants. Catholic words killed thousands of Protestants, and Protestant words killed thousands of Catholics. All imaginable doctrines have in the long, bloody period been made a ground of life or death. Words about baptism, words about the Trinity, words about the Pope, words about transubstantiation, words about the Virgin Mary, words about the Eucharist, words about the doctrine of purgatory, about astronomy, have exposed the body to the stake and the soul to perdition."

In the sermon on the "Influence of Democracy on Christian Doctrine," Professor Swing says:

"This perpetual industry amid external pursuits also diverts the mind from the study of mysteries and to the acceptance and enjoyment of facts, and hence the public mind turns away from predestination and reprobation and absolutism. * * * * * * In this abandonment there is no charge of falsehood cast upon the old mysteries; they may or they may not be true; there is only a passing them by as not being in the line of the current wish or taste, raiment for a past age, perhaps for a future, but not acceptable in the present."

Then on page 86, in a sermon on "Salvation and Morality:"

"Their hope of heaven is based upon faith alone. The righteousness they dream of must be wholly an imputed righteousness."

In another sermon, "St. Paul and the Golden Age:"

"Look at St. Paul's third idea! A new life, a new creature! It will be the development of this idea that will announce the dawn of a perfect civilization and a golden age. The church has tried the religion of dogmas. The Scotch Church reached a creed of 4,000 articles, but that church, and all branches of all churches, have furnished thousands of men for every branch of dishonesty and crime."

In "Soul Culture," page 135, he says:

"It is not the trinity that molds human life, but the doctrine of God. It is not the eternal procession of the Holy Spirit that may shape the human soul, but the fact of an ever-present spirit. That Christ was eternally begot of the Father is a doctrine that cannot be appreciated in any way by man's heart, but the Christ of the New Testament can be grasped and loved, and hence the responsibility and success and beauty of human life will all be related to the latter of these statements, and be wholly discharged from all the former without penalty or cost."

Professor Patton, in concluding his remarks for the day, proceeded to satisfy his audience that a departure from the symbols of the church was an offense to be visited with censure on the offenders. He quoted the case of Heads vs. Sanders, tried by the English Privy Council in 1842, which was the case of a minister who preached against confirmation as practiced by the Established Church. The verdict of the Court of Arches was that the offender be deprived of his ecclesiastical benefice; and, said Professor Patton, according to the reasoning pursued in judging that English case, Professor Swing cannot complain if we put him in the position in which he would have been if, being a candidate for ordination vows, it was known that he had uttered the sentiments with which he was charged. This Presbytery would not ordain a man if, in his last sermon, he proclaimed such views as have been enunciated by the defendant in this case, and by all that is right and just Professor Swing ought to be placed in the same position as he would be were he a candidate for ordination unless a proper retractation is made. But I am aware that there will be those with whom this decision of the English court may not have much weight. I will, therefore, read from the new Digest of the Presbyterian Church, which every man of us will swear by. It is a principle of our form of government that doctrinal truth is of great importance, and that formulated truth is necessary to the existence of religious organizations. I will read the fourth section of Discipline, and I claim that Professor Swing has contravened this principle, and having done so, has made himself liable to censure, and that the knowledge of this fact being before this Presbytery, it will be delinquent if it passes it by without censure. The fourth section is as follows:

"That truth is in order to goodness and the great touchstone of truth, its tendency to promote holiness according to our Saviour's rule. 'By their fruits ye shall know them.' And that no opinion can be either more pernicious or absurd than that which brings truth and falsehood upon a level, and represents it as of no consequence what a man's opinions are. On the contrary, they are persuaded that there is an inseparable connection between faith and practice, truth and duty. Otherwise it would be of no consequence either to discover truth or to embrace it."

If Professor Swing has not ridiculed vital truths and put a falsehood, he has certainly misrepresented them, and I say that it is, therefore, impossible for him to continue within the pale of the Presbyterian Church. Now, we find that principle is not a dead letter; and if it were a dead letter, it is time for us to galvanize it; for in a deliverance of the General Assembly, quoted from the Book of Discipline, page 54, it is said:

"This confession of faith, adopted by our church, contains a system of doctrines professedly believed by the people and the pastors under the care of the General Assembly; nor can it be traduced by any in the communion of our church without subjecting the erring parties to that salutary discipline which hath for its object the maintenance of the peace and purity of the church under the government of her Great Master."

If this instruction was given to the congregation, surely it ought to apply with double force to those who are the acknowledged servants of God and commissioned teachers of the people. In 1825 a subsequent deliverance was made, in the following form:

"The committee appointed on an overture respecting the consistency of admitting to its church ministers who manifest a decided hostility to ecclesiastical creeds, confessions, and formulas, make the following report, which was adopted, viz:

1. That the constitution, as is well known, expressly requires of all candidates for admission a solemn declaration that they sincerely receive and adopt the confession of faith of this church as containing the system of doctrine taught in the Holy Scriptures.

2. That the last Assembly, in a report of their committee, have so explicitly and fully declared the sentiments of the church in regard to her ecclesiastical standard, and all within her communion who may traduce them, that no further expression of our views on this subject is deemed necessary."

The Moderator—Professor Swing, in the passages which I have adduced from his writings, has so traduced by ridicule, by irony, and by insinuation the scriptural doctrines of our church, that the natural effect of such language on the minds of those who hear him can only be to breed skepticism or to lead them to treat those doctrines with contempt. Now, if Professor Swing had come into this court and said, "I admit the charge; I confess I have used uncertain language on vital points, which I regret, and now that my attention has been called to the fact, I promise not to use such in time to come," the members of Presbytery would have felt very different on the subject from what they now do. But how does he act? So far from expressing any regret or having any thing to say by way of retraction he comes into court; he assumes a defiant attitude, and does not retract the sentiments, and goes on to make still more insulting statements in reference to the doctrines of our church. If the public don't believe that the Presbyterian Church does not hold to infant damnation it is not because Professor Swing has not tried to make that impression. If any impression is made on the public mind, it is that the Presbyterian Church, either in its formulated standard or by its representative men, does teach the doctrine of infant damnation. I say, with some knowledge of the doctrine, the representative men, and the history of the church, that such a statement is not true. [Applause.]

The Rev. A. E. Kittredge—I wish to enter my protest against this applause. It has three times occurred. It is unfortunate that such applause is made.

Professor Patton—I am in thorough sympathy with the statement of Mr. Kittredge. Nothing is less desired by me than such expressions. I am glad to know, however, that there are men in the Presbytery who have such an appreciation for the doctrines and standards that at the risk of being discourteous they express themselves in this way. [Laughter.] I say that Professor Swing has traduced our doctrines with respect to future punishment, fatalism, and salvation by faith. We are charged with holding such views with respect to future destiny as to have led to infidelity. Do the Presbytery mean to permit that plea to go on record without giving it their denial? In view of the plea Professor Swing has made before the Presbytery, are you willing to say that he is a faithful minister and a fair representative of the doctrines of the Presbyterian Church as you understand them and as set forth in the good old symbols of the church?

Presbytery then adjourned until this (Wednesday) morning at 9:30 a. m.

WEDNESDAY, MAY 13th.

At 9:30 forenoon, Presbytery re-assembled, very full as to attendance, both clerical and lay. The margins about the judicial settees were crowded by spectators. No previous day had seen a larger number of interested outsiders. And it was a notable point, that Professor Patton's side of the house was better filled than it had been at any previous time since the trial began. His friends, whose faces were elongated at the close of last week, were considerably cheered Tuesday afternoon, and came to the ground in the morning with visages mantled in satisfactory expectation. Professor Swing sat on the front row of seats, quiet and pleasant, as his wont is to look. Dr. Patterson was at his right elbow, three or four little pocket memorandum books and a few sheets of paper in his hand (he "took notes" after the arguments began again), smiling and benign. To the Professor's left sat the Rev. Mr. Wakeman—a thin, gray-haired, and contemplative old gentleman, who has said very little in the case, but contented himself with sticking to a seat, which left no doubt as to which side his sympathies were on, and keeping up a careful attention. The Rev. Mr. Noyes removed himself one row back, took copious notes, and made no remarks except occasional interrogative ones, as to "what page" the prosecutor read from. Dr. Beecher, who is only sitting in Presbytery by courtesy, yet whose voice has frequently been raised in council, removed himself to the Patton end of the middle settee. His very patriarchal visage, long, white beard, and black velvet skull-cap made him a prominent figure, and his shift of sympathy and position attracted unanimous attention.

Little Mr. Brobston and the Rev. Mr. W. F. Wood, of Peotone, Professor Patton's most zealous and worthy supporters, were in their usual places. The Rev. B. E. S. Ely, who has acted (far as Professor Patton would let him) as counsel for the prosecution—whose experience as a California lawyer crops out boldly in the legal points put now and then, sat near Professor Patton, who stood up, facing the Presbytery in front of the Secretary's desk. A little 2x4 table before him was covered with books, each volume presenting a very ragged looking end, by reason of the numerous little slips of paper inserted between the leaves, marking places to be referred to or read. His watch lay open beside the books, and a little pitcher of water stood within his easy reach. He seldom troubled it. His voice, his manner, his look, and his throat were all dry; he rejected the notion of moisture.

It is a question very frequently asked: "What does Patton look like?" To answer this with strict accuracy would be to cause his friends a pang, and to surprise himself. He looks like Death, dismounted. He is every iota the book-man, the introspective student. He is young—not above 35 years of age; his features are regular, and his form erect. But he is oh, so thin, so spare, so feeble in frame, so bloodless. Sunken checks, mild grayish-blue eyes peering thoughtfully through spectacles; heavy, straight hair of the peculiar nondescript hue that is neither brown nor flaxen, but a sort of unimpressive compromise between the two, worn in ordinary shape, not long, nor brushed behind his ears; shadowy side-whiskers that scarcely encroach upon his face; a long, straight mouth, with only the least tinge of color in the lips, and that of a leaden cast; a prominent, acquiline nose. That is his head. He wears black, neat and unobtrusive—the coat hanging loosely about his body—an immaculate shirt front, and a narrow white tie. His arms look longer than they are, on account of their excessive attenuation; his hands are small, delicate, and white. First of all, he is a gentleman. In conversation he is witty, quick, and pleasant. No one can approach him and talk with him without gathering a favorable impression. He is polite in that fine quality of politeness which is the result of "good breeding" from infancy up—the natural, easy politeness of a gentlemen born and reared among gentlemen and ladies. His use of language is superb, and his delivery clear, distinct, and elegant. There is no doubt in the world that he is perfectly sincere in his beliefs, and enthusiastic in the heavy cause he is shouldering. When he becomes worked up in his theme, he speaks with a fluency and earnest vehemence that is remarkable, and commands attention from all within sound of his voice, which is not a whit musical, being parched and full—a sort of dusty tenor.

Professor Swing is his opposite. Nearly every one in Chicago is familiar with his browned, homely, attractive face. During the months he preached at McVicker's Theater his short, firm-built figure became familiar to thousands who never saw him while he officiated in his own church on the North Side. A high, open forehead, protruding chin, mouth that was made to utter warm humanity, deeply-lined cheeks, long, dark hair, worn with negligence—the last man in the world one would suppose full of the tenderest sentiments, the most beautiful and winning language, the smoothest, most charming poesy; yet a good man if ever one carried goodness in his countenance—a man little children would love at first sight and ever after.

He has very little to say. Once in a while he has asked a pertinent question —a playful sounding interrogatory with a sting under its surface. Mr. Noyes has plead his side of the controversy, and plead it well.

It was surprising to see with what eager avidity outside clergymen—shepherds of other denominational flocks—watched the proceedings and listened to the speaker. They stray in and out every day, and crane their necks forward to catch all the points. The Baptists were well represented yesterday: Dr. Ravlin, the Rev. John Gordon, and several others were there. Dr. Thomas, of the first Methodist Episcopal Church, visited during the afternoon.

So did Ald. Dixon. John V. Farwell has been a rather close auditor during the whole trial. Faces of gentlemen whose names are current in Western fame dot the assemblage alway.

It is an historic occasion, and the grave body sitting there as an ecclesiastical court feels the tremendous weight of its responsibility. Barring the debates over the minutes, which used up the forenoons of the two first days, they have been solemn and dignified to a point that was somber.

Court (so to speak) having been opened, Professor Patton arose and resumed his address. He said:

I will resume my address at the point where I left off yesterday at the consideration of the fifth specification. If the allegation set forth in this specification can be proved it is a very serious charge, and one of such gravity that this Presbytery cannot afford to overlook it and pass it by. It cannot be denied that the doctrines stated in this specification form the basis on which all churches which have the right to be called evangelical must stand. One of the elders of the Fourth Church read this specification as expressing his views of what evangelical preaching is. His ideas of that doctrine are embraced in evangelical truth. It is affirmed in the specification that Prof. Swing has omitted to preach or teach these doctrines. Our church has taken special care to invest its ministry with its sanction. When a candidate comes forward to be licensed, he answers in the affirmative that he believes the Scriptures of the Old and New Testaments as the Word of God and the rule and faith of practice, and also that he receives the Confession of Faith as embodying the doctrines taught by the Word of God. When he subsequently comes forward for ordination and is about to assume a pastoral charge, he is called upon to answer another series of questions, by which he promises to preach and maintain these doctrines and the Confession of Faith. Now, if I were to ask this Presbytery what they consider to be a faithful discharge of the duties of the Christian ministry and a full observance of our ordination vows, they would answer without a dissenting voice, the preaching of the doctrines set forth in this allegation. If Christianity has any claim upon us at all, it grounds itself on the fact that Christ saved us by the shedding of His precious blood. Therefore, when we find a minister preaching without making much mention of Christ's blood, when we don't find the scarlet thread weaving its way throughout the whole web of gospel ministrations, I am very apt to be suspicious that something is wrong in reference to his views of the gospel. This is true of Professor Swing, that he says nothing about the blood of Christ, and does not preach that we are redeemed by the precious blood of the Lamb. Another cardinal feature of the gospel system is that we are justified and made righteous by faith. This doctrine is not found in Professor Swing's preaching, and occupies no place in his doctrinal system. Indeed, as I shall hereafter show, he preaches in direct contradiction to this doctrine. I still further affirm that if Christianity has any special claim upon us, if our missionary enterprises are to be carried on with any zeal, then the doctrines that lie as the reason for those enterprises and constitute the basis of all missionary effort are included in this. "There is none other name under heaven among men whereby we can be saved." It was this idea which led Paul to be a missionary to the Gentiles, and it is this idea which constitutes the ground and reason for the existence of the Christian ministry and the perpetuation of the Christian system. I affirm that this doctrine is not taught in Professor Swing's sermons, and will affirm that he has preached the contrary doctrine, either directly or by necessary implication.

There are only three possible standards of faith. There is first the standard of Rationalism, which makes the human mind its own basis and individual judgment the criterion of truth. Another is the Romish doctrine, which makes an organization the standard of faith, and which says that a certain doctrine is truth because a given organization, inspired by God's spirit, and therefore infallible, has said it is true. The cardinal feature of Protestantism is, as opposed to Rationalism on the one hand and Romanism on the other, that the Bible is the standard of faith and practice, that what it says is true, that when it says anything it is sufficient authority and we need not go elsewhere. I affirm that Professor Swing does not teach this doctrine, that the Scriptures are given by inspiration of God, and that they are the only rule of faith and practice.

I will be told in reply that we cannot expect all men to preach alike; you must not undertake to suppress a man's individuality, to model a man in your mould. Certainly not! God forbid. If a man is emotional in his nature, then I like his preaching to show it. If a man is dry in his nature he cannot help it—he must do the best he can. So that would be no reply. I claim that a man can so use his gifts as to preach Gospel doctrines. Then I will be told that Professor Swing is a poet and cannot present those truths with the same strictness and precision that another man can who has made the subject his special business. But I claim that if he is a poet, so was Toplady, and yet he wrote:

> "Nothing in my hand I bring;
> Simply to thy cross I cling."

If Professor Swing is a poet his eloquence would enable him to preach the Gospel with all the more power, and if he has the power, then all the more shame that he does not use it in the service of his Master.

Then, I will be told that Professor Swing is not capable of making strict statements, and that it is an idiosyncracy which makes him unable to express his thoughts with clearness. I deny it, I know better; I know that when he chooses he can be as transparent as glass, and when he chooses he can be as ambiguous as a Delphic orator. I shall be told again that a man cannot be expected to always preach a sermon on some particular doctrine. I have not affirmed that it is necessary to preach doctrinal sermons. I don't care what the subject is, so long as the Evangelical preaching is that of the gospel, and in this sense I do believe every Christian gospel should be dyed in the blood of Christ.

Now, I have affirmed that these things are so, and I offer in evidence the sermons printed by Professor Swing's authority. I defy you to find these doctrines in his sermons. They tell me that these are only specimen sermons, and certainly the most plausible reply the defense can make is that these are but fragments of Professor Swing's preaching during seven years. I reply that if a man publishes a volume of sermons, it is to be presumed that he publishes the volume with the idea of doing good, and in order that they may reach men who cannot be reached by preaching. When these doctrines are wanting in the volume—and this is the only volume put forward over his name—I think it is a fair presumption that he does not regard these doctrines set forth in the specifications as paramount.

But that is not all. They will say "You have not proved that he has not preached those doctrines." I accept the challenge. Then, they tell me it is proving a negative. I accept the challenge, and I do prove it. It is not incumbent upon me in order to establish this negative proposition that I shall have had access to every sermon that Professor Swing has preached, that I shall have heard every sermon, or bring witnesses who have heard every sermon and who would therefore give testimony as to its character. It is sufficient for me if I raise a fair presumption that the accused does not preach these doctrines, and that I do raise this fair presumption I offer all Professor Swing's printed sermons in evidence, and I affirm that in all these sermons those doctrines are wanting. It is a principle in evidence that where a negative proposition of this kind lays the burden of proof on the prosecutor, it is not necessary for the prosecutor to make plenary proof of the same. [Professor Patton here quoted in support of his argument, opinions from Greenleaf, and a decision given by Judge Caton in the Supreme Court. This decision was given in an action for damages brought by an individual against a railway company for killing a mule. At the mention of "the mule," the court burst into a loud laugh.]

Professor Swing having possession of the sermons he has delivered since the fire, and I having established a fair presumption that he does not preach the doctrines I have indicated, the fact may be considered to be established, unless he proves to the contrary. Then, the question is whether the defense has proved that Professor Swing does preach the evangelical doctrines. This averment must be held as proved, unless they have proved the contrary. Have they done so? Let us see. They have produced testimony. The elders of the Fourth Church were called to testify, and they did testify, that in their opinion Professor Swing preached the gospel; that in their opinion he preached the doctrine of the deity of Christ; and the value of their opinions can be determined when I tell you that in proof of that they cited one of the passages which I cited as an instance of Professor Swing's equivocation. They testified that Professor Swing preached the doctrine of eternal punishment, and as indicating the value of their testimony let me remind you that they cited another passage which I read as a specimen of Professor Swing's equivocation. They testified that Professor Swing preached all the cardinal doctrines; and when I asked them when and where, and what he said, the only party who could give any testimony was Mr. Waite, who gave evidence respecting a sermon preached on Unitarianism before Professor Swing became pastor of the Fourth Church. He may have been sound enough then. The only other specific testimony was that of Mr. Lee. And the fact that they chose the printed sermons already offered in evidence to disprove the allegations would imply that they offered this as the very best evidence they had.

The evidence given for the defense by these witnesses as to the sermons was inadmissible, the manuscript sermons being in existence. [Here he quoted a decision given by the General Assembly on Lowroy's appeal, and set forth on 560 page, New Digest, to the effect that the best proof must be adduced, I call for the manuscripts of the sermons preached since the fire. They are in existence; they are all in Professor Swing's house. He can bring them into court to-morrow. He could have brought them into court when previously called upon. If it is true that Professor Swing has preached the doctrines that I allege he has not preached; and if anxious, as I know he is anxious, to disprove these allegations, to set my complaint adrift and turn it out of court, and be acquitted at the hands of the Presbytery, and recognized by the body as still in good standing, as still deserving of the confidence of this court and of the Presbyterian Church—it stands to reason that he would have brought these sermons and flung defiance in the face of his prosecutor, by producing the written testimony of the falsehood of the charges. The fact that he has not done it, in spite of repeated challenges, is demonstration that he cannot do it, and that the allegation is true.

I pass now to the sixth specification. In a sermon called "Christianity and Dogma," printed in "Truths for To-day," the following language is used:

The doctrine of the Trinity as formally stated cannot be experienced. Man has not the power to taste the oneness of three, nor the threeness of one, and see that it is "good." If you, my friend, are giving your daily thought to the facts of Christianity, and are standing bewildered to-day amid the statements of science and Genesis about earth, or its swarms of life, recall the truth that your soul cannot taste any theory of man's origin—cannot experience the origin of man, whatever that origin may have been.

This statement is not an *obiter dictum* on the part of Professor Swing. It is a principle which runs through his theology. He does not say that a doctrine is true in proportion as you can verify it. If he had said that, every man could have seen that it was rationalism; but he says that a doctrine is valuable in proportion as you can verify it by experience. You may fill a garret with theology, and it may be true, but what use is it to me when you have pronounced upon it that it is worthless. And when Professor Swing undertakes to set up this standard as a test of the value of the doctrines, then he has enunciated a principle which lands you inevitably into skepticism. He says you cannot verify the Trinity in your experience, and therefore it is not valuable. This principle relates to every solitary doctrine of the Scriptures which is mysterious. The moment this view is held respecting the Trinity, a door is opened which cannot be shut, for a man comes along and says he cannot see other vital truths and down goes your Christianity. There never was a sentiment uttered more strongly in support of rationalism than this one by Professor Swing: and if there was only this one in his book, it was enough to indicate the drift of his mind and tell you he is not a safe teacher for a Presbyterian flock.

This court, I hope, will not consider it an impertinence if, for the purpose of throwing light on the specification, I go out of my way and state in substance what the doctrine of development is. It is the doctrine in philosophy which more than all other challenges the attention of the Christian students, bids defiance to the history of the Christian church and the historic faith of the Christian disciples. It is the philosophy which in the present day is assuming a position of paramount authority. Applied to the material world, the doctrine is, that all the forms of material existence have developed by a process of evolution from an original ether, whatever that is. Applied to life, it tells us that the highest forms of existence have come through successive transmutations from lower forms of being. Applied to social culture, it tells us that man was first savage; that religion was an after-thought; that he was as unable at one time to worship God as to build a fire; that Christianity is as much the natural growth of the law of circumstances as is steam the natural result of a progress which began with a race which could not build a fire; and when they did succeed in building one, it was by rubbing two sticks together. It is a philosophy that tells that man was at one time without any language, and that, gabbler as he is to-day, at one time he could not talk. It tells us that man first worshipped his grandfather, and that his religion became Polytheism, Pantheism, Monotheism, which culminated in Judaism; and it is Judaism transformed by precisely natural causes which give us the Christianity of to-day. That is positive philosophy.

Now, let me read some passages from Professor Swing, and from some of the holders of these philosophic views, and tell me if any one could not affirm that he had been sitting at the feet of Buckle, and Tylor, and Lubbock, and other evolutionist Gamaliels; that he entertained the view that man in his first stage had no language, and that his position to-day is the result of natural causes, and that the Christianity of to-day is just the outgrowth of the centuries, the blossoming of the flowers of the human heart. Here is a passage from the last work, "Primitive Culture," written by Tylor, who is a representative of culture, looked at from the stand-point of evolution, and the passage might have been written by Professor Swing. Tylor says:

"Looking at each doctrine by itself and for itself as in the abstract time or in time, theologians close their eyes to the instances which history is ever holding up before them, that one phase of a religious belief is the outcome of another; that in all times religion has included within its limits a system of philosophy, expressing more or less its transcendental conceptions in doctrines which form in any age their fittest representations, but which doctrines are liable to modification in the general course of intellectual change, whether the general formulas still hold their authority with altered meaning, or are thereby reformed or replaced."

I will now read a passage from Sir John Lubbock, an eminent English writer, belonging to the same school. He writes in his work:

"The Origin of Civilization and the Primitive Condition of Man;" "The Duke appears to consider that the first men, though deficient in knowledge of the mechanical arts, were morally intellectually superior, or at least equal, to those of the present day, and it is remarkable that supporting such a man he should regard himself as a champion of orthodox. Adam is represented to us in person not only as naked, and subsequently clothed with leaves, but was unable to resist the most trival temptation, and as entertaining very gross and anthropomorphic conceptions of the Deity. In fact, in all three characteristics—in his mode of life, in his moral condition, and his intellectual conceptions—Adam was a typical savage."

In a sermon Professor Swing says: "Low idolatry of primitive man." I do not know what is meant by this term "primitive man," but in the Interior I called attention to the employment of this term, and asked Professor Swing why he insisted on using the language of evolutionists. He turned around and asked me whether I would prefer him to say Adam instead of primitive man. He furnishes me with the conclusion to the syllogism that primitive man was an idolater, and that primitive man was Adam. In another paragraph Professor Swing says:

"The Mosaic Economy was nothing else but a progress; earth had come to Polytheism, to Pantheism, to Feticism. It was the Hebrew philosophy and its immediate result, Christianity, which swept away the iron Jupiter."

Upon an unprejudiced mind the impression would be made that Professor Swing teaches that Christianity developed by the law of nature out of Judaism, as Judaism had already come out of Polytheism and Feticism! Professor Swing may not mean that, but he had two thousand people before him, more or less, when he preached that sermon, many of them men of culture, who would naturally put what he said alongside of what was said by Lubbock, and if they came to the conclusion that Professor Swing and Sir John Lubbock were first cousins, theologically speaking, they would not be doing Professor Swing an injustice. Again Professor Swing says:

"This multitude measures a great revelation of God above that day when earth possessed but one man or family, and that one without language and without learning and without virtue."

Compare this statement with that contained in the first chapter of Genesis, and see if Moses and Swing entertain the same opinions, and whether Moses says that when our first parents, Adam and Eve, were in the garden, they had no knowledge, and could not converse with each other. I must ask Professor Swing to tell us what he means. I have heard that there is one brother in this house who knows what all these passages mean, and I am going to engage him for one week as interpreter if I can not get light anywhere else. What, however, does this language mean?

"The Bible has not made religion, but religion and righteousness have made the Bible. Christianity is not forced upon us; our own nature has forced it up out of the spirit's rich depths."

You can not reconcile that with Christianity. It may be a *lapsus linguæ* or a *lapsus pennæ*, but as it stands, it teaches that Christianity is a development of circumstance, the outgrowth of history. Now, the Bible says "God made man in His own image." If God made man in His own image, then Adam was made in the image of God, and mirrored the perfection of God. Then for any one to say, "In the first human being God could no more display His perfection than a musician like Mozart could unfold his genius to an infant, or to a South Sea Islander," was to tell Moses that he did not tell the truth, for Moses and the Apostles say that God did make man in His own image. I believe that Adam was a great deal more like God than I am going to be for many a day to come.

Professor Swing—May I ask you a question?

Professor Patton—Certainly.

Professor Swing—Do you think Adam had any missionary societies—any asylums of any kind to glorify God with?

Professor Patton—There was not anybody to go to; there were no heathen. [Loud Laughter.]

Professor Patton—I come now to the eighth specification. I will read portions of a sermon called "The Influence of Democracy on Christian doctrine." In this I find passages, which, if they have any meaning, teach that there are no standards by which we can measure eternal verities, by which we can measure moral ideas, are liable to change, and are subject to the laws of all human things. If there is any one hope I cherish, it is that Professor Swing is better than his preaching. I have said this in print, that I honestly hope that his creed is better than the expression of it; but we have to deal only with the expression of it, because it is that by which he exercises influence. Suppose a minister of the Presbyterian Church should stand in his pulpit, and in the presence of his people, who are accustomed to regard the Bible as a Divine revelation, an infallible rule of faith and practice, and who are in the habit of taking the Confession of Faith as embodying the doctrines taught in the Word of God, and believe that the doctrines formulated there are true—what would be the impression produced by such sentences as these?

"When we come to moral ideas, we are compelled to do without any standards." "You may, my friends, at your leisure, seek and find further instances of this modification of Christian belief by the new surroundings of government. Christian customs will also be modified along with the creed."

I tell you there is a standard. I can set my moral watch by the sun of righteousness and know that it is right. Again, Professor Swing says:

"In this casting off of old garments, it no more cheerfully throws away the inconceivable of Christianity than the inconceivable of Kant and Spinoza." "In this abandonment there is no charge of falsehood cast upon the old mysteries; they may or may not be true; there is only a passing them by as not being in the line of the current wish or taste; raiment for a past age, perhaps for a future, but not acceptable for the present."

The inference is that he thinks just as much about predestination as I do about Spinoza—and you cannot get any better idea of it. This Chicago, this new city, with its enterprise and its railroads, cannot be supposed to adhere to old doctrines. "Christian customs will also be modified along with the creed," says Professor Swing. He takes it for granted that the creed is going to be modified, and his only question is as to whether the customs are going to be modified too! This Presbytery will have its own judgment to form in reference to this case. It will be the province of Presbytery to say whether Professor Swing has or has not held to the Confession of Faith, and whether, having departed from the standards of the Presbyterian Church, he still shall have a right to minister at her altar, and be recognized as in good standing. I tell you, the time is coming when you will say, if you suffer this, that you were wrong. The time is coming when ministers of this city will find their own influence undermined by the influence of such preaching as this. You remember the story in classic times of Penelope—we have got Penelope somewhere else. [Laughter.] How, when waiting for the long-absent Ulysses, and pressed by suitors, she postponed the act of accepting a favored one until she had finished a certain web of tapestry, and how she wove in the day-time, and unraveled in the night what she had done in the day. You ministers of Chicago are the Penelope of the daytime, and Professor Swing of your city is the Penelope of the night. You are preaching the doctrines which he is discarding, believing, yourselves, in these time-honored standards, maintaining them in the face of a Godless and scoffing world; and he stands in your presence to tell you he has drifted away from them, while by the adroitness and vagueness of his language and subtle arrangement of his thoughts, leads his people to believe he still is in sympathy with the great doctrines of our faith. Mark you, the time is coming when you will say that the prosecutor in this case was right in what he did, and I will wait for a century, if necessary, for my vindication! [Sensation.]

I will pass to the ninth specification. He has used his pulpit for the purpose of giving countenance to the doctrine of Sabellianism. He gives his public approval to a model Trinity, which is not the Trinity of the Bible, nor of the Gospel. We believe in one God; that the Father is God; that the Son is God, and that the Holy Ghost is God. These are the factors in the doctrine of the Trinity. The question is how to combine. There are two methods—the Sabellian and the Orthodox, or Athanasian. He preaches the Sabellian theory of the Trinity, which is that there is one God, who is viewed in three lights, and appears as Father, Son and Holy Ghost. The true doctrine teaches that there are three persons in one God, the same in substance, equal in power and glory. He has contravened this doctrine which is not a doctrine of to-day. Its history goes back to the 300 bishops who sat in the council at Nice, with the Gospels before them, and formulated it. This Presbytery should pronounce at once against a man who stands up in a Presbyterian pulpit and preaches Sabellianism.

Let us pass to the

TENTH SPECIFICATION.

The first point I shall quote on this charge is the sermon entitled "A Positive Religion,"—Page 189 of "Truths for To-day."

As to this destructive inquiry about God, reducing Him to an oxygen, or an unconscious, unknown agency, we may well recall the fact that there is no moral proposition which may not, by the same devotion to skepticism be stricken out from the catalogue of beliefs. Logic, if well followed, may lead us to doubt whether there is such a thing as honor, such a thing as benevolence, such a thing as mind, such a thing as pure affection. When it comes to a search for perfect assurance, then we soon ruin the moral world, for there is no perfect assurance in it, or any part of it, and hence the logic which seeks that assurance can only destroy. It must come back each evening, saying, 'There is no virtue, no sin, no mind, no God.' When logic informs you and me that God is law, or a widespread blind agency, let us not be deceived, for all it has done is to take away our God. It has not given us a positive origin of the universe, for if positiveness is unattainable, reason will in a few years confess itself to be as uncertain about its data as it is to-day about the data of the Christian. Perfect assurance is just as impossible to a free religionist or atheist as it is to the Christian. Remembering therefore, that there is no moral idea of beauty, or love, or soul, that may not be denied, and remembering, too, that the assurance that there is a God is always logically equal to the opposite belief, why should we not abandon a criticism that only destroys, and clasp to our souls the grand things we possess, and, Christlike, live not to destroy but to fulfill.

I am not charging him with logical attacks upon the being of God. But I take his sentences as I find them; and I find the arguments for and against the existence of God equally balanced. It is our business to take the ground that there is an universal belief in God, and that this belief is corroborated by an array of arguments which make it absurd for him to doubt.

Turn to page 138. This is a sentence I really do not understand. I would not have been surprised to hear it from Matthew Arnold:

"We know not what nor where is our God, or heaven."

I affirm we do know where and what He is; for He "is a spirit infinite, eternal, and unchangeable in His wisdom, power, glory and goodness;" and I am surprised that a preacher in this nineteenth century should lead his congregation to worship at an altar erected to an "unknown god."

I will read to you now what our own symbols say upon the sacraments. Section 1 of chapter 27, says:

"Sacraments are holy signs and seals of the covenant of grace, immediately instituted by God, to represent Christ and His benefits, and to confirm our interest in Him; as also to put a visible difference between those that belong unto the church and the rest of the world, and solemnly to engage them to the service of God in Christ, according to His Word.

"There is in every sacrament a spiritual relation or sacramental union between the sign and the thing signified; whence it comes to pass that the names and effects of this one are attributed to the other."

I would ask you to read with me the specifications, and see whether Professor Swing does believe in the rite of baptism. In the sermon entitled "A Religion of Words" he has said:

Then came the days that brought God an offering of words. Imagining Him to be a God of articles and forms, they repeated thousand of words, and baptized their guilty foreheads in much or little water as an act of salvation!

And now the world awaits the last transfiguration of human worship into a spiritual condition, into a soul lifted above sin, and exulting in a nearness to the image of God. The nations await with tears of past sorrow a religion that shall indeed baptize men and children, either or both, but counting this as only a beautiful form shall take the souls of men into the atmosphere of Jesus, and into the all-pervading presence of God, and detain them there until sin shall have become a hated monster, and perfection of spirit the heaven of this life and that to come. Terms must give place to righteousness and communion with God.

Professor Swing—"I indorse every word of that."

I take it that if the inquiry was started, you would find a great many Presbyterians who neglect the ordinance of baptism, and if every Presbyterian minister should go on and preach that baptism is only a "beautiful form," the Baptist denomination would soon swallow us up, and there would be no more occasion to talk about close communion. [Applause.]

I will read the twelfth specification [which he did.]

I understand why he expresses no doubt on the question of Penelope and Socrates. His theory is that we go to heaven on the strength of our good works. I don't think we are called upon to dogmatize on the question of Penelope. If we believe in the salvation of the heathen without approach to Christ, you cut the nerve of missionary effort and the backbone of Christianity.

We will past to the next specification. When the defense called Dr. Swazey, and I called Mr. Goudy, there was a doubt raised as to whether they heard the same sermon. I hold in my hand the sermon preached at Dr. Swazey's installation. I will read it, and let you judge whether Mr. Goudy's recollection of it was correct.

(The sermon was read at length, as published in the morning papers of May 19, 1873.)

Now I will read the Confession of Faith, chapter 25, section 3.

Professor Swing's sermon, if it means anything, means that the office of Christian ministers has no groundwork in the Bible—that it is an outgrowth of the exigencies of civilization and of the wants of society.

Dr. Swazey said this sermon impressed him very deeply; it seemed to him a getting at the *rationale* of the ministry,—"a digging under," as he said. I should say it was "a digging under"—an undermining of the whole structure of the Christian Church. [Applause to the north.]

Let us go back to page 62 of "David Swing's Sermons." "A religion of words."

"To offer things to God was earth's first form of being religious. The old temples were full of bows, arrows, shields, helmets, and jewels put away from human use by a solemn gift-making to the Gods. * * * * * Good came from this custom, for that spiritual worship is the highest form of religion does not make useless or harmless a form full of material things and ideas. The gift-making worship takes only a second position, inferior, but not useless nor absurd. In Solomon's day not to offer a lamb to Jehovah was to be an infidel, for the religious thought and feeling of the times flowing in that channel, the heart that made no offering was an infidel heart."

I have no objection to his speaking of heathen sacrifices as gift-worship; but when he makes the statements respecting the sacrifices of the Jews, I do most emphatically object. It is a denial of the Scripture statements. The sixteenth chapter of Leviticus informs us it was a divinely appointed ordinance. The great difficulty with Professor Swing's theology is that it robs the Bible of the element of guilt, and takes out the sentence of condemnation, the justification and vicarious atonement of Christ.

Besides this objection to the idea here put forth there are two others—it is an implicit denial of the element of guilt in the doctrine of sin; but it is bound to upset every conception which you will have already accepted as established, for as you judge the sacrifices in the book of Leviticus, will you judge the sacrifice of the Lord Jesus Christ.

The next specification will be the sixteenth. I will pass it for the present, reminding the court of the statements made yesterday in reference to Mr. Mill and Mr. Cousin. We will pass to the seventeenth.

Were Professor Swing to studiously refrain from the use of theological terms, one great objection and difficulty would be out of the way. When he uses them you are not to conclude that they mean in his dictionary what they mean in yours. The necessities of this controversy oblige me to use language by way of antithesis, that may sound harsh to Unitarian ears. I beg they will not think I mean any discourtesy to them. Other denominations use these words: Regeneration, saviour, salvation, justification, divine; therefore, it becomes our duty to scrutinize his meaning when he uses these words. When we say Christ is divine, we mean that He is God.

A spiritual religion announced and a spiritual religion accepted are different matters. A divine being and a few followers may announce one, but the world is always far below the few leading divine souls, and hence, after salvational words are announced, it will continue to be much like this hereafter.

Let us now approach a more warmly disputed proposition, namely: That the divineness of Christ is something essential to Christian system.

I do not know what he means by that. When he speaks of the divineness of our Lord, and in another place of the divineness of Christians, I may be pardoned for saying I do not know whether he believes that Christ is God.

* * * * * * * * * *

I shall take up several of the specifications and group them together; I will not dwell upon them specifically, but I shall allude to them as I go on. I would ask those who have Professor Swing's sermons with them, to read those entitled "Faith" and "Good Works." (The specifications were here read.)

Our discussion is not to-day with the Roman Catholic Church, but the doctrine in issue is the doctrine which Luther defended against the Roman Catholic Church. That is what made Reformation. That is what makes Presbyterianism. And when you depart from it, you leave behind you the cardinal principles of Christianity. I claim that Professor Swing does not preach the doctrine of justification. What is justification? The doctrine of the Catholic Church was that justification means making holy; that a justified person was a holy person, and the issue in the main, with the Roman Catholic Church, was to settle that question, and to deny that justification meant a making holy, and to affirm that it was a judicial act of God, whereby He freely pardons all our sins and accepts us as righteous, as opposed to the mysticism of Romanism. Now, when we come to this, and affirm that justification is a judicial act on the part of God. We find a difference again. They find, for instance, our Arminian brethren going with us thus far, but at this point our paths diverge. They say that justification means pardon. We say it means pardon, and something else besides.

Our standard defines justification as an act of God's free grace wherein He pardons our sins, and counts us as if we were righteous. Did Professor Swing believe that? No; because, if he did, he could not write this sentence: work that is, results—a new life—are the destiny of faith, the reason of its wonderful play of light on the religious horizon. Faith as a believe and a friendship, is good, so far as it bears the soul to "this normal perfection."

[Here he read the definition of "justification," as set forth in the Confession of Faith.]

These words could not be understood to mean justification by faith as believed by the Presbyterian Church, but could only be reconciled as believing that justification means personal character, and taking the ground of the Romanists, and mystics, and Dr. Bushnell, and until he had a direct contradiction from Dr. Swing, I will believe that this is what he means. Professor Swing holds the subjective view of justification by faith as held by Unitarians, as against the objective view held by the Presbyterian Church. When Professor Swing represents the theology of Presbyterianism as a naked assent to an intellectual proposition he gives us an illustration of history repeating itself, for if I read history aright this was one of the points in the controversy in Roman Catholic times in the sixteenth century, that Protestants were claimed by Roman Catholics as believing in salvation by naked assent, and hence arose a distinction in Protestant Latin theology between *fides* and *fiducia*. Faith, as taught in the standards of the Presbyterian Church, is not a naked assent to a proposition, but it is the Lord Jesus Christ.

Adjourned.

THURSDAY'S SESSION.

Professor Patton proceeded with his argument.

BRETHREN: I call your attention this morning to the thirteenth specification, which reads as follows: "In a sermon printed on or about 15th September, 1872, from II Peter, iii. 9, he made use of loose and unguarded language respecting the providence of God."

In support of this allegation, I will read an abstract of a sermon preached by Professor Swing on September 22, 1872, as reported in the *Times*. [The Professor here read the report at length, and afterward the Confession of Faith on the providence of God.] The question I address to the court is this: Understanding this passage of the Confession of Faith as containing the belief of the Presbyterian Church, I ask whether Professor Swing has or has not used loose and unguarded language in reference to the doctrine of the providence of God when he preached the sermon which I have read.

In many of the specifications on which I have commented, the charge is not that Professor Swing believes error, but that he teaches error. I have taken these passages, and so far as it has been practicable have presented the context. All the sermons from which quotations have been made are in evidence, and are accessible to the members of the court. They can see whether I have done injustice to the quotations I have made, and it will be the privilege of the defense, if such injustice has been done, to make it apparent. It was simply impossible that I should read all the sermons through in order that they might justify my use of one or two sentences by way of comment. Now, it might be argued, and, perhaps, the opinion has been expressed before this, that the utterance of error, or the sentences alleged to be error, is a very different thing from direct affirmation of his disbelief of certain doctrines. The point we are arguing in this case is not that Professor Swing does not believe these doctrines. We shall have something to say on that subject under the second charge; but if he does believe them, and yet teaches error, so much the worse. If you can prove that a man is incompetent, that he is ignorant of the system of drugs, that would be a reason for his not administering drugs; but be he ever so well educated, and ever so familiar with the pharmacopœia, if you can prove as a matter of fact that he administers poisons, then I am not going to that shop. [Laughter on the Swing side of the house.] Now, the question with us is, not what Professor Swing believes, but what he says, for it is as a teacher we are making charges now against him. Nor is it necessary that the language used by Professor Swing should be proved to be contrary to the Confession of Faith, or to be incompatible with a construction favorable to sound doctrine, for this Presbytery to make it a subject of judicial action; because, granting that in certain expressions used it is possible that a favorable construction can be put upon it, if the natural meaning of the language and the natural construction which the human mind would put upon it is at once unfavorable to sound doctrine and vital piety, then it is the duty of the court to tell Professor Swing so, to express its disapproval, and do so in terms measured by the offense.

Now that I am correct in this opinion, and that I have the precedents of the Presbyterian Church on my side, let me quote from the digest. This time I will quote from the New School Digest. [Laughter.] [The prosecutor here quoted the decision of the General Assembly in 1763, in the case of Harper, who was charged, among other things, with unintelligible and dangerous modes of expression, which he argued was a parallel case with the Swing case. Next he cited the Balch case, in 1798, in which the respondent was charged with promulgating false doctrine, and met with the disapprobation of the General Assembly. Then the prosecutor cited the case of the Rev. W. C. Davis, in 1810—he having published an objectionable book—to show that "Presbyterians went so far as to tell their ministers that they must not be unhappy in their expressions."]

Again, there is the case of the Rev. Mr. Craighead. What is the point in this case? It is that although Mr. Craighead was charged with heresy, and although he was acquitted of that charge on the ground that the language used was capable of favorable construction, and on the further ground of being capable of that favorable construction, he solemnly disavowed the charge made against him. Nevertheless, the General Assembly pronounced his statements as dangerous, and affirmed that they ought to be condemned. Now, if we are to allow ecclesiastical precedents to have any weight with us, then, even though it were possible that the language of Professor Swing was capable of favorable construction, and he made the most explicit disavowal of the charge of heresy, yet it would be the duty of the Presbytery to express its disapproval of the use of language which has caused widespread distrust of his theological position.

The opinion which I have formed respecting Professor Swing's theology is the result of a very careful study of his discourses, from the fact that I have made his sermons a matter of careful study, and from the further fact that the doctrinal issues involved are of such importance that I feel justified in speaking in such a presence as this, and, I fear, at a wearisome length, on topics of theology, which are familiar to us all.

I left off yesterday with speaking respecting Professor Swing's views upon the doctrine of justification by faith. His position on his doctrine is not a matter of doubt. If the court will read his sermons on "God Works" and on "Faith" the members of Presbytery will be unanimous in the opinion that the views of Professor Swing on this cardinal doctrine of protestantism are not the views of the Presbyterian Church, are not the views which could be accepted by any branch of the evangelical churches. I mean by evangelical churches, such as the Methodist, Presbyterian, Baptist, and Congregationalist and Episcopal. I object to the views of Professor Swing. The objections are grave. The view of Professor Swing on the subject of salvation is, that he only can look forward with joy who can calmly look back, that heaven is a height to which men rise on the deeds of this life; and if I were called to preach the gospel in such a form as that, it would be impossible for me to go to a dying man and tell him to believe in the Lord Jesus Christ and he would be saved. It would be impossible for Mr. LcLeod to go to the jail as he has had to go, and tell an inmate who is paying the penalty of his crime that he would yet be received by Christ if he believed, as Christ said to one who was His companion in suffering, "This day thou shalt be with me in paradise." I object to the views of Professor Swing, because they do an injustice to the righteousness of our Lord Jesus Christ. The gospel which we teach is the righteousness of Christ; of salvation through His blood. It is this gospel which has lent inspiration to every movement whereby the cause of Christ has been furthered. It is the gospel of Charles Hodge, of Albert Barnes, of Charles Spurgeon, of DeWitt Talmage; it is the gospel of the missionary, of the evangelist, of Moody and Sankey, of the Sunday-school—a gospel which is sung by every child who sings:

> "Tell me the old, old story
> Of Jesus and His love."

I will now read a passage from a letter recently received in which reference is made to the revival work which is going on at Edinburgh. The letter has just been handed to me. The passage is as follows:

As we know, Messrs. Moody and Sankey are there, both working and singing. Probably the Lord is blessing their work, and making them greatly useful; but to us they seem merely as a sickle passing through the well ripened fields of grain, white months ago to the harvest. We had ample opportunity during four months in Edinburgh to learn the religious feelings and positions of the people. It is a city exalted as to heaven in point of privilege. Its religious and moral life is a glorious vindication of the excellence of doctrinal preaching. The Edinburgh ministers are not afraid to preach doctrine, and what is called "hard doctrine." They have not failed to declare the whole counsel of God; the trumpet tones of Knox echo in these pulpits still. There is no courting people to church with sensational subjects; no offering of sugar—plain preaching; very little florid rhetoric; no last new opera singer and expensive choir. None of these—merely the truth in Christ Jesus. And what is the result? On Sunday in Edinburgh the streets at service hour, three times a day, are crowded as our streets on the Fourth of July. The last stroke of the bell, and the streets are as deserted as midnight. These mighty throngs have gone into the house of David, to hear "sound doctrine." Edinburgh has been deficient in Sabbath schools, but year after year the church has swelled its numbers from the children of its families, who are always taken to church for the pastor's instruction, and are taught at home by their parents.

I object to the doctrine of Professor Swing, because it is a doctrine which ministers either to self-righteousness or to despair. He teaches us that we are to be saved by our own works; that faith saves us because it leads to a holy love, that salvation means a holy love, therefore, he who expects salvation, and has the assurance of a hope in heaven, is he who is holy, and he hopes for heaven in the ratio of his present holiness. That is not the doctrine that is taught in the epistle to the Romans, wherein it is written that we shall not be saved by works, but by faith. If a man is so constituted that he cannot feel that his own righteousness is enough to save him, then he can only fall down in despair, for the religion of Professor Swing does not offer a hope but that. Instead of Presbyterians teaching "the dark doctrine of despair, I say the teaching of Professor Swing is the doctrine of despair, unless it is the doctrine of self-righteousness. We object to the teaching of Professor Swing upon the subject of justification by faith, in that his preaching makes Christianity simply an exalted morality. The reason why Christianity is better than Hindooism is because the morality of Christianity is better; the reason why Christ is better than Confucius is because the former is an improvement on the latter; the reason why Christ is a better saviour than Socrates is because he was a better man, a greater teacher. "Christ is the *best* Saviour" we ever had.

I come now to the two concluding specifications of the first charge. These specifications have a historic interest as related to this prosecution. The history of these specifications is the history of the relations in which Professor Swing and myself stand to each other. Little did I think when I wrote the editorial of last fall that it would culminate in a scene like this. When I took charge of *The Interior*, I knew of the doubts which had been expressed with reference to Professor Swing's theology. I had seen the newspapers of other churches calling in question his opinions on the subject of inspiration, and entering their protest against the Presbytery of Chicago for sitting in silence while one of its prominent members gave utterance to thoughts in direct violation of the Confession of Faith, and whose tendency was to overthrow the integrity and authority of God's holy word. It was with a great deal of diffidence and with much reluctance I entered upon a re-review of Professor Swing's sermon, and those who followed the discussion, and remember anything about that editorial, will remember something of the spirit in which it was written and the language in which it was couched. If I knew anything of my own heart, it was written in the kindest spirit, in an apologetic vein; if anything was said in it which was calculated to hurt Professor Swing's feelings, I am sorry for it, and I here make this public acknowledgment. I wrote that editorial in the hope that when he replied thereto he would have something to say in the way of explanation, and that his explanatory statements would be couched in such frank terms as would remove doubts, and restore him to the confidence of those who had questioned his expositions. The views expressed by Professor Swing during the controversy were so pronounced in their hostility to what we regard as plenary inspiration, a doctrine which has received the special sanction of the Chicago Presbytery, that I did not hesitate to say on one occasion, that, holding such views, a minister, with the vows of the Presbyterian Church upon him, could not consistently remain in her communion as a minister. Those among you who have watched this controversy, know how it advanced; how one thing led to another, until in a final editorial I did say that there were those who doubted—and I was among those—whether Professor Swing believed even that Christ was God, and other vital doctrines. Those were honest doubts, based upon an honest perusal of his published writings; and it was in connection with the expression of those doubts that I said that I hoped that Professor Swing's published utterances had done him great injustice, and I placed the columns of *The Interior* at his disposal, in order that he might rectify any mistake and correct any false impressions which had gone abroad. If that was not what a manly, Christian course would dictate, then I am at fault, and greatly misapprehend the laws of Christian courtesy and dignified Christian journalism. I have no word to say in reference to those who honestly and sincerely differ with me as to the propriety of expressing my doubts. The expression of these doubts has brought on me a weight of odium which I did not anticipate. Now, the prosecution of this case, I regret to say, has not removed those doubts, but has only served to vindicate me in my own eyes as to the justice of my former position; and I am not only ready to say now that I doubt as to Professor Swing's position, but that, with respect to some of the doctrines, I do not believe that he holds them.

I will now call attention to the questions raised in the twenty-third specification. The following passages from a sermon called "Old Testament Inspiration:"

These thoughts bring me now to the structure of the Psalms of David. Many of them being deeply religious, are suitable to all religious hearts everywhere; there are others that belonged only to the days when they were sung. If it was permitted the Israelites to destroy their enemies, and thus establish the better their monotheism, it was necessary they should sing battle songs, and that much of their hymnology should be military. In days of an American struggle with England, the song of "The Star-spangled Banner" might be useful and truthful. It might impel men along the best path of the period. In France, a few years ago, the "Marseillaise" was rising with power, for it was necessary for the people to check the reckless ambition of Louis Napoleon. These hymns might be confessed to possess a temporary inspiration. That is their good is unmistakable. But let the world and civilization advance, let war become a crime and a barbarism, let peace become not only an article of religion but a policy of all nations, let all its disputes be settled by arbitration and payment of damages, and in that golden age the war songs of America and France become a poor dead letter, and no heart remains so war-like as to sing them. Thus with such psalms as the 109th. They had a temporary significance, depending altogether upon the kind of work the Hebrews had to perform. If it was necessary for them to go to battle, it was desirable that they should have a battle-song — a Marsellaise. If their hands must do bloody work, they were entitled to sing a terrific psalm. But the moment the Hebrew method of life passed away, the moment the war for national existence ceased, that momemt the 109th Psalm lost its value. For as the bloody Hebrew war is over, so is its battle song. There is no logic in perpetuating a war-cry after the war itself has passed away.

That Professor Swing does not believe that the 109th Psalm is the inspired word of God is perfectly plain to any one who is unprejudiced and unbiased, if we read what he said in *The Interior* on Sept. 18, 1873. It is as follows:

The prominence given to the 109th Psalm in my remarks arises only from the fact that it has long been a public test of the value of any given theory of inspiration. This is one of the places at which the rational world asks us to pause and apply our abundant and boastful words. Most of the young men, even in the Presbyterian Church, know what the historian Froude said of this psalm a few years since: "Those who accept the 109th Psalm as the word of God are already far on their way toward *auto-da-fes* and massacres of St. Bartholomew," and while they may for a time reject these words, they will soon demand a theory of inspiration very different from the indefinite admiration of the past.

"It has long been a public test of the value of any given theory of inspiration." What does that mean? It means this: You believe in the plenary inspiration of the Scriptures, do you? Do you believe the 109th Psalm is inspired? That's a puzzler! "It has long been a public test as to the value of any given theory of inspiration." Did it ever bother you, my brethren? Can you not take God's authority even for the 109 Psalm? "This is one of the places where the rational world asks us to pause and apply our abundant and boastful words." We say all Scripture is given by inspiration of God; we say that inasmuch as Jesus gives authority and sanction to the Old Testament in words which distinctly affirm that not a jot or title can pass away or be broken. The authority of Jesus Christ covers everything to which he attaches His signature. There is no boasting about that. The Apostle Paul knew what he was about, and knowing what he was about, could not have based any such argument upon any such Scripture unless the whole Scripture was inspired, and the Apostle Paul's reasoning takes it that all Scripture is inspired, and, therefore, when I quote it I challenge you to say it is boastful. It is simply taking God manifested in the flesh, and the Apostle Paul, God's commissioned servant, as authority on the subject.

Does he believe that the Scriptures of the Old and New Testament, are inspired in such a sense that when you pick up the Twenty-third Psalm, second verse, you can say that it is God's word; that, light upon it where you may, it is God's word; because you have settled the prior question that the Scripture is given by inspiration of God? Does he believe that? If he does, if that is his opinion, if that is his creed, then, sir, of all the curiosities of literature in the history of the world, there never was a greater one in inconsistency than this, which I am going to read.

This is one of the places at which the rational world asks us to pause and apply our abundant words.

Do you know who Froude is? He is not a Christian in any sense of the world. He is a rationalist. His creed is reduced to such small dimensions that it would not take long to count its articles. He quotes Froude, and that in a religious newspaper which goes to some 13,000 or 14,000 people. Would they gather from it that he believed in the inspiration of the Scriptures as it is defined in our standards? He says:

Most young men, even in the Presbyterian Church, know what the historian Froude said of this psalm a few years since: "Those who accept the 109th Psalm as the word of God are already far on their way towards, *auto-da-fe* and massacres of St. Bartholomew."

And the intelligence of this Presbytery is called upon to decide whether such a statement as that can be regarded in a light favorable to his belief in the plenary inspiration of the Scriptures. If that don't mean and is not calculated to mean that he indorses the sentiment he quotes, it don't mean anything, and I will give up reading English and call myself a fool. [Sensation.] You may put this down as a settled fact: that as long as these words stand unretracted in history, they stamp him as denying the plenary inspiration of the Scriptures; and it would be one of the greatest acts of inconsistency ever prepetrated, for this Presbytery, after having pronounced its verdict upon plenary inspiration, and having accepted without debate the report of its committee in reference to two sermons preached by one of its ministers, and remanded that minister to his own Presbytery for discipline, if, after doing that, they should pass a sentence of acquittal, stamping their episcopal seal of approval upon a man against whom can be laid a charge like this.

The inspiration of the Scriptures is valuable as a doctrine because it guarantees the infallibility of the Scriptures. Now, if a man should profess to believe in the inspiration of the Scriptures, and then deny what would give value to that inspiration, I would give little for his acknowledgment.

I wish to know whether this book which I cling to—having cut adrift from Rome, cling to more tenaciously—is the only rule of faith and practice. I wish to know whether it carries with it the signature of Almighty God, and whether it will hold when I take it as my anchor. This is why I wish to know whether this is the Word of God. If a man shall say he believes in the inspiration of the Scriptures, and shall still say that notwithstanding he believes they are not infallible, then the infallibility of the Scriptures goes for naught. He denies the plenary inspiration of the Scriptures; but even if he should retract this broad statement, and say he was in error when he made it, and that he now believes in the plenary inspiration of the Scriptures, I should not have closed the case for the prosecution even then if it was still proved that he does not believe in the infallible authority, when I rest my hopes on what it says, those hopes remain secure. That he does not, I propose to prove.

In his sermon on "Old Testament inspiration" the following passage occurs:

There is, it seems to me, no other conceivable method of treating the Old Testament than that found in the word eclecticism. We must seek out its permanent truths, follow its central ideas, and love them the more because they were eliminated from the barbaric ages with so much sorrow and bloodshed.

The question before us is, What does the passage say? We have heard in evidence—Dr. Patterson said it—that he believes this passage to refer, not to the eclecticism of authority, but to the eclecticism of use. He may have made that statement to Dr. Patterson in such terms that he can have no possibility of a reason for doubt; but he has not made that statement to us—he has not made it to the world. And with all respect and deference to Dr. Patterson, we must submit that in a trial of a case like this we cannot accept such a side statement upon such a question. We do not know what that conversation was, or how they had arrived at that conclusion; whether Dr. Patterson showed him his Confession of Faith, and he said, "these are my sentiments," or whether he showed his Confession of Faith to Dr. Patterson, who said, "That is so."

Dr. Patterson, (rising)—It don't matter how it was done; it was very clearly done.

Professor Patton (resuming, after a mere glance at Dr. Patterson)—That is not a question upon which you, in your judicial capacity, can pass. The sentiment stands out boldly and unrelieved in this passage, that eclecticism is the only system which you can adopt in the interpretation of the Scriptures. We want that statement denied.

But even if he should make that statement, and come to this Presbytery and tell us that what he meant by eclecticism was the eclecticism of use, and not the eclecticism of truth, the case is not closed for the prosecution, because he has said a great deal more than that. In his article in *The Interior* be makes statements from which I shall quote. He admits that the meaning of the word inspiration is vague:

After the Westminster Confession has uttered its conclusions about the Bible being an infallible rule of faith and life, it remains for each mind to find as best it can where that rule lies, and whether the Divine Spirit is always equal in all parts of the Holy Book.

In the course of my controversy with Professor Swing, it had come out that he had some question as to the propriety of the Israelites slaughtering the Canaanites. They did not go to that war at their own charges; and when he intimated his disapproval of the course which the ancient people took, I ventured to remonstrate with him, to the effect that the people were perfectly safe in following a general; and when the general was the Lord God of Hosts, and He was satisfied, we should not complain. He did not accept my explanation; and when he came to review the situation he condemned the Israelites. When I said, "If you do, you must either take that or disbelieve the Bible," he said: "I believe the Bible, but I condemn the Israelites." This is what he wrote in *The Interior:*

The bloody human passion was permitted by God to stand upon the book, because He could make this wrath of man praise Him in the outcome of church life. Your apology here, that God was Himself the general of the armies, and had a moral right to kill non-combatants, is one which has long filled a large place in this debate; but it must be perfectly evident that, in your logic, God is thus made the general in the law of 'eye for eye,' upon the ground that if he has a right to destroy an eye by disease, or a foot by palsy, he has a right to command men to put out eyes, or cut off hands, upon a large scale, here or there. It is barely possible that my discourse may have contained words that should not have fallen upon the ears of a Presbyterian audience, but "it contained no words that made God appear as general in battles that surpassed, in cruelty, those of Julius Cæsar, and no words that bind those battles up in the world's infallible rule of faith and practice. That spirit of warfare was accepted of God from humanity, because He could overrule a human evil for a final good, by tolerance, and not by the way of making known to mankind grand truths which could not have been reached by the light of reason.

If I am at liberty to construe language at all, this sentence means that the Jews, although God had given them an explicit command to go and slaughter the Canaanites, and although in the face of their unwillingness to go God told them He would punish them if they did not go, Professor Swing objects to the course they pursued, and spoke of their wars in disparaging terms. In the face of that statement, but two positions are possible. They are: that God told the Jews to do something which he should not have told them to do; or that the statement that He did tell them to do it is not true—Moses to the contrary, notwithstanding.

It is not only in respect to the wars of the Jews that he is in error. It is in respect to the laws of the Jews. He says they are unjust, and have administered to human depravity.

[Here Professor Patton quoted from Professor Swing's letter in *The Interior* of September 4, which, after taking special exception to the harsh Israelitish laws relative to seduction, concludes as follows]:

"If David's personal character had been preceded by generations which punished over thirty forms of offenses with death, by generations which slew women and children, by generations which punished impurity by a fine of one animal of a flock. And if, reared in this atmosphere, David sent Uriah to the front, and thus secured 'Uriah's beautiful wife,' one certainly should not attribute this immorality 'to any lack of revelation,' indeed, but rather to an absence of that quality of revelation found afterward in the morals of Jesus."

He speaks of the laws of Moses as cruel and unjust; they were given to Moses by God, and if they are cruel the fault is not that of Moses, but of God. In the article on the "Interpretation of the Apocalypse," published in the Sunday-school Teacher for July, 1873, he not only doubts the inspiration of the Old Testament, but of the New.

He cannot be accused of being very partial to that belief to which this Presbytery is pledged.

Let us take one more authority—the Bible. This very book opens with this sentence:

"The revelation of Jesus Christ, which God gave unto Him to show unto His servant things which must shortly come to pass; and He sent a sign by His angel unto His servant, John."

And it closes with this passage:

"And He said unto him, these sayings are faithful and true; and the Lord God sent His angel and showed unto His servant things which must shortly be done. I testify to every man that beareth the words of this book, if any man add unto these things, God shall add unto him the plagues that are written in this book; and if any man shall take away from the things that are written in this book, God shall take away his part out of the book of life.

[This closed his discussion of the case so far as related to the first charge. He thanked the Moderator for the kindness and equity with which he had presided, and for the indulgence he had shown him; and the Presbyters for the patient attention they had given his long argument. He had one apology to make, and made it thus]:

If, in the rapidity of unpremeditated speech, I have crossed the boundary which Christian gentlemen should observe, I hope this Presbytery will forgive me. I do remember that once, at least, since I began this argument, I made an expression for which I wish to make a proper acknowledgment. I did say that this Presbytery ought not to acquit Professor Swing of the charges preferred against him; and I said that if they did, I would impeach the Presbytery at the bar of a higher court. Such a sentence ought not to have passed my lips, and I hope the Presbytery will receive my retraction of it in the spirit in which it is made. [Applause.]

Passing to the second charge, I propose to show that it is true, by the testimony of Mr. Shufeldt, and by his written statements.

The declaration of the accused will not substantiate his innocence; but the admission of the accused is sufficient to establish his guilt. He has admitted on the floor of this Presbytery that he does not receive and adopt the Confession of Faith as containing the system of doctrine taught in the Word of God. I do not mean that he has said that much in so many words, but I do say that his plea cannot be considered in any other way. He says a distinction does exist between Presbyterianism as formulated in past times and the Presbyterian Church actual. I was never informed of that. If we are not to be held to the formulated theology of the Church, then I wish to know what is the basis of Presbyterian faith? Which is the Church actual, the Church of Pittsburgh or the Church of Chicago? He has repudiated those doctrines which "look toward a dark fatalism, and teach that religion is despair." Now, there are no doctrines of fatalism in the Presbyterian Church. It is not for me now to protest against the charge that the Presbyterian Church holds fatalism, but to say that when he referred to those doctrines he could have referred to no other doctrines than those doctrines which speak of God's sovereignty, and he has left a very important element of the Confession of Faith behind him. He says he has left behind him the doctrine of hell, as it is taught in the Confession of Faith with such terrible plainness. He has charged upon the Presbyterian Church the idea that she has pandered to infidelity.

I pass to the testimony of Mr. Shufeldt. While that gentleman revealed a very keen tenacity for that tree about whose branches there was so much discussion, and while there was a great effort made to show that infant damnation was one of the five points of Calvinism that were repudiated, yet he testified that either he had abandoned at least two of those doctrines commonly known as the five points of Calvinism.

Dr. Patterson—Let me call the attention of the prosecutor to the fact that Mr. Shufeldt said these two points were branches of the tree marked "abandoned."

[Professor Patton picked up a newspaper, and referring to it, read Mr. Shufeldt's testimony. Then, resuming his speech:]

He has taught the doctrine of Sabellianism; he gave his approval to the doctrine that Christianity does admit of three offices; and he ridiculed the doctrine of the threeness of one and the oneness of three. It is fair to believe that he believes what he teaches; else that Presbytery, in acquitting him, makes a charge of far more gravity than I prefer against him. He has abandoned the doctrine of justification by faith. I shall not argue that point, because I argued it yesterday. We are led to conclude that he does not believe in it. He does not believe in the doctrine of the inspiration of the Scriptures. If I have not made that clear, I could not make it clear by arguing it a week.

[Professor Patton closed his argument by citing the case of Craighead, and that of Albert Barnes, showing that the Craighead case could not be urged in defence of Professor Swing, unless, (1.) The language complained of is capable, without violence of a favorable construction. (2.) The accused disavows the error which his language is alleged to teach. (3.) And avows his belief in the doctrine alleged to be impugned.

The basis of the Presbyterian Church is the Confession of Faith. The issues between Professor Swing and myself are not issues that could be brought out between any two persons who both held the Confession of Faith. The simple question is, does he hold these doctrines in any sense compatible with an honest construction of the Confession of Faith. They are issues that would have been fought out on the floor of a New School Presbytery with as much zeal as on the floor of an Old School Presbytery. They are issues that go to the foundations of Christianity—which touch the question of the Rule of Faith, which refers to the Trinity—on which we rest our hopes of heaven.

The case now stands with you; you have the evidence and the arguments. You know that it has been proven in this court that he uses equivocal language in respect to vital doctrines; that he has spoken in derogation of the standards of the Presbyterian Church, and with respect to doctrines that underlie the whole system of Christianity; and finally, that he is taught contrary to the doctrine of justification by faith. He says the church actual is something different from the church historic; he admits that he has left many of these doctrines; he has been proven to have departed from many others. And now I leave you to say whether the charges with their specifications are not sustained.

AFTERNOON SESSION.

Long before the hour of re-opening had arrived the chapel was crowded almost to suffocation by vast accessions to the Swing side—for the most part of ladies, who pressed themselves and were pressed forward into every available spot. The Moderator's tap for order hushed the most animated confusion of female voices that ever was heard in that place.

Mr. Noyes immediately proceeded with his argument. He said:

We are confronted to-day by that which, if we are not willfully blind, must appear to all as a "great and serious trouble." Scarcely has the honeymoon passed which followed the happy marriage of the Old and New School branches of the Presbyterian Church, when a new danger arises to threaten our peace. The sound of voices which were raised in joyful thanksgiving to God over that blessed union have hardly died away, when suddenly our hearts are pained and filled with anxiety by the presence of unexpected peril. Upon the married life of these churches, over all of which a spirit of peace and love has been breathed, dark clouds now begin to arise, threatening storm, and wrath and ruin. It would seem that "whom God hath joined together," man is in danger of "putting asunder." Until recently there was peace and happy fellowship within the bounds of this Presbytery. In one branch of the Church there had, unhappily, been strife in the days that are gone; but in the general good feeling consequent upon the reunion, past differences seemed destined to a speedy oblivion; and there was every promise that we should abundantly realize "how good and how pleasant a thing it is for brethren to dwell together in unity." But from our "deep dream of peace" we have been suddenly awakened. How it came about you all know, and I will not take your time, upon which I shall necessarily have to make such large demands, to recount the story. I will therefore proceed at once to the business in hand; and, before entering upon any examination of the argument which has been made before you by the prosecutor in this case, I desire to ask your attention for a little time to the form of the complaint upon which the defendant is arraigned at your bar.

When this indictment was presented the defendant was somewhat peculiarly placed. If his counsel had moved to quash it, there would have been an instant outcry on the part of the prosecutor and his friends, that we were attempting to smother inquiry, and to avoid a fair investigation. If we made no such motion, we felt ourselves in the position of seeming to approve of the indictment as correct, both in form and in substance. We did not wish to move to quash it, nor were we willing to be understood as regarding it rightly drawn. In this state of things I desired at the outset to make an explanatory statement. But to this objection was made, and so the case went to trial. In both the charges here exhibited, and in nearly all the specifications under them, there was such an obvious and glaring defect, either of substance or of form, that, in any purely, equitable, and legal, not to say technical view, they ought never to have been entertained. They should have been turned incontinently out of court. In support of this statement, it will be necessary to consider (1) the nature of a charge, (2) of a specification, and then (3) show how neither the charges of this indictment, nor the specifications by which it is sought to prove them, are such as to make a valid case for trial.

In discussing these points, let it first be distinctly admitted that the extreme nicety and refinement of criticism with which indictments are handled in civil courts, would be quite out of place in an ecclesiastical tribunal like this. And yet it will be admitted by all, that there are certain rules founded on natural justice, which ought to be observed, and held inviolable by ecclesiastical courts. Because an indictment here may not properly be handled in that remorseless way which prevails in civil courts, it does not follow that it may be drawn in such a way as to violate, in its charges and in its specifications, the most obvious principles of justice. But that, in the case before us, this has been done, it will not be difficult to prove.

A CHARGE.

The general term charge may be understood as applying to the whole accusation made against the accused person. This accusation consists of two distinct parts: the first, which is specially called the charge, consists in designating the general offense of which the accused is charged; and the second, which is called the specification to the charge, consists in the alleging of certain specified acts done by the accused, which are supposed to constitute or prove the general offense named in the charge. A charge, it is plain, ought to set forth some one general offense, which is so exceptional in its character as to imperatively call for ecclesiastical censure. The charge must also clearly and distinctly define the offense, so that the accused may know precisely of what he is accused. Vague charges are objectionable, and unfair, to the last degree.

Applying now these principles to the charges in this indictment, what should be our judgment upon them? It is noticeable that they are both negative in form.

The prosecution charges that the defendant has not been "faithful and zealous in maintaining the truths of the gospel," and that he "does not sincerely receive and adopt the confession of faith."

The first charge is indefinite to the extent of not naming at all any punishable offense. Would the prosecutor come into this court and claim that he has been and is faithful as a minister? Such a boast, if he were to make it, would of itself be a swift witness against him for unfaithfulness. You cannot run the line between the faithful and the unfaithful. You cannot find the point where faithfulness ends and unfaithfulness begins; so that this side that point a man may go uncensured of his brethren, and beyond it be justly exposed to their sentence of condemnation. All are zealous, faithful, and diligent in some degree, but in some degrees, also, all come short.

To say, therefore, that a man is unfaithful and wanting in zeal is simply to affirm a fact which is as true of the prosecutor as it is of the defendant, which is true of the members of this court, and of all ministers of the Gospel. "Let him that is without sin among you cast the first stone." This charge does not embrace, therefore, a punishable offense at all. In the Presbyterian Church, a minister who lacks zeal and is unfaithful does not thereby become amenable to discipline. Hence, to make unfaithfulness the basis of a formal charge, is a great injustice. The ranks of the Presbyterian ministry are full of noble and self-sacrificing men; but there is not one of them all against whom this first charge could not with perfect truth be brought. And hence a charge so utterly vague and indefinite as this cannot justly be entertained by a judicial body. Nor is the vagueness at all relieved when we come to examine, as in due time I shall do, the specifications to the charge. Charge 2 is still more objectionable. It arraigns the accused, not for what he teaches, let us carefully observe, but what he *thinks*. It is true, indeed, that the specifications might embody facts that would so reveal the state of the respondent's mind as to show that he does not receive the Confession of Faith. They might do this, but they do not. They contain only the prosecutor's own inferences and conclusions which he draws from Professor Swing's language. The charges are founded upon the supposed state of a man's mind, and not upon any clear and unquestionably heretical utterances from his lips. To judge the heart is the prerogative, not of the prosecutor in this case, not of the members of this court, but of God alone. Let me illustrate what I mean by saying that the specifications under these charges are so indefinite as not to sustain or make manifest what is the offense to which the respondent is to answer. The very first specification under Charge 1 begins with setting forth what? A fact? Not at all: but simply the conclusion of the prosecutor, in this language: "He is in the habit of using equivocal language"—who is the judge of equivocal language?—"to the manifest injury of his reputation as a Christian minister, and to the injury of the cause of Christ. "Specification three:

"He has manifested a culpable disregard to the essential doctrines of Christianity by giving the weight of his influence to the Unitarian denomination, and by the unworthy and extravagant laudation in the pulpit, and through the press of John Stuart Mill, a man who was known not to have believed in the Christian religion."

Is that the setting forth of a fact?—of an act which clearly reveals and manifests to this court the guilt of the respondent? On the contrary, it is the setting forth only of a conclusion of the prosecutor himself.

SPECIFICATION FOUR.

"In the sermon aforesaid language is employed which is derogatory to the standards of the Presbyterian Church."

Again an exhibition of the prosecutor's inferences.

SPECIFICATION NINE.

"He has given his approval in the pulpit to the doctrine commonly known as Sabellianism."

Whatever he may have done in the judgment of Professor Patton, certainly there are multitudes who have made themselves familiar with the facts of this trial as they have been developed, and spread out before you, who do not at all agree with him in the conclusions which he sets forth here, that Professor Swing is a Sabellian, and that he has given his public approval to that doctrine. I might go on through every one of the specifications which are set forth under these charges, and show that they are all, so far as they make out anything culpable, simply the judgments and views of the prosecutor himself.

I come next to speak of the specification. And here, in defining what the specification is, and what it should embrace, I follow the highest authority (O'Brien —Military Law and Courts-Martial). The principles to be stated are, I am sure, such as will commend themselves to the judgment and reason of every member of this body. The specification must always charge the accused with having, at such a time and at such a place, done certain acts which amount, or which are thought to amount, to the offense stated in the charge. "The fact or facts ought to be very distinctly specified or alleged, in such manner that neither the accused nor the court can have any difficulty in knowing what is the precise object of investigation. Every fact in the specification should be such as, if proved, would convict the accused of the charge, or at least might convict him of it." But does any member of this court believe that one-half of these specifications can be regarded as meeting this reasonable requirement? "Any allegation in the specification which, if proved, could not convict the accused of any degree of the crime charged is irrelevant, and should be rejected. Its retention will not vitiate the charge, but it is surplusage, and no evidence should be received thereon. It is always better to reject such matters at first." Again, it is said to be "highly improper that the inferences of the prosecutor should appear in the specifications. The facts alone should be stated; it is for the court to draw the inference. Such inferences of the prosecutor would, however, be mere surplusage, and no evidence should be received on them." "There should be no uncertainty or vagueness in the specification."

These principles, embodied in rules, are so obviously sound, and the construction, in strict conformity with them, of any indictment which is to be tried in an ecclesiastical court, is so clearly important to protect the interests of an accused person, that I need not say a word in commending them to you. And yet the indictment before this body, and on which your brother presbyter has been arraigned, has been framed in conspicuous violation of all these principles. The members of this court have been enveloped in a great cloud of words — words which state next to nothing as regards actual facts, and which insinuate next to everything in the shape of the prosecutor's inferences — and through such a hazy and distorted medium as this they are asked to look at their accused brother, and see if he do not appear an unfaithful minister and a heretical teacher. We have involution and convolution illustrated before us here to such a bewildering extent, that this body might well be adjudged incapable of determining the degree of guilt which should be attached to him who holds to the doctrine of "evolution," or religion's progress and growth. Nor does it help the matter, nor at all serve to lift us out of this haze of indefiniteness, which, like a London fog, envelops us all, that the prosecutor comes and protests in open court, as he did at the outset of this trial, that he cannot make these charges and specifications any more definite; for this is tantamount to a confession on his part that he has no case. [Applause.] If a man were guilty of murder, it would, I suppose, be possible to say so distinctly. If he were guilty of falsehood, the English language is rich enough in resources to enable one to charge that also with definiteness, precision, and even emphasis. And if this respondent at your bar has been guilty of any well-defined and unquestionable ecclesiastical offense, it ought not to be impossible to say what offense, and the statement should be one of fact and not of inference.

But that the charges in this indictment do not give us any light upon this point, I have already shown. That the specifications leave us equally in the dark is that which is now and easily to be shown.

Beginning with the first of the specifications, and assuming the charge to be in proper form, the object of the specifications is to point wherein the defendant has failed in zeal, and faithfulness, and diligence, as a minister. The particular instances in which the lack of these qualities has been manifested should be exhibited in the specifications. We look to see them stand there, and find nothing of the kind.

Specification first is no specification at all. The substance of it is that equivocal language has been used in sermons printed in the *Chicago Pulpit*, the *Alliance*, and in the volume entitled "Truths for To-day." In these sermons, the references to cardinal doctrines are declared to be vague, and it is charged that they have not been unequivocally affirmed. Now the object of specification is to tell a man of what particular dereliction he is accused, that he may deny his guilt in regard to that particular. This specification permits the prosecutor to seek his evidence in any of the volumes of sermons alluded to, while it gives the accused no notice as to the particular utterance or mode of speech which is objected to.

Specification second is that the effect of Professor Swing's offense has been to awaken doubts in the minds of some of his brethren, and to cause Unitarians to claim him. It is further asserted that Mr. Swing, knowing that he was suspected of doctrinal unsoundness, has not declared his position by preaching sermons especially for that purpose, nor in any other way. This specification is remarkable only for what Hamlet would call a "plentiful lack" of definiteness. Men are indicted for crime, but who ever heard of a man being indicted for the effects of a crime? But here the accused is charged with the consequences of his pretended offenses, and that, knowing these consequences, he did not reform.

Now, if the accused had been guilty of an ecclesiastical offense, he should be charged specially with that, and tried upon it, and not, as is here most unjustly done, be arraigned for the consequences of a pretended offense, and for not reforming, though knowing these consequences.

Specification third, in its first averment, declares that the accused has given the weight of his influence in favor of Unitarianism. Now, an influence grows out of acts, and to charge a man with using an influence is charging him with a conclusion. Instead of that, he should be charged with certain specific acts, and he should be punished for these acts, if he is guilty of them, and if they constitute a disciplinable offense, but not otherwise. He is next said to be guilty of unworthy and extravagant laudation of John Stuart Mill. But this is a conclusion which the prosecutor arrives at in his own mind. If the accused has extravagantly lauded Mr. Mill, he did it by the use of certain words, which ought to have been quoted in the specification, and on these he ought to be tried. But instead of this, the prosecutor has drawn his own conclusion from the words which he does not quote, and then seeks to prosecute the defendant on the conclusion which he draws.

In this, therefore, the specification is defective in form. He sets forth the conclusion which the prosecutors draw from the language of the defendant, but not the language itself. It is for the court to draw the conclusions. But may not a man speak words of praise of an atheist? Not of his atheism, for with doing this Professor Patton does not go so far as to charge Professor Swing. "The unworthy and extravagant laudations" of Mr. Mill had respect, as even the prosecutor himself confesses, only to his great abilities, acknowledged by all, and to his fruitful labors in the fields of philosophy, of literature, and of political, moral, and social reform. In all these departments of human effort, it cannot be denied that Mr. Mill was an earnest and conscientious worker. And having been such, is it a sin to speak well of him so far as these labors are concerned? To say that Mr. Mill labored with all his might to tear down and destroy the Christian religion is simply to say what is notoriously untrue. He did nothing of the kind. It was not till his autobiography appeared, almost at the close of his life, that men knew what his opinions were on the subject of religion. He had, to all, except to his intimate friends, if not even to those, kept his opinions concealed. He was not known as an atheist, nor even as an enemy of religion, except in the sense that he was not known as its friend. But even if he had been an open and vindictive enemy of Christianity, should we therefore refuse to recognize his great gifts? Professor Swing may have formed too favorable an opinion of the man, and of his general work. His view is one with which the prosecutor evidently does not coincide, and with which members of this court very possibly may not coincide. But what then? Is it not better to err on the side of charity than on the side of severity? Professor Swing did not fail to see, nor did he fail to point out very emphatically, the defect in Mr. Mill's character. Upon his life, so abounding and so magnificent in its labors in behalf of philosophy and reform, he wrote the word "vanity" as his final verdict, in broad and legible characters, and even though you suppose that his judgment of him as a philosopher, as a political economist, and as a reformer, be a too favorable one, are you going to regard this as an ecclesiastical misdemeanor which required a formal censure? I have not so poor an opinion of this court as to believe that they will for one moment entertain such a thought. No, sir. Professor Patton is wrong. He is wrong in thinking that the religion of Christ is to be commended and advanced by treating every unbeliever in it as a heathen man, a publican. He is wrong in himself insisting upon the principle of refusing to commend what is commendable in another, simply because he is not all that we know he should be. Not so did the Saviour, for He commended one almost warmly for the good qualities that he possessed; but He did not omit to say, "One thing thou lackest." Lacking that, he lacked all things. It is not in any important respect different from this, that Professor Swing has spoken of John Stuart Mill. He has not, therefore, done in this matter what amounts even to an indiscretion, least of all to an offense, and hence all the prosecutor's ingenious and skillful pleading does not deserve, as I am persuaded it will not receive at your hands, any serious consideration.

Professor Swing is next charged with having said, in substance, in the *Lakeside Monthly*, that Robert Patterson and Robert Collyer preached the same doctrines. This also is a conclusion of Professor Patton, and one which does manifest violence to the language which the defendant employed. He said that the two ministers preached practically; and to infer from this that they preached the same Gospel, and that the gospel is mutable, is about as reasonable as to assume that two men are declared to preach the same gospel because they both preach earnestly, or both preach from manuscript, or are both eloquent men.

In like manner, the prosecutor's comments upon the words "local gospel" grossly perverted Professor Swing's meaning, as if he had said that the gospel was one thing in Pittsburgh, and another in St. Louis, and still another in Chicago. I submit that no fair-minded man, reading another for the sole purpose of getting at his meaning, would be in danger of mistaking the meaning of these words. He would understand them as referring to the different modes of presenting the gospel, and not as signifying a different gospel for each. In this sense, the local gospel where I preach, and the local gospel where Professor Patton preaches, are very different from each other; and I suppose they always will be, unless — which is exceedingly unlikely— the prosecutor comes to adopt substantially my methods of stating and illustrating the truth. [Applause.] Mr. Moderator, it is hard to be patient with a critic so unreasonably captious, so grossly unfair, so absurdly whimsical, as the framer of this indictment has shown himself to be. I say, unhesitatingly and reverently, that if he were to subject the language of Christ to the same torture that he applies to Professor Swing, he would have no difficulty at all in making Him out a teacher of false doctrines. [Applause.] There is, then, nothing in this specification that is definite except one act, and one saying. The act is that Professor Swing gave a lecture in aid of a unitarian church, and the saying is that he considered religion a model of virtue. But neither the act nor the saying amounts to an offense.

By no fair construction can this act of lecturing in aid of the chapel, erected in memory of Mary Price Collier, be taken out of the domain of Christian casuistry and private conscience. There is where it belongs, and there is where the adjudication must be held, and not in this court. You may say, Mr. Moderator, that you would not perform such a service, and it would be your right to decline any such invitation, if you were to receive one. But you have no right to impeach the motives, still less to demand the formal censure, of a brother who, in the exercise of his own judgment, and in conformity with the decisions of his own conscience, renders this service when asked to do so. So great and good a man, and so sound a theologian as the venerable Dr. Hodge, gave his countenance and support publicly to the Roman Catholic Church, on a memorable occasion which we all remember. Yet it has been the fashion with Protestants — and I presume the prosecutor has followed the fashion — to denounce this Church as "the mother of harlots"— that great Babylon whose exemplary and terrible overthrow is set forth in the visions of the Apocalypse. Liberty of private judgment must be allowed here. Because you think that temperance means total abstinence, you must not arraign the man who cannot see exactly with your eyes. Because you count it an offense against good morals and Divine law to ride in the street-cars on Sunday, you have no right to indict before the Church a man who may happen to think and act differently. Because you believe it to be a sin against God and man to use tobacco, you must not therefore undertake to set up your own private opinion as the rule of faith and practice for others.

Besides, if it is a disciplinable offense for a Presbyterian minister to help Unitarianism by lecturing—and it is simply a begging of the question to say that it does—is it not equally a disciplinable offense for a Presbyterian elder to keep on sale Unitarian and even infidel books? The lecturer did his work without pay, but the bookseller carries on his trade for the purpose of honorable and private gain. No, sir. You cannot adjudicate on a question of this kind. It is a gross invasion of a private right to undertake to do so. So much for the act which this specification sets forth as an offense.

How is it with the saying? Professor Swing is arraigned for saying that the gospel is a mode of virtue. Well, is not that a good definition of the gospel on its practical side? It certainly is not a mode of vice. The language does not refer to the gospel in the abstract, or as a system of doctrines received by the understanding, but it sets forth that Gospel by its fruits. It declares that the effect of the Gospel is to make men virtuous, to lead them to holiness, and to prepare them for a better life hereafter. When, therefore, the prosecutor criticises and carps at this language, as if there were no natural nor even possible explanation of it which would make it accord with evangelical teaching, the presumption is at least a fair one that he believes in a salvation that is divorced from morals.

Having spoken an hour, Mr. Noyes said he was too much exhausted to go on; and the Presbytery therefore adjourned until half-past nine Friday morning.

FRIDAY, MAY 15TH.

PROF. SWING'S PLEA.

The Chicago Presbytery met again, at the First Presbyterian Church, and again devoted its energies to a hearing of the arguments on behalf of the defense. There was, as usual, a large attendance despite the inclement weather. The court was called to order at 2:30 o'clock by the moderator, Rev. Mr. Mitchell, and after prayer the floor was tendered to Rev. Mr. Noyes for a continuance of the argument, which he cut short on Thursday in consequence of illness. Instead of Rev. Mr. Noyes, Prof. Swing advanced, dropped his overcoat, and made his bow. His appearance behind the pulpit was greeted with great applause. He spoke as follows:

MR. MODERATOR: It was the understanding among my brethren that the burden of this matter should not fall upon me, both on account of my ill health and distaste for it, and up to this morning I supposed I should have nothing to say; but my counsel having very poor health, I have thought it best to assist him this afternoon by speaking before you for the space of perhaps an hour, and touching upon some of the points which, perhaps, I could clear of doubt more easily than he could himself. I know not what may be the etiquette of the case. I hope the prosecutor will consider it as no breach of etiquette. I do not know the exact duties of the prisoner at the bar, [laughter] but would state that the ground I will pass over will not be passed over by Brother Noyes, and thus time will be saved, —at least not lost by our both speaking.

I thought it would be my pleasure to fulfill the words of Lucretius, "that it is the province of some to sit upon the calm mountain summit and see the poor sailors struggling and toiling in the storm and waves beneath;" but the illness of my counsel has disturbed my repose, and has compelled me to go down into this battlefield. I shall, I hope, not be compelled to go beyond the skirmish line, for the sound of war frightens me [laughter], especially when the war is waged for conquest, or for the extension of slavery beyond its present limits. As some statesman said he would not want to tell a lie for anything less than an empire, so it does not seem desirable to go into a theological fight where the price of victory or the pain of defeat is exceedingly small. Xenophon says of Clearchus that, notwithstanding his bright armor and royal robes, yet, when the baggage wagons got entangled or stalled, he would put his own shoulder to the wheel, going himself into the mud. The theological baggage wagons upon my side of the house are blockaded to-day, and, like the old general, willingly I descend into the mud. [Laughter.] Let me ask your attention to Stuart Mill. When he died, our statesmen had just been breaking their hearts over the pursuit of presidential honors. Greeley and Chase had both died of grief over lost honors. In such an hour I thought it a piece of good fortune that I could hold up before the public a name that found sufficient honor and sufficient object of life in the greatness of personal character. And hence I said:

"If it were not for such men as Mr. Mill coming here and there in human life, we might fail to know what that thing called soul is. I do not know where, in the public men of our land, we can see so well the picture of human dignity. Swayed out of balance by a love of office and gold, disturbed by a storm of bad passions, our public men reveal the soul, not in its nobleness, but in some shape that begs for pity and forgiveness.

"Our great men are all said to die disappointed, and half broken-hearted, because they fail to catch a four-year bauble from the tumultuous crowd. To run for president, and then die in glory or in cloud, according to the counting of the votes, has become a brief history of some of our greatest men. It is a sad remembrance of Mr. Greeley and Mr. Chase, that their failure to reach a great office turned their days into a winter of discontent.

"All over our land it seems to be forgotten that a human soul may be something to which no office can add anything, and from which no political defeat can take anything away.

"God has in no way connected human greatness with a ballot-box.

> "The boast of heraldry, the pomp of power,
> And all that rank and fortune e'er gave
> Await alike the inevitable hour;
> And paths of glory lead but to the grave."

"From such a scene it is sweet to turn to a man who might have honored any office, but whom no office could have honored. Nothing lasting for four years could have added to a soul great before that four years and great afterward. Mr. Mill could scarcely have known when an earthly honor came to his forehead, or when it departed. Like Marcus Aurelius, whose laurels of virtue were greater than the throne of the Roman empire, Mr. Mill's own forehead was nobler in itself than it could have been rendered by all the political wreaths of his generation.

"True greatness never reveals nor cherishes much ambition, for the gift of mind and the possession of a profound character leave little for the soul to wish or for earth to give. Hence in the blessed life of the Saviour we perceive no trace of popular ambition, but everywhere simple greatness of spirit, as if that were the supreme destiny of rational being.

"Oh, what an era would begin in our land, if, instead of waiting for something outside of self to come to us and honor us, our citizens should unfold the glory within them, as a flower sends forth beauty and perfume from its own opening heart."

And then, this was the chief point: that the glory of such a mind and of such a philosophy as Mill possessed came to him through Christianity; for though Mr. Mill was not a Christian, yet Christianity had always been all around him and had forced him into every virtue he possessed; had given him the entire character of the nineteenth century; just as Lady Hester Stanhope, flying to the south land to escape England, carried with her everywhere English customs and English thought. So Stuart Mill, though an atheist, carried, in all his thoughts and in all his life, every germ of Christianity except his personal belief.

Mill's character was all wrought out in a Christian atmosphere although his father vainly tried to shield the child from the influence of the great religion of Jesus Christ—tried in vain. And then I said what a liberal world need regard most was, not that he was not a Presbyterian or a Methodist, but that the poor unfortunate man had no trace of any kind of religion in his soul. We would have been thankful if he had had any form of religion in his heart.

Now, while I was thus dealing with Stuart Mill, what was my prosecutor doing? Had he called together 2,000 to tell you how Stuart Mill had been sent to perdition from all eternity? Was he faithful as a great public man to his trust? That is a matter of opinion. But it is my impression that he was praising Agassiz, not because he held an orthodox creed (Oh! no, that was not what his liberal world rejoiced over), but he was rejoicing because, upon some occasion, that great naturalist had acknowledged a supreme being, and just barely escaped being an infidel. And did the prosecutor avail himself of Agassiz's death to preach at McVicker's that a prayer is only offensive to God unless it be connected with a belief in the Deity, or expiatory atonement of Christ? Did he rise to the greatness of the occasion and inform the community that there was no hope for Agassiz's soul? Did he come forward with his ordination vows upon him and hand over Agassiz to perdition in the following language from the confession of faith: "Much less can men, not professing the Christian religion, be saved in any other way whatsoever, be they ever so diligent to frame their lives according to the light of nature, and the law of that religion they profess; and to assert and maintain that they may is very pernicious, and to be detested."

And yet, in his paper, that went to 14,000 families, he held up Agassiz as a Christian and scientific man.

Let us pass to a second offense alleged by the prosecutor: "We know not what nor where is our God, our heaven." This sermon was preached to show the reason why the religious world had always been full of debate. It came partly from the fact that moral ideas have no such definiteness as is enjoyed by mathematical ideas. There has never been one set of men to hold that twice two make four, and another set to hold that twice two make five, because these ideas are fixed. But there has been one set of men to hold to the theory of an expiatory atonement and another to hold to the theory of a propitiatory atonement because men have no slate and pencil by which to fix these ideas beyond all debate, no pyramid upon which to measure these things. The prosecutor had expounded the confession of faith and declared that he had a standard. But unfortunately the whole religious world are not Presbyterians, and unfortunately these Presbyterians, who are here to-day, do not understand it alike.

Therefore we do not mathematically know what our God is, and we are not called upon exactly to know. You do not know it as you know that two and two are four or that they are not five; and hence the debates and discords, just such as has gathered us here to-day.

But the prosecutor has not arraigned *me* only for this dreadful idea that we do not know mathematically about our God. He has not arraigned me alone.

If the Holy Spirit was so unfortunate as to furnish poor me with such a text as that of the sermon "Clouds and Darkness are Bound About Him," the prosecutor knows where to lay his charges and specifications in this particular. It is intimated in Job that no one by searching can find out God, and hence when the presbytery shall past sentence upon me I shall insist upon their making Job and the 97th psalm *particeps criminis* in this case—[applause and laughter]—and if in such good company as Job and the Psalmist, I should not much fear the prosecutor of this case, he need not be much surprised. [Laughter.] I will anticipate the reply of the prosecutor. I will not wait for him to rise to explain. He will plead that the bible was written before the confession of faith and that the Psalmist was in doubt about the nature of God and that Paul shrank before the mystery of heaven, saying "eye hath not seen, nor ear heard," because they lived before the Westminster confession had been formulated—[laughter]—at Westminster, and expounded at Chicago. In the revised editions of the bible, when readers shall come upon my text, "clouds and darkness are round about him," they will no doubt see a marginal reference "for refutation of this idea see Prof. Patton's charges and specifications." [Laughter.]

But to be serious again. Prof. Patton points to the confession of faith and reads: "God is a spirit." Well, does the prosecutor know what a spirit is? It is to be hoped he will elucidate this point and also tell us where heaven is, for he will not be so unkind as to arraign a brother for want of information when he himself possesses it and refuses to deliver it to me, and to the presbytery. A young man stepped up to a clergyman east and asked him if it was possible to know all about God. The clergyman, who was a droll fellow, as Trowbridge says, replied that personally he had no such knowledge, but that there was a man out in Minnesota who knew all about him. [Laughter.] Well, now, brethren, if we have this information at some point nearer than Minnesota, it ought to be forthcoming —[laughter]—and free to all.

Let us pass to another idea that has perplexed the prosecutor: "This multitude measures a great revelation of God above that day when earth possessed but one man or family, and that one without language, and without virtue." "In the first human family God could no more display His perfections than a musician like Mozart could unfold his genius to an infant or to a South sea islander." Now the meaning of that passage is this: I know not how he may understand it, but the sermon was upon the days that are past. "Ask, now, the days that are past. Look into history——" and I found, in looking into history, that the glory of God unfolds itself as the human race advances. "The 6,000 years past are the great unfolding of the Almighty; not in the Darwinian sense, nor in the Spencerian sense, but in the Christian sense. Adam, however innocent, and however beautiful in his character, as I believe he was both innocent and beautiful, had no cities, no arts, no eloquence, no poetry, no cross of Jesus Christ, no benevolence, no charity for the multitude. Hence God no more unfolded his perfections in Adam than Mozart or Beethoven could make known their vast realm of music to an infant or a savage. It is the grand opening up of the world that gives us the glory of God; the manifold glory of God. The many-pictured glory of God is all thrown forward and made visible by this ever-unfolding earth, and from the very moment God created Adam his own glory went marching forward."

If the prosecutor knew the meaning of the illustration, he would know that this language would not imply that Adam was either an infant or a savage. It simply means that God's glory is too large a spectacle to be cast upon Adam alone. It required all the 6,000 years of humanity combined together to reveal this wisdom, and power, and grace, and manifold glory of God. Why, the prosecutor has taken the cross of Jesus Christ out of the world, and has the world just as great in Adam alone as it is in the whole human race.

And then I went on to illustrate, or to apply this thought: "So each individual cannot gather up the glory of his life in any one year. It must lie all over his past. It is all his past he must drag along after him, and if he has for 50 years fed the poor and blessed them like a Saviour, or if he has cared for the slave like a Wilberforce, all his life, or preached like a Paul or a Wesley all his life, he will go into futurity with all this glorious record back of him." And here the bible must be arraigned, for it says "their works do follow them" and the converse was shown to be true, that if a human soul spent life in seeking gold only, or in seeking wicked pleasures, or in buying and selling slaves or even in prosecuting heretics, that long life thus spent would come dragging after the soul into eternity. And I said that "no man can go to heaven gloriously unless he can look sweetly back." If this be heresy, Mr. Moderator, write me down as a heretic, and make the letters large and plain. Why, even old Livy said, "You must keep continually looking at the past, because," he says, "things that are past may be repented of, but they never can be erased." And one of our own poets says: "To morrow you may do your worst, for I lived yesterday." And old Martial says: "Did'st thou say thou wilt live to-morrow? He is a wise man who lived yesterday."

To-day is the sublime part of life, because it is continually making that yesterday which will always follow us, go where we may, for glory or for shame.

And hence, I rebuked the young people present for always living in the future, and paying no attention to the past. And I quoted from Dryden to them, saying:

"Trust on and think the morrow will repay;
The morrow's falser than the former day;
Lies worse, and while it says you shall be blest,
Steals all the pleasures that you once possessed."

Let us come now to the dear Penelope and Socrates. [Laughter.] My brethren, you must excuse me for treating this case with something like levity, for it has not in it to me one particle of solemnity.

Now that sermon was all regarding the value of being above saying or seeming. It was on Soul Culture. The idea was that the value of life lies not in what creed one says over and over, but in what creed one lives. And hence I said: "A soul with a defective creed may be higher and may be nobler than a soul which knows more but which disregards all its precepts"—an idea I have heard all my life in the Presbyterian church.

Dr. MacMaster, whom the prosecutor succeeds, legally and chronologically, said that he believed that "somewhere on the confines of heaven would be found Socrates and Penelope." And I think our general assembly, a few years ago, offered a premium to some one who would produce the best tract upon the condition of the heathen in the future world; and Dr. Smythe, of South Carolina, who took the prize said, "All those heathen who live up to the light of their best knowledge might hope for happiness beyond."

I did not say how great was the happiness of Penelope or Socrates. But the prosecutor has unwittingly arraigned Jesus Christ. I fear my zealous friend or enemy, friend I guess, does not read his bible as much as he does his confession of faith. But, no wonder, for he says: "We must guard against too great attachment to scripture phraseology, and must wait to have our religion well formulated." [Laughter.] Regarding Socrates and Penelope we shall now read from the words of Christ. Did you know He has spoken of them? He has. "Woe! unto thee, Chorasin (Catherine II.), for it shall be more tolerable for Tyre and Sidon (Socrates and Penelope) in the day of judgment than for thee." Now we again anticipate the objection of the prosecutor. He will say this scripture was announced before the confession was formulated,—[laughter]—and that my ordination vows were upon me. Well, in subsequent editions of the bible, readers will find a marginal reference upon this passage from Christ, "For refutation of this passage about Tyre and Sidon, see Prof. Patton's on Socrates and Penelope, chap. 10. sec. 24." [Laughter.] But let us pass to other things. The learned prosecutor after unfolding to you the evolution theory of Spencer and others, says, as usual, Mr. Swing holds these, and yet I am, I believe, the only Chicago minister who has published a sermon, in part, against that theory. It is singular that while I only have published a sermon against the evolution thereof, I should be the one arraigned for not doing it. While the prosecutor was proving the divinity or deity of Christ, I don't known which, from the date Anno Domini, claiming that no nation would reckon its years from anything less than a God, while he was thus learning the divine origin of Mahommed and of the Olympiads of Greece, and of Romulus and Remus, I was on the same Sunday trying to overthrow the Spencerian theory of evolution. Here is what I said: "It is not, certainly, a myth that there is a human race; and hence, there must have been a first pair in this long series, and this first pair must have had a first home and a creator just at hand; and this pair must have made their first move in virtue or sin; and from what sin we now see in the world, not much doubt can remain as to what line of conduct this first pair followed, and that they early left a paradise of virtue is the verdict of history. The theory most in conflict with this bible picture of primitive man is the almost popular notion that man is a gradual result of progress in the animal kingdom, and never had a paradise, but is on the way toward one, from a cellular and electric starting point a million years back. Against this theory, however, rises up the fact that in the thousands of years of history no animal is showing the least sign of passing over into that moral consciousness, that selfhood which so wonderfully distinguishes man. The highest order of brutes are doing absolutely nothing toward forming a language or toward reaching that consciousness of 'me' and not 'me,' which joins man to the divine; there is no effort visible on the part of the most intelligent *quadrumana* to build a schoolhouse or start a country newspaper; and if in the historic period no progress whatever has been made, and that too with the advantage of human association, what could they have done in two historic periods? If 6,000 years give nothing, what will 6,000,000 years give? The best reason I can myself bring to bear upon this matter leads me to see man setting forth as man and setting forth from a creator; hence he had a place which we may call Eden, and lowly reason may join the bible in giving it river banks and trees and flowers and the song of birds."

The prosecutor has read my sermons tolerably well only. Let us pass now to the 109th psalm. I am very glad to see that this matter has at last been put to rest. The prosecutor has wholly given up all that he claimed here. It was my theory you know, that this was a special psalm, no part of the perpetual hymnology of the world not inspired for all times, like the 23d psalm or the 90th. My theory was that it was an adaptation to a military age, when the church advanced, not by persuading its enemies but by exterminating them; a psalm dictated by the Almighty for an age a hundred or five hundred years or more, and that Christ has announced the perpetual law the everlasting law of life, when He has said that you shall pray for your enemies and bless them that persecute you and despitefully use you.

My point was that, as Christ repealed a divorce law which was divinely given for a certain period only, so He did, by His person, repeal also a psalm full of curses, and took it away from everlasting hymnology of life; that the same God who passed a bad divorce law, could inspire a bad psalm also, and that when He recalled the one, He could recall the other. And though I may be mistaken, yet my principle is founded right on the inspiration of the bible.

But this idea that it was a perpetual psalm, the prosecutor has at last given up, for he says now that the 109th psalm was written as a curse upon Judas Iscariot.

This is all I want. Only his theory is narrower than mine, for my theory was that it was used by the Jews as a military hymn for hundred of years, and then, by divine command, applied also to Judas Iscariot. But if the prosecutor tells us that it was even too bad for the Jewish people to sing, and that I laid dormant a thousand years waiting for a great traitor like Judas to come, before the psalm should spring into life, I have not in my heart any reason to object. And Judas being now dead, the psalm has been abrogated from Christian hymnology, I trust,—expired by limitation,—[laughter]—if Judas is indeed dead. [Laughter.]

I know not whether anyone needs a word with regard to those Hebrew wars, but I will make a remark or two regarding them. My position all along has been this: That God in the bible revealed two forms of His will; that in some parts of the bible He expresses Himself absolutely, as in the Sermon upon the Mount. He there announces everlasting principles for all the human race everywhere, but that in other parts of the Old Testament God accepts of a temporary kind of morality, and that God was everywhere influenced by the presence of man, and was not promulging His own abstract law, but was everywhere accommodating Himself to the presence of a sinful race; and hence, all through the Old Testament, it is not God alone that is marching along—it is God and a wicked race. And hence, when he permitted or ordered the Israelites to go up and destroy the Canaanites, it was not God acting absolutely and announcing a great principle of action, but it was God acting under the influence of the presence of those wicked Israelites; not investing those wars with or evolving them from His divine mind, but permitting them, tolerating them, just as He did the old divorce law and all the wickedness of that era.

This is my position on that point. But when Christ came to the New Testament, there He announces an era of peace—everlasting peace. He began to unfold Himself, not as a deity restricted by the presence of sinful man, but as a deity all glorious in his own right, and in His own name unfolding the everlasting in Jesus Christ. I hope I am theologian enough to understand this, and hence I said that young men are coming along now who want to know about these things; and they all know what infidels say. They all know what Mr. Froude has said about the 109th psalm, and hence they want a theory to be handed them by our theological professors and our clergymen which will save them from the infidelity of Froude and men of that class. Here, the prosecutor says, I indorse Froude. This is simply nonsense. What I plead for is, that men of learning like Prof. Patton, having his high position, shall elaborate some theory of revelation that a young man can take to his heart—[applause and laughter]—and not say, when some one asks him, "What about the 109th psalm," "You go and mind your business, young man; that is inspired!" [Laughter.] That is what I call the theory of admiration. [Laughter.] A young man comes to him and says: "What about those bloody wars where the Israelites went out and destroyed the Canaanites, men, women, and children?" and he replies, "Young man, the bible is inspired. It is the word of God." Now is not that horrible? That makes infidels—covers the world with infidels. And yet, there is an explanation of all the difficulties of the Old Testament, which it is the duty of every clergyman having the vows of Jesus Christ upon him to unfold to the young men of this age and crush Froude to powder beneath their logic—not their malice.

Then I observe, too, when it came time to build the temple, God would not let David build the temple at all, because he has made his hands so bloody in these wars. It seems that God Himself did not like those wars, and He let Solomon build it, because He wanted a man of peace, whose hands were not stained with blood.

Now, Mr. Moderator and brethren, I come to the point where I shall point out to you the difference between the prosecutor's theology and my own, in some respects. And as he justly quoted, yesterday, the aphorism from Newman's Grammar of Assent, that there are times when "egotism is modesty." I shall repeat it here, because I do not wish to pretend that anybody holds the views I shall express here other than myself. I shall not pretend that they are accepted or welcome in the whole presbytery. They may be a weakness, and hence to stand by them alone is an egotism that is modesty. The remarks about to be offered will explain my position as to faith and infidelity and to Old Testament inspiration and to the call for the ministry. My idea is this: Prof. Patton's theology all proceeds from God as a simple despot. Mine from God as a reasonable being. By Prof. Patton's theology, I do not mean the Presbyterian theology, or the Calvinistic theology, it is infinitely worse than both,—[laughter],—but I mean his own personal theology, as he has unfolded it since he came to this city, and, latterly, to this trial. One of the eighteenth century philosophers said the universe is an enormous will rushing into life. The theology of the prosecutor of this case is nothing but the picture of an enormous power rushing into a moral world. It is power; it is force. You dare not subject his Deity to any question whatever.

As Luther said, "It is the glory of human faith to suppose God to be just when he damns the innocent." So the theology of my friend is one that does nothing but look down to earth and say, "God! God!" As though God could not be thought about, or prayed to, or spoken to. But who this God is, how He acts, upon what basis, he dares not inquire, because it would be "rationalism" if he did—he so fears rationalism. When, therefore, a young man comes to this form of theology and humbly inquires about the slaughter of the Canaanites, or the 109th psalm, and says, "How shall I answer Mr. Froude and show him and all the bold infidels that my church is a sensible, reasonable church?" the answer is, "Go, young man, and tell Froude that he was foreordained to be damned! Go! and if you raise such an inquiry again you will soon be in a similar condition." [Laughter.]

Now, I hope I do his theology no injustice—I have studied it well and thought over it. This is his method with regard to the inspiration of the Old Testament. So with salvation by faith. You dare not ask what faith is—whether it is a natural or moral excellence—that has induced God to crown it with such glory in the New Testament, in the Christian religion. Any inquiry on this point, is *rationalism.* It is your business to believe, and there terminates your inquiry. I have read it all over, and read it long.

Now, on the opposite, I believe a theology which not only believes that God is a sovereign, but that he is a reasonable sovereign, and that beneath all his commands there will, for the most part, be some beautiful reason visible, ever unfolding itself.

Faith, therefore, is clothed with judicial worth, because it possesses such an intrinsic worth in the mind and in the heart, such power it has to carry the mind forward, to cheer up the heart in dark hours, and to transform us into the likeness of Jesus Christ. Looking out and seeing this faith that it had the power to take the whole world into its arms and all remodel it; therefore He said, "By faith ye shall be saved." He did not go forth as a tyrant or as a despot, but as a reasonable loving father of us all.

God has pronounced intemperance to be a curse. No drunkard shall inherit the kingdom. This being announced, all the scientific men go to work and find a reason for this curse. It is a judicial act, and hence they seek a reason. They seek it in the mind, in the blood, in the burnt-up coatings of the stomach, in the inflamed brain, in the loss of money, in the loss of mind, in the ruin of the wife and the children.

Yes, God having said, "The intemperate man shall be punished," men look into this intemperance to find the reason of this punishment. But when God pronounces the woe upon the infidel, you must not inquire about the natural drift of this infidelity. That is rationalism!

You dare not ask whether it wages any war in the soul such as intemperance does in the body; whether it closes the gate of moral sense and shuts out a world from the heart; whether it shuts out Christ and heaven from the soul; whether it be a natural damnation like intemperance as well as a judicial one. Oh! no. If you do this, you will be arraigned before the Presbytery for not regarding your ordination vows.

Well, brethren, if my ordination vows impose upon me to live a life of ignorance and stupidity, destitute of all inquiry, the sooner you relieve me of these ordination vows the better. ["Amen!" and applause.]

The fact that intemperance injures men by God's decree does not debar me from looking into the natural operation of that intemperance; and the fact that God saves a soul by faith, and condemns a soul for infidelity, does not debar me from looking into the natural quality of that belief and that unbelief. But, according to the theology of the prosecutor, infidelity may be a virtue, for all I know, and faith may be a vice. All he knows is that God forbade the one and commanded the other. And there he stops. His theology always terminates with the fact. It dare not ever ask a single question. It is just, "Believe and be saved. Believe not and be damned." That is all there is of it. Hence, I say his God has marched right through his theology; has no sweet reasonableness, but is only an enormous will rushing out like a hurricane to the fields of His own dear children, trampling alike over their cradle and their grave.

Now I am as firm a believer in salvation by faith as the prosecutor in this case, only his faith is but a despotic command from the Almighty. Mine, I feel, is from a God, all-wise, unfolding His wisdom to His children. Hence my faith is one clothed not only with good works, but clothed with sense. [Applause.]

This dreadful hostility to reason has robbed Prof. Patton of almost the entire world, apart from his little narrow church world.

To say that man was a religious being before Christianity, and that religion was not forced upon man as it might be forced upon the brute world; that it was demanded by man's nature, and was a flower that came naturally right up out of his heart, is something that greatly angers him. Religion is something born right out of the heart because man saw before him a heaven to be gained and a hell to be shunned. He was a moral creature. Prof. Patton, in his own inaugural, says a man is religious at bottom. He ought to have made the sentence end in "religious" and put the "at bottom" in the beginning. But that is a small matter. [Laughter.]

He says there is no fitness, that we know of, naturally, between the soul and Christianity simply; God came in the days of Christ and planted Christianity because He wanted to. The time had come for doing it. There was nothing in man to suggest any such kindness. There was nothing in the human family to render natural such a gift from God. The gift of Christianity to the world was just like giving speech to a corpse, or giving wings to a clod, a pure act of omnipotence. Thus, in the theology of our friend, on the opposite, you will perceive nothing but an enormous will that explains nothing. It is a great foreordaining power, destitute alike of intelligence and humanity.

By pondering this over, you will find what the new school theology is. And furthermore, it would seem that this enormous will does not touch the world anywhere between Adam and Christ—anywhere, scarcely: for when I attempted to show that God laid the foundations of the Christian ministry when He made man, and that, as He set Moses apart for a law-giver, and Aaron apart for a white-robed priest, and David apart for a king, and Daniel apart to be a prophet, and thus, in the deeply religious nature of His children laid the foundation of the Christian ministry for that differentiation of man which Christ afterward so reinforced with the truth of His gospel and the power of His cross, our prosecutor absolutely arraigns me and says the ministry began at year one Anno Domini, and refers me to his Confession of faith.

The Christian ministry, or the ministry, began at the advent. That is, in his theology, after 4,000 years had passed—after tens of thousands of ministers of God's own religion had ministered at the altars, from Abel to Samuel, and from Samuel to the very day of Christ. Then God came and established the ministry, not on account of any need of his church or of mankind; not on account of any desirableness in the office that there should be a division of labor; not for any reason whatever, visible or invisible, but just because this great Being, which the prosecutor supposes to be God, so desired—God so wanted it. That is all. God so compassed the situation, and so concluded and so ordained.

This is the theology that makes infidels. Thus God is separated from all those four thousand years between Christ and Adam, and is waked up, at last, from a long neglect, and concludes to found a religious ministry.

Now, although the prosecutor made the accused out to be an infidel, a Brahmin, and a evolutionist, and a Sabellian, and a Unitarian, yet the accused, with all these faults upon him, can show to this court a better view of Providence, a more universal, a more careful and delightful Heavenly Father than the prosecutor can present.

The God of my friend seems only to come to this world once in a while, and then as a clap of thunder strikes it, and then withdraws again for a thousand years. [Laughter].

His Creator came suddenly, and laid down Christianity as though in a night. He had not been preparing for it at all in those four thousand years. He suddenly invented the ministry also, and introduced it for the first time at the advent of the Saviour, "See Confession of Faith," he says [laughter] whereas my Providence has been holding and building up that ministry for six thousand years, right along, without any intermission—no rest. When he gave man a religious nature, when he placed heaven and hell before him, and when he called the sons of Levi to the altar and decorated them in white, spotless robes, this Providence, which I believe in, has been all along, from the earliest morning of earth, right close by His people-building up this holy ministry, in Whose name we came here to-day.

And now, since in our century the prosecutor holds to the idea of an imperfect Providence, for the most part coming to His church alone. [Laughter.]

His own witnesses here, Mr. Goudy and Mr. Miller, join with him in separating God from such beings as Lincoln and Washington, and indeed from all the human marching host, and in employing God only in looking up young men for theological seminaries in our church [laughter and applause] thus giving us the world of the atheist, except so far as the church is concerned. But in the theology of our friend, if theology that can be called which has everything in it except God, the providence of the Almighty must undergo a more painful limitation. I do not mean he is conscious of this, I am speaking only of his theology.

Now, we know this: That the prosecutor will deny that God could call any heterodox clergyman to the pulpit. The advantage of having the Deity to superintend this work must lie in his supreme advantages for knowing the true theology and the pure heart. Hence, we cannot suppose God calls a heterodox minister to the pulpit. Hence all heterodox clergymen must be set aside from the care of God's special providence. If in the ministry, they must come in only as Sumner came to his office, or Wilberforce to his.

So the Professor has limited God's special providence still more yet, to only the orthodox clergy; and when he proved not long ago, in his paper, that he that rejects infant baptism, as not orthodox, you see how he is limiting the care of God in this direction. And thus we must cast away from God's special love and call all those who hold not our standards.

And then, furthermore, he excludes all elders as having never been called to this holy work; excluding such men as Geo. H. Stewart, and J. V. Farwell; and all women such as Miss Smiley—[laughter]—and all revivalists such as Moody, for I believe he was not an ordained minister. And thus we have him narrowing down the providence of God, until we find, in looking around here and there that it is caring for a few clergymen left in Zion's great church. My friends, when I look upon such men as Sumner and Burke and William Wirt and Wilberforce, and feel that they came into being only by an ordinary providence or else through God's neglect, because those elders did not know whether Mr. Lincoln was called or not,—he came, perhaps, by God's neglect,—and when I look upon some clergyman,—and am told that these clergymen came by some miraculous method, let us pray God that he may return to an ordinary providence hereafter. [Long continued laughter and applause.]

Now, my brethren, I have but two remarks to make, and one is this: The prosecutor called your attention to Penelope, who in the day-time wove her woof and in the night-time unraveled it. I thank him for thus recalling this, for it has been several years since I have read the Odyssey. He is the greatest Penelope of all in this matter, for whereas, my brethren, on one day he proved to you, in a whole day's long argument, that I did not believe in hell, he yesterday showed you that I held a religion without hope—a religion of good works, he said. Where can you find hope in that. Now when you come to condemn me I don't want you to condemn me for holding both a religion without hell and without hope. [Laughter and applause.] Take one or the other. Again he proved to you, by a long argument, that a Sabellian is a man who fully identifies Jesus Christ with God. The truth is a Sabellian is, *par excellence*, a believer in the deity of Jesus Christ. In the theology Sabellian, Jesus Christ is nothing else than the Great Father, having for the moment become the Mediator, and for the moment having become the Holy Spirit. Thus the theory of Sabellius is the theory above all others that makes Jesus Christ the very God. Having toiled all that day to show that I was a Sabellian, he toiled all the next day to show that I was a Unitarian—[laughter]—that religion which of all others separates Jesus Christ from God.

And now, my brethren, I want you when you come to make up your verdict, not to make me both of these characters. [Laughter.] I could bear it to be either, perhaps, but I could not bear to be both. [Applause.]

MR. NOYES arose and took up his argument again, as follows:

Mr. Moderator: When I felt compelled to ask on yesterday afternoon for an adjournment, feeling unable to proceed farther with my remarks, it will, perhaps, be remembered that I had reached and spoken somewhat briefly upon the third specification in this indictment. Without undertaking this afternoon to go through these in their order, I shall take occasion to ask your attention, first in the remarks which may be able to offer to the fifth specification, which asserts that the defendant in this case omits to preach the doctrines commonly known as evangelical. I will read the specification:

Being a minister of the Presbyterian Church, and preaching regularly to the Fourth Presbyterian Church of this city, he has omitted to preach in his sermons the doctrines commonly known as evangelical—that is to say, in particular, he omits to preach or teach one or more of the doctrines indicated in the following statements of Scripture, namely: That Christ is a "propitiation for our sins," that we have "redemption through His blood," that we are "justified by faith," that "there is no other name under heaven given among men whereby we may be saved." That Jesus is "equal with God," and is "God manifest in the flesh?"

that "all Scripture is given by inspiration of God." and that "the wicked shall go away into everlasting punishment."

To say that a minister in the Presbyterian Church omits to preach or teach the doctrines that are set forth in this specification is, you will agree, to bring a very serious accusation against him. And if I supposed that the defendant in this case were guilty of the thing alleged in this specification, I certainly should not be here to-day to undertake to plead his case, to correct grave mistakes and misrepresentations concerning his views. It is only because I believe, and know, and can prove, that the doctrines which are here set forth in scriptural phrases are preached and taught by him, that I am willing not only, but count it a privilege and honor, to stand here and plead his case before you.

This specification, as you have already heard, asserts that the defendant omits to preach these doctrines. If we are to understand by this that he omits, that he fails to preach these doctrines by many of making set and formal discourses upon each of them, we readily admit that this is true, so far as concerns the documentary evidence which is before this court. But if the specification means that Professor Swing has not interwoven all these subjects into his sermons, and taught the truth concerning them, then the charge is utterly denied. And by the testimony which has already been spread out before this court from the lips of living witnesses, that charge was proven to be baseless; and as I shall presently be able to show, can be abundantly proven to be baseless, from the very sermons which have been read in your hearing here, and by which it has been attempted to prove that he does not preach these doctrines.

The prosecutor, in all his arguments, seems to have gone upon the supposition that Professor Swing's language is the language of heresy—unless we grant him the benefit of the assumption that he is a Presbyterian. Well, I think the most of us; the most of the members of this court, will be ready at the outset to grant him the poor benefit of such an assumption, namely, that he is a Presbyterian; and that that assumption will be permitted to stand until it is clearly demonstrated that it is not true. Surely, the respondent has a right to this assumption.

One of the prosecutor's arguments would seem to indicate that he had perceived the weakness of his case. He made at the outset the term "evangelical" a test word. He assumes, in specification seventeen, that the evangelical sense of terms is the standard by which to judge the language of the defendant in this case; the same thing is assumed also in specifications four and five. Let me read specification seventeen:

In the sermons aforesaid, he employes the words used to indicate the doctrines of the Bible in an unscriptural sense, and in sense different from that in which they are used by the evangelical churches in general, and the Presbyterian Church in particular; that is to say, that he so uses such words as "regeneration," "conversion," "repentance," "Divine," "justification," "new heart," "salvation," "Saviour."

Without stopping to put such a specification as this on grounds which were set forth in the remarks that I was enabled to make here yesterday, I ask you to consider how much basis there is for making such assertions as are put forth concerning the defendant. I ask you notice, in reading this specification, and specifications like to this which may be found in this indictment, that the defendant meets the prosecutor on his own ground, as you will find his language set forth in the new volume of sermons, pages 138 and 139.

A Member—What is the sermon?

It is the declaration of the defendant at the opening of this case before the Presbytery. He says:

I admit the extracts from sermons and writings, but I would ask the Presbytery to consider the entire essays [which we proposed to do]—the whole of the discourses from which the extracts are made.

I own myself to be what, before the late union, was styled a new-school Presbyterian; and deny myself to have come into conflict with any of the evangelical Calvinistic doctrines of the denomination with which I am connected; and I beg permission to enter, as a part of my plea, the following statements, etc.

Let me in this connection, while I am reading from this declaration, call your attention to what is here said with reference to a charge that has been continually made against him in the course of the prosecutor's argument, that he was a Unitarian.

The names of Channing and Elliott and Huntington and Peabody, in the pulpits of that sect, and the Christ-like lives of thousands in the congregations of that denomination, utterly exclude from my mind and my heart the most remote idea that in showing that brotherhood any kindness I am offering indirect approval to persons outside the pale of the Christian religion and hope. The idea that these brethren are doomed to wrath beyond the tomb, I wholly repudiate. It is, indeed, my conviction that they do not hold as correct a version of the gospel as that announced by the Evangelical Alliance a few years ago, yet I am just as certain that the blessed Lord does not bestow His forgiveness and grace upon the mind that possesses the most accurate information, but upon the heart that loves and trusts Him. It is possible that the venerable Dr. Hodge, of Princeton, holds a more truthful view of Jesus than may be held by the distinguished Peabody, who has just lectured from his Unitarian standpoint before the Calvinists in the Union Theological Seminary, but we can point to nothing in the Bible that would indicate that heaven is to be given to only the one of these two giants who may possess a clearer apprehension of the truth. It may be assumed that God grants the world salvation only on account of the expiatory atonement made by Redeemer, but that God will grant this salvation to only those who fully apprehend this fact in an idea not to be entertained for an infant, for this would give heaven only to philosophers, and, indeed, only to those of this small class who shall have made no intellectual mistake. Looking upon the multitudes who need this salvation, and seeing that they are composed of men, women, and children who know nothing of the distinctions of formal theology, we cannot but conclude that paradise is not to be a reward of scholarship, but of a loving, obedient faith in Jesus Christ.

That, it would seem, ought to satisfy the mind of the prosecutor upon that point. But it does not satisfy him, for, seeing that his original demand is met, he shifts his ground, changes his test, and throws the evangelical sense entirely aside. Then he attempts to show that the evangelical terms employed by the respondent are also used by Unitarians, Universalists, and Arminians—used by them when they speak with reference to the same subjects; and from this he leaps to the conclusion that therefore (you see the connection) Professor Swing is an Unitarian! In this way he could make the accused not an Unitarian only, but an Universalist, a Roman, an Arminian, a moral theorist, and whatever else one may mean who is so unfortunate as to use evangelical phrases. By this method he might with perfect propriety classify the inspired writers with heretics; by this method, who of all the ministers of this body, or of any other Presbytery in the church to which we belong—who of them all could stand?

But after he has resumed his own test— namely, that of the evangelical sense, proposed by himself in the charges which he has drawn and which he has presented here, and on which the defendant is arraigned—after he has removed this test, because it would seem that he himself saw that he had lost his case by it, what does he next do? What is the next great feat in logic which we are called upon to witness and admire? He assumes that the accused must use certain technical terms manufactured especially by him, such as "the deity of Christ," "Christ is God"—terms which are not in the Bible, which are not in the Confession of Faith, and which are rarely used, as I venture to say, by the ministers of this body. If the accused speaks of inspiration, of regeneration, of a new heart and life—these will not serve this purpose—not even when the accused declares, as he has distinctly done before this body, that he uses these good old Bible terms in an evangelical sense.

In our innocence we have supposed that Bible preaching was gospel preaching; but evidently it is not so, according to the arguments that we have heard in this court. It is heretical, it is Unitarianism, if these phrases which the prosecutor insists shall be the test words by which to ascertain the orthodoxy or the heterodoxy of a Presbyterian minister—he insists upon these terms, and these terms are not found in the Bible—and so that is an Unitarian book. Well may the Unitarians thank the prosecutor for coming to their help in his plea that they use evangelical terms. Now, if they will only adopt Professor Patton's new terms, as some of them would have no hesitation or difficulty in doing, they might claim him as in accord with them. How would this logic sound: "Professor Patton speaks of the deity of Christ; Sabellians admit the deity of Christ; therefore Professor Patton is a Sabellian." [Laughter.] This is the logic—precisely this—which he applies to Professor Swing. Again, the prosecutor comments on certain language of the respondent as if he understood it perfectly, without any possibility of mistake or error. He can see heresy in it. There is no doubt in his mind but it is there;

but still, conscious that he is torturing that language, and perhaps having his pity awakened as he sees how it writhes in his logical machine, and anticipating the evangelical sense which we may put upon it, he takes another turn; he appears before this body in the character of one who can understand this language. Now, I submit that the prosecutor does not understand certain language used by the defendant does not prove that his regular hearers do not understand him. Who are the most likely to understand him. Who are the best interpreters of his words, as they are spoken from Sabbath to Sabbath? Certainly we ought to agree with his regular hearers. His elders, who have been before you here, and upon the witness stand have testified one and all, and consistently, to the same evangelical preaching which they have heard from week to week, and from month to month, and from year to year, during all the seven years past. And these were men whose theological knowledge, as you will all remember, drew from the prosecutor a compliment. Let us ask, What it his next display of art? To compliment them in his argument? By no means; rather to discredit their testimony, and to pronounce it worthless, on two grounds: one, that they are untrained in the discussions of theology, and the other, that they are prejudiced—that they have a personal interest in this prosecution, and so deep a personal interest in it as to make them incompetent witnesses. Hence, he would make it appear to this body that the pastor of these elders had beguiled them with his unevangelical and Biblical language. O, what is our Bible to be worth after this? A pious-hearted man reads in his Bible words such as those embodied in the fifth specification, or such as these: "The Son of Man is Lord of the Sabbath;" "Jesus Christ came into the world to save sinners;" "We believe and are sure that thou art Christ, the son of the Living God," and then those of this argument of the prosecutor, and says, "What can all this mean? Unitarians and Sabellians use just this evangelical language, and therefore this must be—there is no escape from the conclusion—this must be an heretical book."

Having followed, in this way, and taken up some of the prominent points that were put before you in the argument of the prosecutor; having recalled your attention to some of the leading moves, if I may so speak of them, which he took in the conduct of that argument, it would seem a fair inference from all this, that he must have felt hard pressed by the evidence which was given by the elders, or he would never have so manipulated the term "evangelical." And this court will readily detect the art of the magician in whose successful hands not only the sermons of our preacher, but the very Bible, would lose their meaning and their power to save souls.

Let me ask you to give attention to some elements which will disprove the charges of perversion—of omission and perversion.

Upon the subject of regeneration, let me ask your attention to a passage found in the volume of sermons last published. It is at page 47, and is as follows: "It is not worth while, therefore, to quarrel about the Bible, when it says: 'I was born in iniquity,' 'The heart is deceitful,' 'The heart is desperately wicked,' and 'Man must be born again.'" The conspicuousness of Christ, of Paul, of Penn, of the great Elliott among the Indians, shows that the Bible is only a picture of human life, and that men do need to be born again. You may quarrel with theologians if you wish, who have taken Bible texts into their laboratories, and have re-appeared after long stirring of the crucible, having in their hands some strange compound of mysterious color and questionable use; but with the plain Bible—with its words, 'ye must be born again'—let us have no debate."

You will readily understand in advance the answer which the prosecutor will make to this language—that it was used in a unitarian, or an evasive, or a disingenious or dishonest sense. Let us attend, however, to the words themselves:

"It was the effort of the old chemists to turn all things into gold, but the old theologians seemed to have possessed the faculty of changing gold into all things else; and taking a pure, priceless truth from the Bible, were wont, unconscious of its worth, to join it to their amalgam and then emerge with a poor oreide—their very faces meanwhile crying out the old "Eureka." With these we may dispute, but as for the simple words of the Bible, they are the world's facts. They are the mirror which reflects back to us nothing but our face, with no charm nor deformity left out. Those words are deeply written on all generations, and their meaning is only too vivid. It makes the heart and the head to ache. Let us confess that one of the most prominent facts of society is its moral weakness, its depravity. It ought to be born again."

At page 48 he says:

"This sentiment is not true to the letter, but it shows what Christ meant, when he said: 'Jesus is to be born again.' He meant that the soul must be hurled into being a second time. Its first life was a failure; it ought to be reborn, so that a new genius, a new drift might be possible." * * * There are several Christian sects which do not sufficiently magnify this idea of conversion, or new life. They believe in it, but do not make it the great central thought of their teaching. With the Methodists, the Presbyterians and the kindred schools the first effort is to help to convert men, and hence their great question to the candidate for membership is, "Do you feel that you have undergone a change of heart? Do you hate sin, do you love holiness?" And persons enter the Church or remain out, according to the responses to these inquiries. It matters not if some assert a change who have really met with none, and if some assert a falsehood knowingly. The questions are exactly in the line of the world's reform; they are the great questions to be asked. Hence, the religion that most particularly asks them, and most longingly seeks affirmative answers, will always secure better results than a church that passes them by in silence, and answer that all is well in the soul." At page 49, he said: "The perpetual effort to build up a new spiritual life, the unchanging conviction that the soul needs a profound reform now, and the accompanying belief that such a new drift of being may be found by the heart, has all the advantage to be found in all direct effort toward result. The mere Rationalist will assure you that the quantity of education or wealth in a land will be as the quantity of zeal, and longing, and will-power in those two directions."

At page 21 there are the following passages: "Christianity silently points to Jesus Christ; pass it not by. O, may this generation, while it is passing along, number among its transformations the transformation of your hearts into the image of the Saviour, that when, after a few years, it shall have strewn all your bodies like autumn leaves upon the earth, it may waft your spirits, redeemed and sanctified, back to your Maker."

The counsel then quoted passages from the sermons in respect to "Salvation by Christ" and "The Person of Christ." He cited from "Salvation and Morality," pages 102 and 104; also from the sermons on pages 107, 179, 239 and 240, all of which were strongly in support of defendant's position.

At 5 o'clock an adjournment was taken until Saturday morning.

SATURDAY, MAY 17th.

Presbytery opened at 9:30 o'clock this morning, in a very crowded condition After very few preliminaries,

MR. NOYES

took the floor, and proceeded with his argument, as follows:

MR. MODERATOR: No one regrets more than I do that the course of the prosecutor in his argument has imposed upon me the necessity of taking far more of your time than I presumed it would be necessary to take, before the case was taken up for argument. Not that the arguments which he presented were of a character that could not be overthrown, but simply for the reason that the arguments were deftly inserted in the evidence; and that you were asked to adjudicate upon this case upon the argument, and not upon the evidence. And so I shall be obliged to consume a very considerable portion of time still to come in reading from the documentary evidence. I must be permitted also, before proceeding to this presentation, to call attention to a fact (which certainly could not have escaped any member of this court), that the manner in which the documentary evidence was read by the prosecutor was such as in itself to cast ridicule upon it. The contrast was very striking and noticeable between the dignified and respectful manner in which he read, for instance, from James Freeman Clarke, and the contemptuous and scornful manner in which he read from the sermons of Professor Swing. And I could not but be reminded of a story in that connection which I heard long ago, and which goes to show how the whole force of any passage may be changed by mere inflection or emphasis. In the good old colonial times of Massachusetts, it is said that a certain minister of the gospel had an unspeakable contempt for the private and official character of the then acting governor of the commonwealth. It was a custom then, (and Brother Kittredge can say whether it is not now), for thanksgiving proclamations to be read from the pulpit. And it was the custom of the Governors to draw up these proclamations in due form, and after signing their names as witness to the document, would add the words, "God save the commonwealth." This minister, determined to have an expression of his contempt for the Governor (whose name escapes me, but whom we will call, familiarly, John Smith), read the proclamation in due form; and as he came to the signature, and the prayer following it, said: "John Smith Governor? God save the Commonwealth!" [Laughter.]

This, Mr. Moderator, illustrates, to my mind, fairly, the manner in which this documentary evidence was presented to the court by the prosecutor—so far, especially, as relates to the manner of the presentation: as to the garbling of it, here and there, I have already referred to that.

I shall begin my reading this morning from "Truths for To-day," upon the seventy-third page. I shall begin the reading of extracts which will set forth the views of the defendant upon faith and attendant doctrines, and which will show how certain doctrines are assumed, or only briefly stated. For example, the doctrine of the inspiration of the Scriptures, of the Trinity, of the divinity of Christ, and the like:

"No man can preach Christianity without being a doctrinal preacher."

It is made one of the offenses of the defendant that he condemns and ridicules the doctrines; but the passage which I am about reading does not give any such sound as that.

"No man can preach Christianity without being a doctrinal preacher; and no man can acquire a Christian or a religious heart except by the obedience of doctrine. Doctrines sustain the same relation to Christian character that mechanical law sustains to the Cathedral of St. Paul, or that the law of sound sustains to church chimes, or the music of the many-voiced organ. The attempt to separate Christianity in any way from its own announced doctrines is as pitiable a weakness as it would be to invite engineers to bridge a vast river by emotional action, wholly separated from any creed of mechanics. Having reached the inference that Christianity is founded upon doctrine—that doctrines are its State laws, and that all preachers must be doctrinal preachers, and all Christians doctrinal Christians, let us look now into the quality of these doctrines, which all must teach and obey. When we shall have found these we shall have escaped a thing which the wicked world fears or suspects—a group of human dogmas supporting some church *de facto*, secured by a usurpation in some dark night, and shall have found what the wicked world ought to love, a church *de jure*, founded by the Almighty and sanctioned by the longings of the soul, and by the experience of all generations. In seeking for these doctrines we may permit Christ, the Founder of Christianity, to supersede reason and point out a path for His followers. But the moment He has uttered our text—that 'Those which men can subject to experience are the doctrines that be of God'—reason rises up and unites its voice with that of simple authority. The doctrines of Christianity are those which may be tried by the human heart. This is declared often in the Divine word. From the words of Solomon, "Fear God and keep His commandments, for this is the whole duty of man," to the Saviour's words of the text; from the Psalm, "O, taste and see that the Lord is good," to the deeply spiritual passage where Christ compares Himself to bread to be eaten by the soul, there is one prominent idea—that the doctrines of religion are those which can be converted into spiritual being, making the spirit advance from childhood to the stature of Christ."

Upon page 76—"But when the Bible says: 'He that believes shall be saved,' it unfolds a doctrine; for human experience, taking up this faith, is wholly transformed thereby, as a desert is transformed by rain and sun into a paradise. Faith is man's relation to Christ, in an intellectual sense, in a belief in the proposition. Just as the student's love of knowledge is his relation to all study and wisdom. Faith is the union between the cluster and the vine, between the rose and the nourishing earth. Separate the rose and it withers—never reaches its bloom. Hence, he that believeth not is damned, because, the chain that should have bound him to God being broken, his moral world sinks, and goes down in the darkness, like the virgin's oilless lamp when the joy of the marriage feast was near. If God is the life of the world, then the soul that separates itself from Him by unbelief would seem to have broken the chain of perpetual being."

On the 77th page—it is evidence that I present, not argument.

"Appealing, therefore, to the range of human experience, we must declare faith, repentance, and conversion to be unavoidable laws of Christianity, not having come into it by any council of Catholics or Protestants, but direct from God, who poured into the human mind its reason and into the heart its love. Not so easily can we persuade reason to admit, as a matter of public experience, the idea of a mediator. We waive the inquiry as to reason's voice, because we are seeking not what the public confesses, but Christianity itself holds that may perchance be a matter of experience, may be tasted and thus be seen to be good. Under this head of doctrine open to experience, we must include the notion of a mediator, for we find millions of hearts glad in the feeling that there is a daysman between them and God. Millions who have passed away have gone, after a joyful life in this mediator, to a peaceful death in Him. The hymns of many ages from the tombstones of the Christian catacombs, where a few sweet words were written, to the 'Lamb of God, I come, I come,' of our century, the experiénce of man as a mediator has rolled along like Daniel's vast bird song over the forest of Chiassi. When we sing the hymn, 'Jesus, lover of my soul,' or 'Rock of ages, cleft for me,' and look into the faces of those borne upward by this sentiment, we know that this idea of a mediator belongs to human experience, and hence is to be enrolled among the doctrines of any true Christianity. Let us approach now a more warmly disputed proposition—that the divineness of Christ is something essential in the Christian system. The Trinity, as formerly stated, cannot be experienced."

Is that a denial of the Trinity? On the contrary, this passage distinctly assumes the doctrine of the Trinity. It is assumed as a fact, and being assumed as a fact, the deity of Christ is assumed as a fact.

Man has not the power to taste the threeness of one, nor the oneness of three, and say that it is good. Man cannot do his will here with reference to this doctrine of the Trinity, and know of the doctrine whether it be from God. It is not conceivable that any one will pretend to have experienced three persons as being one person, the same in substance and at the same time equal.

This doctrine, therefore, is not to be rejected nor denied, but to be assumed.

It belongs to the simple region of fact, and not to one of experience; and hence the distance between that idea, and the idea of faith or penitence is the difference between a fact and a perpetual law. But while human experience cannot approach the Trinity, it can approach the divineness of Christ; for if Christ be not divine—and what that phrase means we have already been made aware of by the language which I have read before—I wish you would give attention to this passage, which was so dangerous and heretical in the view of the prosecutor, and one which he quoted to a witness and asked his opinion as to whether it was an evangelical sentiment:

"For if Christ be not divine, every impulse of the Christian world falls to a lower octave, and life and love and hope alike decline."

Now, take the passage in its connection. I have read what goes before, and I will read what follows immediately after:

"There is no doctrine into which the heart may so inweave itself and find anchorage and peace as in this divineness of the Lord."

And then, assuming all the while the doctrine of the Trinity to be a fact, Professor Swing goes on to say:

"Christianity bears readily the idea of three offices."

Does "offices" mean manifestation and bearing, in the dictionary which the prosecutor uses? If it does, I would like to know what the dictionary is.

"And permits the one God to appear in Father, in Son, or in Spirit. But when the divine is excluded from Christ, and He is left a mortal only, the heart, robbed of the place where the glory of God was once seen, and where the body was once seen rising from the tomb, and where the words were spoken, 'Come unto Me all ye that labor and are heavy laden,' the heart thus robbed is emptied of a world of light and hope."

Now, interpret this sentence in the light of the respondent's declaration which he has made before this Presbytery, and it is to the effect that he holds the doctrine of the Trinity in the evangelical sense. And so interpreted, the doctrines here set forth are not heretical. If they be, there is more than one heretic belonging to this Presbytery.

I will read also, continuing on the same line of thought, from the eightieth page:

"In presence of such experience, to make Christ only a frail human is to strike Christianity in its heart's life; and hence, among the great laws of the Christian religion, selected by the measurement of our text, we must include the divineness of our Lord. As a result of the experience here given, that the doctrines of Christianity are such as may be tried by experience, hundreds of what the world calls dogmas are excluded *from any enumeration of essentials*, and must stand only among the facts, or alleged facts, of Christian history, and not among religious laws of life and salvation. God does not ask you to taste the tasteless, nor to experience that which lies beyond the sight or sense; but to cast yourself into the laws of faith and conversion, and repentance, and love, and hope, and of the divine Lord, and upon these be carried by a new recreative experience over to a new world, called a new heart here—called heaven hereafter. If we base our religion upon a revelation, we must find in it not only the existence of a doctrine, but the relative value of a doctrine. We need not go to the Bible for a truth, and to man for an estimate of the value of the truth. The comparative value of a truth is to be learned from the guide that pretends to lead the human race. For example, if the doctrine of a faith plays a more prominent part in the Bible than the doctrine of infant baptism, such also will be the order of their usefulness (does the prosecutor deny this?) And if the three offices of God, as Father and Redeemer and Spirit, are made more prominent than the idea that these three persons are one God"—and to this certainly no one would demur—I don't find any firmer statement of that idea anywhere in the Bible—is it not a statement, fair and unequivocal, of the doctrine of the Trinity.

"Then what mankind will need most will be the three influences, God as Father, God as Saviour, God as Holy Spirit; and what he may make secondary is the enigma of three in one; for why make prominent things which are not conspicuous in the inspired guide? By this estimate of Christianity, illustrated in this discourse, you who are afar off, and unwilling to come nearer to this Saviour, may at least find a method of discriminating between a church weighed down by a hundred declarations and one simple religion of Christ, which announces but few laws, and those all measurable by your own experience."

On page 83, "Truths for To-day," we find the following:

O, skeptical friend! O, Christian, too! Fly each day from the debate over simple events or entities in religion to the laws of being that may be tasted like sweet fruit, and which confess themselves at once to belong to the nature of God and man. It is in this realm of experience the millions of earth become one.

On page 101 the following passages occur:

The evidences of Christianity must be weighed by a mind not averse to virtue, not averse to the being and presence of a just God: by a mind not wholly wedded to exact science, but full of tender of sympathy with man, and pity for him if his career of study and love is to terminate at the grave; by a mind capable of looking away from the market place and from the pleasure of sense and of beholding the vast human family flashing their angelic wings afar off beyond these humbler times and scenes. The evidences of Christianity must be weighed by a soul capable of sadness and of hope. Not simply must the books of theologians be read for, and the books of skeptics against, the doctrines of faith, but the genius of earth, its little children, its joys, its laughter, its cradle, its marriage altar, its deep love crushed often in its building, its final white hair, its mighty sorrow, embracing all last from its Christ to its humblest child in its black mantle, must be confessed in its inmost heart; then when to such a spirit the common arguments of religion are only whispered, the sanctuary of God would seem to be founded in eternity, and men here and angels elsewhere will throng its blessed gates.

Let us now revert to faith as we find it on page 242:

Faith is evidence of the soul's attachment to a being.

It is not assent to a proposition, but attachment to a person.

At page 245 the following is stated:

If there were enough truth—truth of morals and redemption—in the Mohammedan and Buddhist system to save the soul, faith would be the law of salvation within those systems.

You will remember that this is embraced in some of the specifications. You will remember also that the prosecutor called special attention to that little word "if." I approve his suggestion and commend it to you in this connection. It is a question of fact that is stated. There is no salvation in those systems mentioned; if there were, then faith would be the law of salvation in them, and yet they require a belief. But Professor Swing does not here say that salvation by faith is not peculiar to Christianity. On the contrary, by any fair and reasonable construction of his language that is just what he does say. He says:

"Faith comes into Christianity, thus not by the exceptional decree of God, but by the universal law of nature."

Let us look at this doctrine of Divine sovereignty, as there is some reference to it in this passage.

Now, men have always differed in opinion on the question whether there is a natural element in faith or a reasonable element, and, whatever the opinions herein expressed on that point, I submit that there is no heresy.

I now return to page 105. I ask your attention in this connection to a passage in "Faith and Works." Let me first say that Professor Swing is planting himself here square upon the text which he announces for his discourse, and he is opposing those who pervert it.

"Paul says, 'Faith works by love;' he insisted on good works, as he sets forth in his Epistle to Titus, seventh chapter, eighth verse, and in First Timothy, sixth chapter, seventeenth and nineteenth verses."

Upon the one hundred and fifth page we find the following:

"The doctrines of salvation by faith must, therefore, be so stated and held as to leave society its friend, trusting faith rather than fearing it, and must be so stated and held as to leave other doctrines of Christianity some reason of existence. * * * There are always those with whom some one doctrine has eclipsed all other truths of the Bible."

And now if the prosecutor calls in question these doctrines as set forth in the passage I have read, I beg to refer him to the last number of the *Interior*, of which he is the editor, [laughter] wherein it is said:

"No great principle must be taken by itself, and herein is where so many mistakes are made by many thinkers. The principle or law of gravitation by itself would plunge the solar system into the fiery billows of the sun and give us a grand cremation of worlds. So Luther was so filled with the grand doctrine of justification by faith that he ignored and contradicted the necessary fruits and purposes of faith. But he reformed his opinion as he pursued the study of the word. The wildness of all extremists, the meteor-like rush away from harmonious systems of truth which we so often see in the world of thought, results from taking a single truthful principle and following it without regard to other principles which bear upon it."

A second Daniel come to judgment! [Laughter.]

Observe the *Interior*—unless we say it is vague and ambiguous—asserts that good works are the purposes of faith, which is parallel to that charge that Professor Swing teaches, that faith saves because it leads to a holy life, because he speaks of works as the destiny of faith. Oh, what is the *Interior* coming to? If we cannot trust it. What and whom can we trust? [Laughter.]

[Turning to page 111, the counsel read at length from the sermon on "Good Works," and said:]

Before I again resume the reading of Professor Swing's sermons I desire to call attention to an opinion given by Dr. Hodge with reference to the doctrine of the Trinity, an opinion which may be found recorded on page 290 of the Presbyterian Reunion Memorial Volume. It is as follows:

"If a man comes to us and adopts the system of doctrine taught in our confession we have a right to ask him. 'Do you believe there are three persons in the Godhead, the Father, the Son, and the Holy Ghost, and that these three are one God, the same in substance, equal in power and glory?' If he says 'Yes,' we are satisfied. We do not call upon him to explain how three persons are one God, or to determine in what relations in the awful mystery of the Godhead are indicated by the terms Father, Son, and Holy Ghost."

In specification 21 Professor Swing is accused of denying the doctrine of Justification by Faith, as held by the Reformed churches and taught in the Westminster Confession of Faith. On page 120 of "Truths for To-day," you will find these words:

"That grand text which helped revolutionize the Christian world in the sixteenth century, 'The just shall live by faith,' having by its final word set us free from Romish error and despair, ought now by its initial word to help to set us free from public and private neglect of a virtuous character."

It is evident from this passage, said Mr. Noyes, that Professor Swing uses the word "faith" in the reformed sense of the term.

[The counsel for the defense then read passages, without comment, on pages 248, 251, 252, and 271, of "Truths for To-day," to show that Professor Swing preached that "faith produces works and character."]

At pages 80 and 81 of the sermon "Value of Moral Motive," in Keen, Cooke & Co.'s book, the following passage occurs:

"There was something in the times of Calvin and Luther, and on to Jonathan Edwards, that enabled the motive of punishment to be very influential for good. To inquire whether anything would have done as good service would be about like the inquiry whether some other method of light and heat might not have been resorted to by the Creator that would have made our existing sun unnecessary. It is certain that 'the terror of the Lord' wielded a mighty influence on the past centuries, and the same impulse of virtue will be always extant and active, but to the millions of a subsequent age a new impulse is liable to arrive, and expressing itself in the words, 'the love of Christ constraineth us,' may, for a time, be a complete universe to the existing heart."

At page 13 there is a very strong, and I think unequivocal and unambiguous, statement of the doctrine of God's sovereignty.

The doctrine of God's absolute sovereignty is just as true as it was in the days of King Œdipus or of Calvin. It will always remain a confessed fact that God's will must be a supreme will of the world, but while this is confessed, yet we do perceive that our age is a fact passes over the great absolutism in silence, compared with the age of Athens or Geneva, and God's love and sweet Fatherhood become more visible than His absolute despotism."

The idea of Almighty love is brought prominently forward, and the idea of Almighty power and divine sovereignty is left in the background.

And now I bring to an end my readings from Professor Swing's sermons. I might extend them indefinitely. But I feel that the documentary evidence I have already presented is simply overwhelming; and that if there is any one in this body who is not satisfied with it, "neither would he be convinced though one rose from the dead." I ask you to consider this evidence, give it that weight to which it is entitled on account of the clear and unequivocal statements of evangelical doctrines which it contains. Brethren, I know that you have not failed to find these doctrines as I have read them; and that you will not, in making up your verdict, be influenced by any fear of Professor Patton's contempt of your intelligence, for you remember that he has warned you in advance that if you do find the evangelical doctrines in these sermons he will believe that you do not know what these doctrines are yourselves. I challenge the prosecutor to find a statement in Professor Swing's sermons that cannot be explained as evangelical.

Before I pass from the consideration of the indictment, there are two things that I have to say. The first, that the opening statements of my argument have been abundantly proved, both by oral and documentary testimony. I said there was nothing in this indictment from beginning to end, so far as the specifications are concerned, except the inferences of the prosecutor. Taking these away, there would be nothing left of the complaint. And these, as I have shown, ought never to have been admitted into the indictment at all. The complaint, on the very face of it, is defective throughout, either in substance or form. The form is vague, or the substance is only shadow cast by the dark thoughts which the prosecutor has entertained of Professor Swing's language. I shall not, therefore, follow him in his vigorous and brilliant pleadings as he passed from one specification to another, perverting the language of the defendant, and so making it to appear that its teaching was false and dangerous. I speak to intelligent men, who can judge of the plain and obvious meaning of language as well as he.

But there are two of the specifications on which, before I leave this part of the subject, I desire to offer a few words. They are specifications 23 and 24. The address of the defendant yesterday must have met and removed any doubts which any member of this court may have entertained upon this subject. But I desire to recall to mind two statements which have been submitted in evidence. The first was made by Dr. Patterson when he was upon the witness stand. His testimony was distinct and emphatic, to the effect that Professor Swing had explained to him that in his use of the word eclecticism, he meant only an eclecticism of use. And when the prosecutor said, as he did say before you yesterday, that Dr. Patterson's statement was not evidence, he simply impeached the veracity of the witness.

I do not think that this court will sustain that impeachment. The one assumption upon which as a basis or foundation the prosecutor has raised the whole splendid superstructure of his argument is this: that the respondent at your bar is a liar. [Sensation.] To sustain this assumption, in other words, to keep the foundation under the argument, and so prevent its tumbling down into shapeless ruin, all risks must be accepted. The defandant's categorical averments must be emphatically denied, and the supporting testimony of responsible witnesses must be fearlessly contradicted. And all this as a direct defiance of the authority of the General Assembly, which has declared that an accused party shall be accorded the poor privileges of defining the meaning of the language which he employs. Fully corroborative of the testimony of Dr. Patterson are the statements which the defendant made in his letter to Dr. Judkins. [Counsel here read the letter, which has already been published in the *Inter-Ocean.*

Passing now from the documentary to the oral testimony, to which I have so far made only incidental reference, I need not make any extended review of it. Of oral testimony, the court will agree with me when I say that the prosecutor had absolutely none. In this respect the trial, on his part, proved to be a broad farce! [Sensation.] His own witnesses turned out to be strong witnesses for the defense. Especially was this true of Mr. Thompson and Dr. Patterson. Nor will the prosecutor's great skill in special pleading at all avail to break the force of Dr. Patterson's testimony. He was a ministerial brother who early fulfilled his duty to his misrepresented and maligned friend. He did not shun him, and nurse his doubts until he should be ready to give them voice and send them to every part of the church, but he went to him in the spirit of love. What he learned in these interviews he has declared to this court. His testimony cannot be in the least invalidated by any attempt to pervert the language which he employed in his letter to the *Interior*. The circumstances under which that letter was written are a sure guide to its right interpretation. Professor Swing had been publicly accused as having, in heart, gone clear over to the enemy's camp. The air had been filled with suspicion against him. On every hand men were speaking to each other their fears. In this state of things Dr. Patterson, obeying a very manful impulse, wrote to the *Interior* expressing strongly his disapprobation of its course toward Professor Swing. Knowing that the latter was openly charged with expressing the truth in his ministry, he said that "in so far as he failed to preach the central doctrines of the gospel, his preaching was seriously defective." Was that saying that he disavowed these doctrines? Not at all. It was only saying that if he did, and in so far as he did, his preaching was seriously defective, and to that position the Doctor probably holds to-day.

But the prosecutor undertakes to impeach the testimony given by the elders of the Fourth Church. Well he might, for it bore mightily against him. He insists that parol testimony has no value when written sermons may be had in evidence. I have two things to say in reply: These elders are the "living epistles" of Mr. Swing's ministry. On the theory of the prosecutor, that they have been fed on the poison of false doctrine, and on that alone, I think that Professor Swing himself must admit that they showed themselves to be pretty sound and healthy Christians. It is hardly worth while to be fed on "the sincere milk of the word," if false teachings can make such orthodox Christians.

The very same sermons from which Professor Patton sucks only the deadly poison of false doctrine are the sermons from which these plain, uncaviling men extract the honey of truth. That which is deadly to him is nourishing to them. That which fills his soul with trouble fills theirs with light and peace, and joy in the Holy Ghost. That which makes him "black with astonishment," to use the expressive words of the old prophet, makes them radiant with joy. That which fills him with sorrow and sighing inspires them to go on their way with songs. I ask your attention to this, Mr. Moderator and brethren of the court. It is a curious phenomenon. It is worth studying for the lessons it may yield. Can "a fountain send forth at the same place sweet water and bitter?" We know it cannot. But where is the bitterness then, of which the prosecutor so loudly complains? It must be in him, and not in the fountain of whose waters he still persists in drinking so copiously. The oral testimony of these elders thus becomes very strong. It shows that the impressions which they received are totally different from the impressions which Professor Patton received from reading them or garbled portions of them. The sermons are the same, and yet they are not the same. But then, where is the common-sense man who does not know that the best way by which to test the nourishing quality of—roast beef, for instance, is to eat it, and not to analyze it? And so, business men, who are laden with manifold responsibilities and cares, need to feed upon the truth; and it is not for the cloistered theologian to demand that they shall be skilled enough first to analyze it, and see if it be tainted with error before they feed upon it.

This is one form of my answer to the prosecutor's special pleading against the admissibility and value of this evidence. My other answer will serve to correct a mistake into which he seems to have fallen. We have in no instance set out to prove the contents of a paper. The one thing which we have aimed to do is to establish before this body the thoroughly evangelical character of the defendant's preaching. This, I think, we have abundantly done, and by the testimony of men who sustain prominent business and social relations to this community, and whose moral and Christian characters are without a stain. Professor Swing often fills out his sermons by the addition of extemporized passages; his teachings in the prayer meeting are all extemporaneous; and we have proved that his teachings are not, as this indictment falsely charges, heretical, but evangelical and fruitful.

Nor is it a generous thing in the prosecutor to undertake to break down this testimony by attempting to show that the witnesses are incompetent by reason of prejudice or self-interest. He has not a shadow of evidence to support his allegations. The men whose testimony he impeaches are well known in this community, and it will not anywhere be believed that their testimony can be invalidated. That they are deeply interested in this prosecution, as officers who are responsible for the character of the teaching which the congregation "over whom the Holy Ghost hath made them overseers," shall receive, is undoubtedly true; then, indeed, might their evidence be regarded as without value. But that they are prejudiced is utterly untrue.

The only witnesses for the prosecutor who gave his case any shadow of support were Messrs. Goudy and Miller. I have not sought, nor have I any thought of seeking to discredit their testimony. One of these gentlemen I know well and very highly esteem. I think both of them will regard me as doing them a favor if I say that they do not range themselves among the admirers of Professor Swing. But their testimony is not for a moment to be questioned on any ground of prejudice. Neither is the testimony of the Fourth Church elders to be questioned.

Perhaps I ought to say a word of the testimony of Mr. Shufeldt, but it shall be only a word. I do not imagine that any member of this court regards that testimony as establishing anything. Mr. Shufeldt confessed that his recollection was very uncertain. While he was sure that certain branches of the tree were broken off, yet whether those branches represented any of the five points of Calvinism was a matter of doubt.

And now, Mr. Moderator, before I proceed to speak of certain points in the argument of the prosecutor, there are some other matters to which I must refer, as having a decided bearing upon this case. It is my duty to refer to certain facts which are properly a part of this case. And one of these matters of history is, that during all the long period which intervened between the first opening of the newspaper discussion on "Inspiration," and the exhibition of charges against the defendant, the prosecutor never once went to Professor Swing to try the effect of a fraternal conference in bringing them into a fraternal and doctrinal agreement. I am aware that he says it was not a private, but a public, offense with which Mr. Swing was charged. But this plea fails to meet the facts of the case, as I shall show.

The specification which connects with it the name of Mr. Collier as a witness is a very serious matter. Such a charge, if proved true, would blast the name of any man, no matter how potent the name might previously have been. But who is the man against whom this grave charge is blurted forth to the world? He has lived in this community for seven years. During all this time his good name has never been sullied by the breath of scandal; never have evil words been framed against him until they were framed into this indictment by the prosecutor in this case, and perhaps by another hand which is said to have lent its best cunning for the work. Of accused and accuser or accusers, therefore, the words of Cowper are strikingly descriptive:

"Assailed by scandal and the tongue of strife,
His only answer was a blameless life;
And he that forged, and he that threw the dart,
Had each a brother's interest in his heart."

Mr. Moderator, it is an inspired declaration that "a good name is rather to be chosen than great riches;" and in the same volume of living truth we learn that "a good name is better than precious ointment." In view of these divine testimonies, I leave it with this Presbytery to say whether the hasty publication of this report was not a wrong to Professor Swing.

I must also put on record the expression of my regret that Professor Patton did not feel moved to seek a conference with elders of the Fourth Church very soon after he found himself wrestling with doubts as to Mr. Swing's orthodoxy, and especially when, at a later day, he found fear that this loved pastor was at heart an unbeliever in evangelical doctrines, and a dangerous teacher; he would have found in all these elders very intelligent Christian gentlemen, who are keenly alive, not only to the good of their pastor, but also to the welfare of their church, and to the interests of the Presbyterian Church at large; he would have discovered that they are discreet in counsel and sound in the faith. They would have given an instant and respectful hearing to the utterance of his anxieties and fears. And considering the danger that a popular pastor going astray himself should lead his people astray also, it is certainly to be regretted that Professor Patton should have entered upon this prosecution without so much as attempting a mediation. Surely, if the pastor must be given up as hopeless, it were worth while to try and save the church; but this was not done. I do not speak of these things otherwise than with sorrow. I think it must be submitted that this deplorable breach of the peace which we witness now has, at the least, been inconsiderately brought about. Every means of private mediation should have been tried and exhausted beforehand.

But I pass from these animadversions, which I have no pleasure in making, but which my duty, in this case requires that I should make, to ask your attention to the argument which the prosecutor has made in support of his indictment. As an honorable opponent I am glad to bear witness to his ability, if not to the candor displayed in it. Grant him the assumption which is the underlying basis of all his plea, and there is no escape from the conclusion to which that plea conducts you. That assumption is, that the defendant in this case is not a truthful man. If the members of this court believe this assumption of the prosecutor, then the present indictment ought to be dismissed, and a new one framed on which the defendant should be charged with falsehood. But I know they do not believe this. It is singular that the prosecutor should distinctly declare, as he did on this last day of his argument, that he did not believe the respondent's declarations before the Presbytery at the opening of this trial. For many months previously he had appealed to him through the *Interior* to give to the world an explicit affirmation that he held to the evangelical creed, and then he, the prosecutor, would be satisfied. When at last an opportunity was offered and improved for making that explicit declaration, the prosecutor characterized it as a "candid statement." But it seems that a candid statement may also be a false statement, for Professor Patton now declares that he does not believe the defendant. It is his conviction of his insincerity and untruthfulness, then what is the animus of this whole prosecution? It is this assumption which lies at the very foundation of the prosecutor's whole argument.

Professor Swing's sermons readily and naturally admit of an evangelical meaning. They not only admit of that, but they are full of Gospel truth. His elders testify that he preaches the same doctrines that they heard all their lives from Presbyterian pulpits; and yet, in the face of these testimonies, the prosecutor labors three days to prove that the defendant is not evangelical. I submit that such an argument, however plausible and brilliant, does not challenge any very serious examination. The argument cannot be true, if the defendant is true; and the defendant cannot be true if the argument is true; and in either event, there is no case on this indictment. But there are some considerations which the prosecutor's argument suggests, and which are of great importance in their bearing upon a right adjudication of this case. One of these is that every man's words should be interpreted with reference to the relations which he may sustain toward any body of Christians. Language spoken by an Unitarian would not be used to convey the meaning which the same words, when employed by a Presbyterian minister, would be designed to convey; the standpoint of the two men being different, their views will be different on vital matters, even though those views may be expressed in substantially the same language.

Mr. Moderator, I do not know, but I have an impression, that in your preaching you generally speak of the divinity of Christ, and seldom or never of the deity of Christ. Shall we, therefore, begin to suspect you, and whisper our fears to one another with bated breath, or publish our doubts in a newspaper? If you do say "Divinity of Christ," then you say no more than an Unitarian would say. No, sir. Divinity of Christ means from your lips and from the lips of Professor Swing, one thing, and from the pen of James Freeman Clarke it means quite another thing. These statements, so obviously true, will help us to see how grossly unfair the prosecutor has been in attempting to trace an identity of view between Professor Swing and Unitarian thinkers, because they alike use certain terms, such as "divinity of Christ"—calling Christ "divine," "Saviour," etc. These are the very terms which Presbyterian ministers use, so far as I know, almost universally. It is, then, to the last degree unfair to single out one of them, and undertake to disgrace him before the Church for using those terms which are the common speech of our ministry. Not less unworthy and reprehensible were the efforts of the prosecutor to establish a similarity of views between Professor Swing on the one hand and such men as Tylor and Lubbock on the other.

During our late civil war, we had two classes of men among us. One class comprised a mighty multitude; the other a small handful of people. Both classes talked of loyalty, of devotion, of devotion to the country, of love for the flag. But, sir, this language, though the same, was not the same. It did not mean the same thing; and in order to be certain what it did mean, you had first to ascertain to which of the two classes the speaker belonged. When you knew whether he belonged to the party of Unionists or Southern sympathizers, then you knew what he meant by loyalty, and love for the flag. And so it is with respect to theological divisions to-day. Unless you interpret a man's words by the relations he sustains, there is not a minister in this Presbytery who would stand the test to which the prosecutor has subjected Professor Swing. There is not one of you all who has not, time and time again, uttered paragraphs substantially the same in phraseology as those which any Unitarian might utter; but you are not, therefore, Unitarians. Professor Patton says he believes the Gospel. So do the Free Religionists say the same thing. Are they, therefore, alike? God forbid! and yet they are, if using the same terms makes men alike. Let us not hear any more of a kind of pleading so wholly irrelevant to the case, and so unfair to the defendant.

[A long extract from an article in the Princeton *Review*, by Dr. Henry Smith, of Princeton College, bearing in precisely the same line of thought Professor Swing was taken in task for following, was here read; and, being finished, recess was taken until 2 o'clock p. m. It was then about 12:30.]

AFTERNOON SESSION.

At two o'clock, Presbytery having re-assembled, the Rev. Mr. Wisner said that ample proof had been offered the court of the inadequacy of the English language as an adequate medium for the expression of thought in an unambiguous manner. He, therefore, moved that it be supplanted in the Presbytery by its great sister, the German language, which had no such defect. [Laughter.] An effort was being made to have the language taught in the public schools of the United States.

The motion was seconded amid much merriment. It was shortly afterward tabled, and the proceedings of Presbytery will continue to be conducted in the "ambiguous" English tongue.

Elder Williams asked Presbytery to make arrangements for the installation of the Rev. Dr. Hurd as pastor of Highland Park Church.

The call having been read and accepted by Mr. Hurd, the Revs. Walker and Taylor, with Elder Williams, were appointed Installation Committee.

Dr. Blackburn moved the appointment of a committee to consider the question as to how the vote on the Patton charges should be taken, and report to the court. He explained that the motion was not made with any wish to introduce any new method, but in order to facilitate business.

The Rev. B. E. S. Ely strongly opposed the motion, and threatened to read and submit an elaborate plan on voting, which, he said, he had prepared.

The motion was tabled.

The Rev. Mr. Noyes thereupon resumed his address for the defense.

There is another reason, he said, for entertaining the motion submitted by Mr. Wisner, in the fact that it seems not yet to be understood what is the doctrinal position of Professor Swing before this body. [Laughter.] We have been told that he had omitted altogether to state what his creed was; that it was not possible to find out from the declaration read before this body what his views really were, and for the reason, as was alleged, that he had not given them any distinct statement of his views, but had simply said on what grounds he would be ready to meet the skeptical, and educated, and sinful world. In his declaration he said: "Holding the general creed as rendered by the former New School Theologians, I will, in addition to such a general statement, repeat to you the abstracts of belief upon which I am willing to meet the educated world, the skeptical and the sinful world, using my words in the evangelical sense: The inspiration of the Holy Scriptures, the Trinity, the Divinity of Christ, the office of Christ as a mediator when grasped by an obedient faith, conversion by God's spirit, man's natural sinfulness, and the final separation of the righteous and the wicked."

In the Presbyterian Memorial Volume, Dr. Musgrave, in the course of some remarks, says:

"There must of necessity be difference of opinion. So long as men think at all they will differ in some respects. We understand there is to be allowed in this reunited church a reasonable degree of liberty."

That is all the defense asked—that men are not to be made offenders for one word, that we shall discourage needless prosecutions, for there is always danger that prosecution will degenerate into persecution. In the report of the Committee on Reunion, page 279, there was the following language: "At the same time as we interchange these guarantees of orthodoxy we interchange guarantees of Christian liberty. Differences always have existed, and been allowed, as to modes of expressing and theorizing within the reach and bounds of one accepted system." In view of these testimonies, I submit whether it is proper and respectful for the prosecutor to come before this body and declare, as he did in his opening argument, that if you were loyal Presbyters you would have resented the expression of belief which was made on the part of the defendant in making his plea. To say that this trial does not bring up the old issues of New and Old Schools, is to say what all the intelligent world knows to be the reverse of the fact. It does bring up these issues. These are the only issues that are before this body: and I say here, under a deep sense of personal responsibility to God, that if the respondent is to be condemned on the platform which he has distinctly laid down before you, while I do not speak at all in the language of threat, but only in the language of sorrowful foreboding and prophesy, I believe it will rend again this church which has so recently and so happily been reunited.

And now I ask that the printed and oral evidence which has been submitted in this case may be adjudicated upon with distinct and constant reference to three facts; first the decision of the General Assembly upon the case of the Rev. Mr. Craighead. The points of this case are two. The Presbytery first says. "Here it will be important to remark that a man cannot on trial be convicted of heresy for using expressions which may be so interpreted as to involve heretical doctrines, if they may also admit of a more favorable construction."

The next point in that case was that the Presbytery decided that no man can be convicted of heresy by inference or implication. It is not right to charge any man with opinions which he disavows.

The second fact which the court should hold in view was the respondent's own declaration, which is to the effect that he does receive, and receive in the evangelical sense, the very doctrines for the rejection or omission to teach which the defendant is arraigned at the bar of this court.

The third fact was the testimony of the elders of the Fourth Church, which is confirmatory in every particular of the documentary evidence.

A final word in regard to the alleged ambiguity of language:

I count it providential that the prosecutor should have fallen into such a palpable and gross mistake in the use of language as that into which he did fall in drawing up this indictment, as regards the language employed with respect to Mary Price Collier. His own friends misunderstood utterly the meaning which he said he intended to convey by the language he used. I submit, therefore, that if the defendant is to be censured by this court for using equivocal language, that vote of censure should also include his prosecutor for being guilty of the same offense. [Laughter and applause.]

At the close of the address of defendant's counsel, the Rev. Mr. Ely moved the adjournment of the court until Monday morning, when the prosecutor should proceed with his review of the case. This motion was, however, voted down, and a resolution passed extending the sitting to such an extent as might be occupied by the prosecutor, he having intimated that he would not require more than about four hours for his address.

PROFESSOR PATTON,

who appeared to be physically worn out with his exertions during the trial, then entered upon his review of the case, remarking at the outset that the defense would have the opportunity to reply only in the event of new matter being introduced, but this he would carefully avoid doing. The Professor fulfilled his intentions, and his remarks were strictly confined to the points previously discussed at length. He affirmed that both charges were true, and his previous doubts as to the defendant's theology, he said, were strengthened by the two declarations made by the defense. There was not one distinct statement in Swing's sermons that Christ was God, and therefore specification 5, relating to the doctrines, was distinctly proved. He did not call Swing an Arian, but it was singular that during a seven years' ministry, and believing in the deity of Christ, he had not brought forward one sentence which would silence the allegation.

Giving the most favorable construction to Swing's language, it still remained true that the question of Sabellianism had not been explained, though he did not affirm that Swing was a Sabellian. But he did affirm that the defendant had been unfaithful in his ministry, for he had given his approval to the doctrine of the modal trinity. He had arraigned the Presbyterian Churches and the Council of Nice, and had put forward a doctrine which would, he (Swing) thought, save the trinity and at the same time meet the objections raised against the trinity by Unitarians. The sermon was an attempted reconciliation of the doctrine of the three persons of one God, with Unitarian views. Did Swing believe that the three persons in the Godhead are equals? That was the question.

The Rev. Mr. Noyes—He has said he does.

Professor Patton—Nor had the defense been more successful in showing that Professor Swing agreed with the Confession of Faith respecting justification; and his sermon, "Faith," proved this to be true. Swing declared yesterday that he believed in salvation by faith; but the point was whether he believed in justification by Faith, as taught by the Presbyterian Church? He never mentioned the righteousness of Christ as that by which man is justified.

The prosecutor then propounded an elaborate doctrinal proposition on the question of faith, and, turning round to Brother Barrett, one of the clerks, asked his concurrence thereto. The jovial-faced clerk looked amazed at the problem submitted for his solution and gave up the enigma, amid the laughter of the audience.

Professor Patton then proceeded to review Professor Swing's expressions respecting the inspiration of the Scriptures, and declared that so soon as you spoke of the faith of the people in the infallibility and inspiration of the Bible, rationalism would be established. Professor Swing had not denied the accusations brought respecting his views on the 109th Psalm, but said that God did make a bad psalm, and therefore he could not believe that God inspired all the Scriptures. Summing up his argument, he declared that notwithstanding the ability of the accused, and their friendship for him, the Presbytery would be doing an act of violence to the Presbyterian Church if they permitted him to go on, unimpeded, in his dangerous course. Professor Swing distinctly stated that the Presbyterian Church actual is one thing and the Presbyterian Church historic is another, and that his church is the church actual and not the church historic. They did not know, however, what the doctrines of the actual church were, but they did know the views held by the historic church. Professor Swing had no right to call himself a New School Presbyterian, for he did not adhere to their doctrines, and this view was held by the New York *Evangelist*, a good representative of New School theology.

Turning to Brother Young, the prosecutor said that if Young had used Swing's language he would have thought the brother sound, but he could not give Swing the benefit of the doubt.

He proceeded to read extracts from the defendant's sermons, until Mr. Noyes requested him to read the context. This caused a "scene."

Professor Patton declared with vehemence, "I will not be interrupted."

The spectators on the south side of the room loudly hissed this remark, while the prosecutor's friends on the north applauded stoutly.

The Moderator endeavored to restore harmony by remarking that he would not have allowed the prosecutor to be interrupted, had he thought he did not wish to be.

The Rev. Mr. Carden demanded of the Moderator his ruling as to whether he would permit hissing by the public.

Said the Moderator, meekly: "You must remember the Moderator is a small man."

There were peals of laughter at this remark. When the merriment had subsided the Moderator denied his intention of being funny, and told the inquiring member that the Chair had no authority except such as Christian courtesy gave him.

The Rev. Mr. Eddy protested against the prosecutor's declaration, remarking that it would be a novel practice in a Presbyterian court if a speaker was not to be interrupted by members who wished to ask questions.

The Moderator hoped that all these demonstrations of opinion and feeling would cease.

Professor Patton said that interruptions threw even a cool-headed speaker off his guard, and he ought not to be interrupted when the court had compelled him to proceed. He re-affirmed his original statement, without, he said, meaning any discourtesy.

Then he resumed his argument. He had not proceeded far when his friends moved an adjournment, but this was voted down. After some further remarks by the Professor, and the motion to adjourn was again moved by a member on his side of the house, Mr. Young rose and explained that the motion was submitted, as it was feared by the Professor's family and friends that he would break down if he proceeded further.

Professor Patton, who was evidently suffering severely from physical exhaustion, said he had already spoken during eleven hours in that assembly, and his friends had submitted the previous resolutions on account of his prostration. He didn't wish the Presbytery to now grant an adjournment, he would not have an adjournment, but would go through with his address.

He did close his address, at the close of which he called upon the Presbytery to perform its duty, as the Presbyterian churches everywhere were watching this trial, and declare David Swing not fit to be any longer a minister of the Presbyterian Church. When he had closed, his friends gave him a round of applause. The court then adjourned to Monday morning.

REPORT ON THE VERDICT.

The committee appointed to prepare a statement of reasons for the final judgment of the Presbytery in the case of the Rev. David Swing, report as follows:

Both of the charges against Mr. Swing are negative in form, and devolve upon the prosecutor the labor of proving a negative. Much depends in this case upon the character of the statement of the questions at issue. It is not the question—

1. What we may believe for private reasons in regard to the real views of Mr. Swing. We must be governed by the evidence, not by private opinions, in our judgment as a court.

2. It is not the question what Mr. Swing may do in the future. We are confined to the evidence of what he has said or done, or failed to do or say.

3. It is not the question whether Mr. Swing occupies such a position or habitually uses such expressions in his preaching as are satisfactory to us all. He may assume an attitude in relation to exceptics or errorists which some of us deem too liberal, and he may employ many expressions which to most of us seem not sufficiently guarded, and yet be guilty of no heresy, and of no such unfaithfulness as constitutes an ecclesiastical offense. The question as it regards a kindly treatment of errorists is one about which our church has no positive rule or judgment.

4. It is not the question whether the views of Mr. Swing in regard to the relative importance of formulated theology are or are not correct. A man may judge erroneously on this point, and yet hold all the essential doctrines of evangelical Christianity and of the Calvinistic system, and preach the gospel with fidelity.

5. It is not the question whether Mr. Swing is right or wrong in his opinion regarding the extent to which our church at this day actually holds to the letter of our formula faith, or insists upon the propositions contained in our confession. He may for himself sincerely receive and adopt the confession as "containing the system of doctrine taught in the holy scriptures," and yet be mistaken as to the sense in which the church requires its ministers to hold the Calvinistic system.

6. It is not the question whether Mr. Swing's judgment in regard to the best style of preaching is strictly correct or not. There are great varieties of judgment on this subject allowed by our churches, inasmuch as we have no authorized definition of what faithful preaching is. Only such styles of preaching as studiously and designedly avoid Christian truth, or clearly inculcate essential error, can be justly regarded as involving an offense in the ecclesiastical sense.

7. It is not the question whether Mr. Swing has been unfaithful, as all imperfect men are in preaching different truths more or less out of their due proportions; for on this point we have no absolute standard of ecclesiastical judgment.

8. Nor is it the question whether Mr. Swing has been claimed by Unitarians, or suspected of error by some orthodox people; for all this has been true of sound men who were not specially unfaithful, but were either unfortunate in their modes of expression, or surrounded by persons who were for one reason or another inclined to misconstrue their words, or position. Such circumstances do not by themselves prove either error of doctrine or ministerial unfaithfulness in such a sense as constitutes an ecclesiastical offense.

But the questions are only these:

1. Whether it has been conclusively proved that Mr. Swing does not personally hold all the doctrines that are by our church regarded as *essential* to the system of doctrine taught in the confession and in the holy scriptures.

2. Whether it has been proved beyond a doubt that he has been unfaithful in the discharge of his ministerial duty in such a sense as to constitute an ecclesiastical offense.

These questions the Presbytery has answered in the negative, for the following reasons:

1. Mr. Swing's position, as a Presbyterian minister who has solemnly professed to receive and adopt our confession as "containing the system of doctrine taught in the holy scriptures," and has engaged to perform all his ministerial duties with fidelity, obliges us to regard him as orthodox and faithful until the contrary is incontestibly established, not by inferential reasonings from his statements, but by undeniable and direct proof. But such proofs, in our judgment, have not been produced. The alleged evidences, to be conclusive, require us to assume that Mr. Swing has been artfully and systematically acting the part of a willful deceiver, who ought to be indicted for the most wicked and shameless hypocrisy. But we dare not assume such a ground without overwhelming evidence.

2. Mr. Swing has denied the charges against him in his declaration; has affirmed that he is a New School Presbyterian, and has asserted that he holds in the evangelical sense "the inspiration of the holy scriptures," "the trinity," the "divinity of Christ," "the office of Christ as a mediator," when grasped by an obedient faith, "Conversion by God's Spirit," "man's natural sinfulness," and "the final separation of the righteous and the wicked." This denial, and these affirmations, if sincerely made, oblige us to regard Mr. Swing as occupying on all the points of the evangelical and Calvinistic faith substantially the same ground as the former New School theologians, whose views of Calvinistic doctrine, as set forth in the Auburn declaration and in their writings, were recognized by both general assemblies, at the time of the reunion, as not inconsistent with the integrity of the Calvinistic system, and with a sincere reception and adoption of the confession of faith as *containing the system of doctrine* taught in the holy scriptures. We by no means contend or believe that it was implied in the reunion that the great body of the church *endorsed* what was called the New School theology, as held by such men as Drs. Richards, Benson, Spear, and Hickock, and Albert Barnes. What we say is, that after the Auburn declaration had been affirmed by the Assembly at Albany, in 1868, to "contain all the essentials of the Calvinistic creed," and when all the theologians of the New School church whose views had been long before the world were freely received into the united body, and the church in which they had been not only tolerated, but honored, was pronounced "a sound and orthodox body," it was clearly understood that the doctrines of what was called the New School theology were to be allowed in the reunited church as not inconsistent with a sincere acceptance and adoption of the confession of faith as containing the system of doctrine taught in the holy scriptures. And in our jugdment it has not been found that Mr. Swing has departed further from the letter of the confession than many other New School theologians, who were recognized as in good standing at the time of the reunion. It is conceded on both sides that a subscription to the letter of the confession on all points, or even to all the propositions in the confession, is not essential to good standing in the reunited church. The doctrines of particular and general atonement, and the different views that are held among us in regard to the lawfulness of marrying a deceased wife's sister, are not alike consistent with the letter of propositions of the confession. But they are alike allowed in the church, as not destroying the integrity of the system embraced in our confession: and so of many other points of difference among us. But Mr. Swing has not, so far as has been shown, discarded any teachings of the confession which are essential to the integrity of the system taught in the symbols of our church. The doctrines which he avowedly discards in his declaration are not held by any school in the church, and he only implies in that declaration his adoption of the New School in preference to the Old School of theology.

3. It has not, in our judgment, been proved from the published writings of Mr. Swing that he discarded any essential doctrine of the Presbyterian church. The principal specifications bearing directly on this point are the 9th, 18th, 19th, 20th, 21st, 23d, and 24th, under charge first, and the four specifications under charge second. Specification 9th alleges that Mr. Swing has taught or given his sanction to Sabellianism. But the language quoted is consistent with a belief in the church doctrines of the trinity, and this doctrine of three persons in one God

is distinctly recognized in "Truths for To-day," p. 81. Besides, it has been proved by parole testimony that Mr. Swing does avow his belief in the doctrine of three persons in one God. Specification 18th charges that Mr. Swing denies in effect the judicial condemnation of the lost. But of this we have seen no proof. The statement that unbelief "does not destroy the soul by an arbitrary decree," may be fairly understood to mean that God does not assign damnation to disbelievers without good reasons, which reasons are found partly in the very nature of unbelief. There is no denial, expressed or implied, of a divine judicial sentence upon the unbeliever. Specification 19th alleges that Mr. Swing teaches that faith saves because it leads to a holy life, &c. But he does not say that this is the only relation of faith. He does not deny that faith has a supernatural origin, when he affirms that it acts naturally, or in accordance with the nature and laws of the human mind. And we do not see that any of the statements quoted in the specification contravene any fundamental doctrine of the scripture or the confession. He does not discuss in the sermon quoted the whole subject of faith, but simply considers its relation to a holy character. Specification 20th accuses Mr. Swing of teaching that men are saved by works. But it does not follow that he denies that there is another sense in which men are saved by faith in the Saviour's atoning sacrifice. Indeed, he expressly says in his sermon on faith, p. 239, that "Pardon and atonement form parts of the great salvation." There is a sense in which men are saved by works, as the apostle James explicitly teaches. Specification 21 alleges that Mr. Swing denies the doctrine of justification by faith, as held by the reformed churches and taught in our confession. But Mr. Swing, in showing that works—that is, a new life,—is the destiny or end toward which faith operates, does not deny that judicial justification is a reality in the Christian system. On the contrary, he asserts, as we have seen, that "pardon and atonement are parts of the great salvation." Like James, in speaking of good works, he treats only of the necessary place which a new life holds in the matter of salvation. Specifications 23 and 24 allege that Mr. Swing denies the plenary inspiration and the infallibility of the scriptures. But it appears from Mr. Swing's letter to *The Presbyterian*, and from his explanations before this body, as well as from private statements of his views in evidence before us, that he believes in the plenary inspiration and the infallibility of the bible, and only adopts some peculiar modes of interpreting and applying Old Testament teachings and the book of Revelations, about which our confession says nothing.

Specification 1, under the second charge, alleges an offense which was known, when the charges were brought forward, only to a few persons,—a private offense, —and which has not been proved. Specification 2 under charge second has not been established by any clear evidence. Specification 3 under that head failed because the memory of Mr. Shufeldt was altogether uncertain, and because there was at best but one witness. And specification 4 failed because even if the quotations were fairly made they only show Mr. Swing's relative estimate of the practical importance of the doctrines referred to, and not that he disbelieves these doctrines. The proofs of the prosecution are all inferential and indirect, and even by his inferences we do not admit as clearly made out. The accused is entitled to the benefit of the more favorable interpretations which his language seems to us to admit of. Besides all this it appears from the testimony of the elders of the Fourth Church and of other witnesses that Mr. Swing has not taught the doctrines charged upon him in any of his lectures, but has explicitly taught the contrary; and that he has in private conversation explicitly disavowed his belief in those doctrines.

It should be added that the evidence from Prof. Swing's sermons before this body goes to show that he does believe the doctrines of divine decrees and nearly all of the other doctrines which he is charged with denying.

For all these reasons we have judged that the second charge is not sustained by any clear and satisfactory proof. And for the same and like reasons we have decided that the first charge has not been sustained. A few additional circumstances may be stated for our judgment regarding the first charge. Under this head we take into account not only the position of Mr. Swing as a Presbyterian minister, and his explicit denial of guilt and his affirmations of substantial agreement with New School Presbyterians, in which we are bound to assume his entire honesty, until the contrary is clearly proved; but the particularity of his mind and style, the special object which he had before him in many of his discourses, and the character of the audiences whom he has chiefly addressed in his Sabbath services since the fire. Mr. Swing deals largely in illustration and the use of metaphorical language, and often rapidly groups together many particulars which are only very generally related together, and, although not a mystic, his thought and style are often mystical, and, therefore, more or less obscure. It should be remembered, also, that he avows his sense of the necessity of less theological and more practical preaching; also that his audiences since the fire have consisted largely of persons who were not convinced of the divine authority of the scriptures, and whom he was, therefore, induced to address frequently on the reasonableness of Christianity, in the hope of gradually preparing them to admit its divine authority. This accounts for the fact that during this period he has dwelt less upon the central doctrines of the gospel in his discourses on the Sabbath, reserving his more explicit instructions for the benefit of his own people, for his Wednesday evening lectures, as his elders tell us he has done. With these facts in mind, it is not difficult to understand many things in his sermons which might otherwise seem hardly consistent with an earnest evangelical purpose.

It has not been shown that he has intentionally used vague or equivocal language in regard to important doctrines; or that he has declined to explain his meaning when misunderstood, in such a way as to prove him ecclesiastically unfaithful. His treatment of Unitarians, and his discourse on the life and character of John Stuart Mill, we attribute rather to his kindly and charitable habits of mind than to any disposition to give his sanction to fundamental error. For he has often in his sermons declared that a religion which makes Christ a mere man as the Unitarianism of our day almost uniformly does, strikes the sun from the centre of the system; and as to Mr. Mill, he only commenced his philanthropy, which he expressly attributed to the Christian influences of which he was unable to divest his mind. Mr. Swing does, indeed, ridicule the manner in which some of the more difficult doctrines of religion have been often defended and propagated by persecution and force, and he once speaks of the doctrines of predestination and election as not important in their relation to "the historical features of an age." But while he deems the prominence sometimes given to such mysteries unwarrantable, it has not been shown that he treats contemptuously the doctrines themselves.

The allegation that he has omitted to preach or teach several fundamental doctrines is not sustained in any sense to show that he has been intentionally unfaithful. For it has been shown that he has frequently recognized these doctrines in his preaching or lectures, excepting those which are seldom touched upon directly in most of our Christian pulpits; and that his reference to those doctrines, interpreted in view of his evangelical stand-point, are to be regarded as carrying with them an evangelical meaning. His sermon on experience as a test of scriptural doctrine in contradistinction to the doctrines of the church "as formally stated," though liable to be misunderstood, has not been proved to teach any radical error. He has expressly disavowed the doctrine both in his sermons and before the Presbytery. The allegation that he has made false and dangerous statements regarding the standard of faith and practice, it is not established by the passages referred to, when considered in their construction, although the language used is in some instances liable to be misapprehended. In regard to the being and attributes of God, we do not find any language of Mr. Swing that is clearly of false and dangerous import, although some expressions are perhaps not sufficiently guarded against misconstruction. The specification in regard to baptism does not seem to be sustained by any sufficient evidence, and the allegation respecting Penelope and Socrates is not supported by unquestionable proofs. For, taking the language quoted in its most unfavorable sense, it asserts a doctrine which is held by some confessedly sound Presbyterians, and which is not regarded by them as contrary to our confession. Specifications both 14 and 15 have not been established in such a manner as to prove unfaithfulness in the sense of an ecclesiastical offense. Indeed they seem to rest on a misapprehension of Mr. Swing's meaning. Specification 16, to say the most, is only supported by an appeal to language carelessly used, such as we often find in the writings of good and truthful men. Specification 17 has not been established in such a manner as to prove an ecclesiastical offense. It thus appears that none of the specifications have been so substantiated as to make out clearly an ecclesiastical offense.

The legal principles applicable to this case are clear. No man can be justly convicted of heresy by an unfavorable interpretation of his language, when it admits of a more favorable construction than the prosecutor has put upon it, as we have seen.

Every man is entitled to the benefit of his disclaimer of doctrines attributed to him which he denies that he holds. And we have seen that Mr. Swing does deny that he discards any doctrine that is essential to the system taught in the confession as held by New-School theologians, and heretofore acknowledged as allowable by the authorities of the church.

No man can be justly convicted of error by inferences from his teachings, which inferences he refuses to acknowledge, however logically the conclusion may be drawn, and much less can anyone be held responsible for inferences which do not follow by necessary consequence from his position.

But Mr. Swing is accused by the prosecutor on almost every point, on the ground of inferences which do not seem to follow unavoidably from the language used.

It is a just maxim in our ecclesiastical law that no man should be convicted of an offense, so long as there can be any doubt of his guilt.

But it seems to us that there is, to say the very least, room for some doubt in regard to the guilt of the accused in this case. For these principles see the cases of Craighead and Barnes' digest.

In view of all these considerations, some of which are deemed more weighty and some less weighty, by different members of this body who voted with the majority, we are clearly of the opinion that the several specifications have not been sustained.

In rendering the judgment we by no means indorse all the expressions and sentiments of Mr. Swing, or assume the responsibility of defending his peculiar style of preaching. We would be understood as simply pronouncing our judgment on the points involved in the indictment, according to the evidence that has come before our minds in the progress of this distressing trial. All of which is respectfully submitted.

R. W. Patterson.
A. Swazey.
R. E. Barber.

Throughout the entire proceedings of the Presbytery in this case, the reader will observe that reference is made to the work entitled "Truths for To-day." This beautiful book is published by Jansen, McClurg & Co., Chicago. Price $1.50. It contains the following Sermons: "Religious Toleration, or Charity." "The Golden Rule." "Righteousness." "Christianity and Dogma." "Emotion and Evidence." "Good Works." "The Great Debate." "Charles Sumner." "The Lost Paradise." "Positive Religion." "Christianity as a Civilization." "St. Paul." "Faith." "St. John." "Immortal Life." "A Reasonable Orthodoxy." (The latter preached May 3d.) The complete official report of the trial is being prepared by a committee of the Presbytery, and will be published immediately by the above firm.

PEN-PICTURES

—OF—

PROFESSORS PATTON AND SWING.

By Rev. Charles L. Thompson.

We who have so many great things are now about to have the greatest trial for heresy of this generation. The Presbytery of Chicago is the cynosure of very many eyes, religious and irreligious. It is an ill wind, etc. The daily press has taken to religious matter as if to the manner born. They fairly revel in religious interviewing, and plume themselves on leaded "leaders" settling by a final "ipse dixit" the fundamental principles of ecclesiastical law. The Confession of Faith is furnished as a condiment at a hundred thousand breakfast tables, and liberal doses of the "Digest" are given out to help digestion.

We are just beginning to see what a popular subject theology is. It only needs the dress of gossip to make it supremely attractive. Meantime pushing past this whirl of newspaper dust that fairly darkens the air, how stands the matter within the Church? Rev. David Swing is arraigned at the bar of Presbytery by Prof. F. L. Patton on the double charge of unfaithfulness in his ministry, and not sincerely adopting the Confession of Faith.

Who are these men? Both bear the title of professor. Both are good preachers, and good fellows, and somewhere in that neighborhood the resemblance ends, for these two men are singularly unlike. A word about their *personnel*, physical and mental. If you happen into the Fourth Presbyterian Church at half-past ten of a Sunday morning you will see on the pulpit platform a very quiet, unassuming man, of medium height, weight and age, with smooth face, brown hair combed back, friendly eyes, well-molded forehead, good-sized mouth, and heavy jaws—that is Prof. Swing. When he begins the service you perceive he is not a graceful man. His voice has a singular drawl, yet not wholly unpleasant. Its tones are persuasive, and suggest a gentle spirit. He does not stand erect, but half leans upon the desk, and reads the Bible, or engages in prayer in subdued and measured tones. You will not listen long till you conclude there is not much self consciousness there. As the sermon proceeds you become interested. Uncouth manner, awkward gestures, and poetic thought have a fitness about them that makes an attractive *tout ensemble.* You become aware as you are quietly borne on from sentence to sentence of a mind that sees things in large and general relations. There is a certain indefiniteness of statement that suggests a long perspective of thought. There is no clank of surveyor's chain, but only the sliding in and out of the object glass that adjusts your vision now to one focus, now to another, but always to a beautiful picture. When he closes you perceive he has led you through a very pleasant land, shown you some stimulating truths, and perhaps grounded you in certain broad principles which underlie the separate forms of church life or doctrine. He has not analyzed much, but he has created a good deal, and leaves you to make your own arrangement and application. As you leave the sauctuary you will probably have some such impressions as these: That man has not striven after any effect, but his thoughts run in his own mold, and have been before me in a form unhackneyed. He has not clearly asserted any new proposition, but he has been climbing to a broad view that holds within its picture-lines many propositions. He has not specially defined truth, but he has suggested certain views which may lead me to a definition. In a word, he has not exactly preached to me, but he and I have had a ramble in fields that hold within them the possibilities of a good harvest. And, especially, I think the vital force of that sermon was in a tender, earnest sentiment, a kind of implied friendship between us, and an implied aspiration in his heart and mine toward a higher life. And if you should thus judge you would not greatly misjudge the preacher.

Step over now into a neighboring church. A tall, slender, straight young man looks directly at you through a pair of spectacles, and announces his text in clear, positive tones, that at once suggest deep conviction, and that man is Prof. Patton. He is so very thin he looks uncomfortably frail, but he comes down on his text with a solid emphasis that indicates no disposition to spare the flesh. He has no notes. There is no introduction to his sermon. He plunges straight into the argument in phrases far enough from stilted, and in clear-cut propositions which are far enough from dullness. His tone is conversational. His manner and matter are exceedingly frank and manly. His process of thought, logical and unhalting. The sermon is doctrinal, but not bony. It has life-color, and is rounded off with apt and fresh illustrations. From first to last he goes fluently on. The thoughts succeed each other in such bright movement no attention can flag, and when he suddenly closes, you realize that you have got quite a body of divinity to meditate upon. As you walk out of the house, very likely you will say, Well, this man, in sincerity, frankness, manhood, the same as the other, is his intellectual antipode. If the other was a picture, this is a surveyor's chain flashing in every solid link. His convictions are deeply cut, and earnestly put. He will stake his life on the truth he sees and speaks. It is lively, rattling logic, brought down to date. Calvinistic Young America. And if you should thus judge you would not greatly misjudge the preacher.

These are the men who stand before each other, and the public, in a contest in which each is sincere and honest, and in which it should be the prayer of every Christian mind (knowing no man after the flesh) may the end be for the truth and the glory of God.

Dr. Powers in the Independent.

The Rev. H. N. Powers, D. D., of this city, in the last number of the New York *Independent*, thus speaks of Prof. Swing:

He has tenderness and he has strength; he has learning and he has sentiment; he has common sense and he has piety; and with his poetic vision and ardor are blended such holy and penetrative sympathies as enable him to use his resources in a way more helpful to some than could be possible with even greater intellectual ability and a less characteristic spiritual mold. It is this peculiar constitution that enables him to appreciate well the hindrances to reason alone and to faith alone; but, while he ignores neither the laws of matter nor of mind, and, therefore, never treats flippantly or disdainfully the facts of science or the perplexities of the intellect, he never forgets the nature and needs of the soul—he never forgets that "Christ came that we might have life, and that we might have it more abundantly." Spirit is the absolute fact with him, and it is the commanding vitalities of Christianity that engage his heart and inspire his ministry.

www.ingramcontent.com/pod-product-compliance
Lightning Source LLC
LaVergne TN
LVHW021357110826
845150LV00007B/1682

9781425513498